B.J. Kidd

The Thirty-Nine Articles

Their History and Explanation, Vol I, Aritcles I - VIII

B.J. Kidd

The Thirty-Nine Articles
Their History and Explanation, Vol I, Aritcles I - VIII

ISBN/EAN: 9783743399600

Manufactured in Europe, USA, Canada, Australia, Japa

Cover: Foto ©ninafisch / pixelio.de

Manufactured and distributed by brebook publishing software (www.brebook.com)

B.J. Kidd

The Thirty-Nine Articles

Oxford Church Text Books

The Thirty-nine Articles

THEIR HISTORY AND EXPLANATION

BY

THE REV. B. J. KIDD, B.D.

KEBLE COLLEGE
TUTOR OF NON-COLLEGIATE STUDENTS, OXFORD

IN TWO VOLUMES

VOL. I

ARTICLES I-VIII

RIVINGTONS

34 *KING STREET, COVENT GARDEN*

LONDON

1899

INTRODUCTORY NOTE

THE author wishes to express his obligations to the works of Archdeacon Hardwick, Dr. Maclear, and Dr. Gibson on the Articles, obligations which it is impossible, in so short a compass, to acknowledge in detail.

CONTENTS

Part I.—History of the Articles.

CHAP.		PAGE
I.	The Growth of new Doctrinal Formularies,	1
II.	The Doctrinal Formularies of the reign of Henry VIII., ...	15
III.	The Forty-two Articles of the reign of Edward VI., ...	25
IV.	The Thirty-nine Articles of the reign of Elizabeth, ...	38

Part II.—Explanation.

Article I.,	. . . .	65
,, II.,	. . . . .	69
,, III.,	. . . .	80
,, IV.,	. . . .	83
,, V.,	. . . .	89
,, VI.,	. . . .	93
,, VII.,	. . . .	103
,, VIII.,	. . . .	109
Appendix—The Latin Articles of 1553 and 1563 (I.-VIII.), ...		113
Index, ...		117

THE THIRTY-NINE ARTICLES

PART I.—THEIR HISTORY

CHAPTER I

THE GROWTH OF NEW DOCTRINAL FORMULARIES

§ 1. **Creeds and Articles.**—There have been two periods in the history of the Christian Church in which it was necessary to make doctrinal statements about belief. In the 4th and 5th centuries, such statements took shape as Creeds; while the 16th century cast its tenets into the form of Articles. So far as Creeds and Articles are alike attempts to reduce belief to formal statement for the sake of avoiding error, they may be said to owe their origin to a common impetus. Both periods were times of active speculation on religious subjects: so much so that the chaff of the market-place at Alexandria ran as naturally in that direction as the jests of an ale-house bench in London. 'Well, my friend, have we one Unbegotten, or two?' was an Arian witticism to be paralleled only by the Anabaptist's joke at the expense of the Sacrament, 'Is it anything else but a piece of bread, or a little pretty round robin?' Behind such levity lay serious unsettlement, which both Creeds and Articles were framed to meet. Moreover, they met it in the same way, by setting up a ring fence round the common heritage of truth. This is the reason why Creeds, and even Articles, are necessary. They are not desirable in themselves; and it would certainly have been a happier thing if the Church could have done without any formal expression of her

Faith. But it was impossible. Like a common which is perpetually being contracted by the encroachments of persons who quietly fence bits off for their own use, the Faith at these two epochs was suffering loss from the depredations of heretics who deprived the Christian community, say, of the right to worship Christ, as did Arius; or of the right to a real incorporation into, and maintenance by, His Body, as did the Sacramentaries of the 16th century. In either case the Church had to protect the religious interests of her members. She had to vindicate their right to share in the whole of the common heritage of the ancient Faith; and she did so by recourse to formularies. She set up her fence, and her notice to trespassers; not however to narrow down the limits of truth, but on the contrary, to save them from contraction, and to secure the ancient freedom and latitude for all her children. Thus it is because they are the products of two over-speculative ages in the history of the Church, that the Creeds and Articles, though influenced by philosophical language and built up in some measure by its assistance, are eminently unspeculative. So far from supplying, their set purpose is to exclude, explanatory theories of the truth. It has been pertinently said of the Creeds, that 'they were the *negation* of explanations. . . . The Church held that all such explanations, or partial explanations [as Arius and others proposed for the doctrine of the Trinity] inflicted irremediable impoverishment on the idea of the Godhead which was essentially involved in the Christian revelation. They insisted on preserving that idea in all its inexplicable fulness.' So, by the Articles, as in the doctrine of the Sacraments for instance, the whole truth has been preserved free from the encroachment of explanatory theories, *i.e.* by the same negative policy of a ring fence to secure the integrity of the Christian's territory and free access for him by an open door. Thus the Creeds and Articles are akin in a common impulse and a common purpose.

But there are marked differences between them, not to be overlooked :—

1. *In origin.*—The Creeds grew. The Articles were made. It is true that the Creeds took shape under the

stress of heretical speculation, and that certain clauses were expressly added, and on definite occasions, to meet special perversions, as, *e.g.* 'Of one substance with the Father,' to exclude Arianism at the Council of Nicæa, 325 A.D. But the Creed, both in substance and arrangement, had its origin in a period long anterior to the age of controversy, and in needs much simpler than the exigencies of negativing heretical conclusions. The form of the Catholic Creed suggests, by its threefold division, its origin in connection with the Baptismal Formula; while the early custom of the delivery and rehearsal of the Creed, belonging to the preparation of converts for baptism at Easter and Pentecost, indicates the positive use made of it in the missionary work of the Church. Certainly the Creed went on receiving additions and developments, to meet the aberrations of heresy, for a considerable length of time. It did not reach its complete form in the East till the 4th century, and in the West till the 8th. But in two points the process of its formation is distinct from that of the Articles. (*a*) These developments were, in the main, unconscious additions, and can only be assigned conjecturally, if at all, to any place or time. (*b*) The type which the Catholic Creeds, with all their variations, follow, represents a body of positive truth which was everywhere received as traditional before the age of doctrinal developments began. Thus the clause 'Of one substance with the Father,' which was the first addition made to exclude a particular heresy, was simply inserted into the formulary proposed by Eusebius of Cæsarea, which was none of his own composing, but 'the faith which he had received from the bishops who preceded him, first when he was being instructed as a catechumen, and afterwards when he was baptized. . . . Such also . . . he had taught, first as presbyter, afterwards as bishop.' The Articles, on the contrary, were deliberately framed to meet definite errors prevalent at a particular time; and were withdrawn or retained accordingly.

2. *In contents.*—The Creed is a summary collection of simple statements. The Articles are conceived and executed on quite a different scale, occupying many pages,

and covering, as they do, a large area both of theology and politics. The Creeds do not touch upon a Christian's duty to the State; for the ancient Empire, whether it persecuted or favoured him, left him no choice in that matter, and such questions were not raised. It was only when the authority of the Mediæval Empire and the Papacy was breaking up, that elements of disorder appeared, and forced the Churches of Christendom to take a side as to the authority of the magistrate and kindred questions. Thus the state of society in the 16th, as compared with its condition in the 4th, century accounts for one notable addition in the contents of the Articles by contrast with those of the Creed. But this is not all. The Creeds are theological and historical. The Articles are anthropological and controversial. The second paragraph of the Creed,—that in which we profess our belief in God the Son—is certainly the largest, and, if we have regard to the elementary creeds contained in Scripture, such as 'Jesus is Lord' (1 Cor. xii. 3), the oldest also. We should note that in contents this section is historical rather than doctrinal. Its statements, if looked into, are, in the main, assertions of such facts concerning our Lord's Person and teaching as would have come within the range of the Apostles' experience, and would of course carry with them the belief in the Father and the Holy Spirit set forth by way of introduction and supplement in the first and third paragraphs. The Creed then preserves to us the facts of their Lord's Person and teaching to which the Apostles witnessed. It is historical rather than doctrinal; or, if doctrinal, it preserves doctrines only so far as they are bound up in that which He was and did and said. It needs but a glance, and no proof, to see that the Articles are essentially a series of doctrinal, and even controversial, statements. Further, where the Creed is doctrinal, it is theological. It deals with the being and the operations of God in Creation, Redemption, and Sanctification. The Articles, on the contrary, expend most of their energy in anthropology. They deal with Sin, Faith, Works, Justification, and the Means of Grace.

3. *In authority.*—Obviously, while the Articles are only

of local and temporary import, the Creeds are of universal and permanent authority. The various English Articles, for instance, were put forth on the authority of the synods of a local or national Church. This is frequently made clear in their titles, as also the fact that they were intended to meet a temporary crisis. Thus the title of the Ten Articles of 1536—the first of our series of reformed doctrinal standards—runs:—'Articles . . . to stablish Christian quietness . . . approved by the . . . whole Clergy of this Realm'; where nothing beyond a local authority and a temporary object is claimed for them. That is all that is claimed for the last of the series—a much more systematic and, as it has turned out, more permanent formulary; for the title of the Articles of 1571 follows just the same lines:—'Articles whereupon it was agreed by the Archbishops and Bishops of both provinces and the whole clergy in the Convocations holden at London in the year of our Lord God 1562, . . . for the avoiding of the diversities of opinions, and for the stablishing of consent touching true Religion.' To compose the religious differences of recent years in England, was all that the Articles aimed at; and they emanated from a certain local synod in a certain year. It might be said that the Nicene Creed emanated at a certain date from a certain place, and was intended to settle a particular controversy. True; but (a) the Council of Nicæa was an Œcumenical Council; (b) the formulary which it accepted was not a new one composed then and there, but the long-standing traditional Creed of the East with one pointed addition, 'Of one substance with the Father'; while (c), and here we touch the essence of the contrast between Creeds and Articles in point of authority—its doctrinal decisions acquired universal authority, because they were adopted by universal consent. For the same reason, what we call the Apostles' Creed enjoys an equal authority with the Nicene, superior to that possessed by any series of Articles, because, though not drawn up in an Œcumenical Council, it rests upon the basis which gives all such Councils their credit, the basis of universal consent. Western in form, it is in substance one with the Catholic Creed of the East. The names of

'Western' and 'Eastern' Creeds are, in a sense, misleading. The latter became known as the Nicene Creed, because of its connection with that Council. But when, from that time forward, distinctive names began to be given to particular formularies, the Western Creed, which hitherto had none, retained the appellation of 'The Apostles' Creed' once common to all. There is really but one Creed, Apostolic and Catholic. In both these points, Articles contrast with the Creed. They do not represent the fulness of apostolic doctrine, but only such parts or developments of it as were wanted by their compilers to meet a temporary need; while, again, they rest for their authority upon adoption by some local synod, and not, as do the Creeds, upon adoption by Catholic consent.

4. *In purpose.*—The Creeds are formularies of faith. They are for learners. 'I' [West] or 'We' [East] 'believe' is the key to their use. They are for instruction; and so from early times have been used in the services of the Church. From the first they were recited by the convert at his Baptism; from the 5th century onwards they established their right to a place in his great act of worship at the Eucharist. Thus the Creed is the layman's treasure. Its verities are at once the ground of his privileges in Baptism, and the guide to his intelligent adoration in the Eucharist. No further statement is required by, or required of, him for his salvation. But the Articles are a formulary for teachers. As their title says, they are 'Articles of Religion'; or, as we might say, tests to keep teaching within bounds. They deal with consent, *i.e.* with the office of the intellect; not with belief, or the province of faith. They mark out the lines along which official teaching is to proceed, and set the limits which it is not to overstep. Thus they are negative and exclusive of error, where the Creeds are positive and inclusive of truth. They aim at peace and comprehension; 'the Creeds represent decisions. Their whole purpose is to determine. There is no doubt, on the other hand, that except where the Articles simply express over again the mind of the ancient Church (as in 1-9, 33-34), or pointedly exclude certain mediæval abuses (as in

30 and 32), or Reformation excesses (38, 39), the purpose which governed their wording was to avoid an issue rather than to seek it—to shelve questions, leaving a large tract of open country, rather than to decide them. This characteristic of the Articles is at once their weakness as formulas and their strength as temporary safeguards:' but it is specially indicative of their purpose.

Thus in *origin*, *contents*, *authority*, and *purpose*, the formularies of the two epochs, when the Church had to define her beliefs, are widely divergent. It is of importance to notice then, that

§ 2. **Articles are a characteristic product of the Reformation.** That movement was not one but manifold. There are three great names associated with its inauguration abroad, Zwingli, Luther, and Calvin : and their several cities, Zurich, Wittenberg, and Geneva became the centres of very different types of teaching. It is true that in their attack on the reigning system, all three leaders chose for their weapons certain common principles, such as the sole authority of Scripture in matters of faith and the equal right of each baptized believer, as a priest, to interpret them for himself. But there the agreement ended. They differed in the thoroughness with which they applied these 'principles of the Reformation' both to practice and doctrine. In church ornaments, for instance, while the Lutherans or Protestants were willing to retain everything that was not expressly forbidden in Scripture, the Swiss or Reformed excluded everything but what was positively enjoined. So, in doctrine, the principle that the Bible and the Bible only is of authority in matters of faith was corrected on Luther's part by reference to the test of his favourite tenet, Justification by Faith only, and on Calvin's by reference to that of the Divine Election. The time came when the Catholic powers dropped their political rivalries, and began to take the reforming movements seriously. Called upon to defend themselves, the reformers drew up apologies, such as Zwingli's *Fidei Ratio* and the Augsburg Confession, presented to the Emperor Charles v. in 1530 at the Diet of Augsburg ; or again, such as Calvin's *Institutes*, 1536, dedicated, for a similar purpose, to Francis I. of France. Then it was that divergences began to appear; and their appearance had been already assisted by the failure of well-meant attempts at common action, such as Philip of Hesse tried to secure between Luther and Zwingli at the Conference of Marburg in 1529.

That meeting revealed deep lines of cleavage between the Saxon and Swiss reformers upon the presence of Our Lord in the Eucharist. Hence, during the period at which our Articles were in the making (1536-1571), we find on the Continent a large crop of **Confessions**, as they were called; for it had become necessary for the reformers to define their own position against one another, as well as against the common enemy. Occasionally, too, there arose formularies of comprehension. It is to one or other of these purposes that every specimen of the Confessional Literature of the 16th century may be traced. Articles and Confessions are therefore a product peculiar to the conditions of that age. Thus the **Augsburg Confession 1530**, which was originally no more than 'Master Philip's (*sc.* Melanchthon's) Apology,' as Luther called it, for the new teaching, after serving as the basis for common political action between the Lutheran princes (1531), was generally accepted as the first of the Lutheran Symbolical ($\sigma\acute{\upsilon}\mu\beta o\lambda o\nu$ = a creed) Books: and the series went on developing, whether for the purposes of conciliation or exclusion, until the Lutheran doctrines attained their final exposition in the **Formula of Concord 1577**. Thus the period of the formulation of the Lutheran tenets (1530-77) corresponds roughly with the period during which the English Church restated her beliefs (1536-1571): yet only at two points did the Lutheran influences reach our Thirty-nine Articles, and then but indirectly. 'The compilers of the Forty-two Articles in the reign of Edward VI. drew largely from the Lutheran formulary of 1530; but such derivation, instead of being direct, took place entirely through the medium' of the *Thirteen Articles of 1538*, which were drawn up by a mixed body of English and German divines. Again, when Archbishop Parker and his friends took in hand the revision of the Edwardian Articles, 'no small part of the fresh matter in the Articles of 1563 was borrowed from a Lutheran document, itself in turn an echo of the Augsburg Confession,' known as the **Confession of Würtemberg**, presented to the Council of Trent in **1552** by the ambassadors of that state. So much for the development of the Lutheran formularies, and their connection with our own.

It is of less importance, for the history of the Thirty-nine Articles, to trace the modifications and affinities of the Swiss formularies. They were grounded, not in form but in doctrine, upon **Calvin's Institutes 1536**. Such was his influence, that in a few years the reforming movements of German Switzerland, which had their centres at Basel and Zurich, were brought into line with Calvin's own masterful theology by the **Consensus Tigurinus 1549**, (Consent of Zurich). This document is of importance because, by securing the advance of the earlier (or German) Swiss reformers to Calvin's doctrine of a Virtual Presence of Our Lord in the Eucharist, it consolidated the 'Reformed' theology, and so prepared the way not only for the final formulary of union between Zurich and Geneva called the **Second Helvetic Confession 1566**, but also for those national Confessions, such as the Scottish (1560) from which, along with the Helvetic, the Puritan party in England drew the inspiration of its attempts to improve upon, or rather improve away, the Thirty-nine Articles. Such attempts are to be met with in the **Lambeth Articles 1595** and the **Westminster Confession 1646**. Thus the development of Calvinistic formularies deserves mention for a reason opposite to that which gives Englishmen an interest in the growth of the Lutheran series. While the latter successfully exerted an indirect influence upon our formularies in the making, the former tried, but unsuccessfully, to supplant them once made.

Both the Lutheran and Calvinistic formularies, however, while possessing features in common with the great Roman Catholic formulary known as **The Canons and Decrees of the Council of Trent 1563**, contrast with our Articles in two notable directions. The doctrinal decisions of this Council, which are contained by way of exposition in the

Dogmatic Chapters accompanied by Canons anathematising all teaching to the contrary, are a restatement of the traditional theology of the Middle Ages in a modified but *systematic* form. Exactly so the *later* Lutheran and the Calvinistic formularies are *systematic* theological treatises. This cannot be said of the Thirty-nine Articles, which do not pretend to cover systematically the whole ground of Christian doctrine. They are 'Articles,' not a 'Confession'; and this is a characteristic difference between English and Continental restatements of doctrine in the 16th century, this absence or presence of elaboration into systematic form.

But, after all, this feature is not quite universal abroad, for the Augsburg Confession is not a systematic treatise; and the arrangement of the Tridentine decisions, though it is based upon a systematic exposition of the Seven Sacraments, presents an orderly whole quite different in method from the other continental Confessions. Nevertheless all the Protestant and Reformed Confessions, by contrast with our Articles, and, in this respect, with the Canons and Decrees of Trent, have one distinguishing mark about them. Where least systematic, each is held together by revolving round *one central doctrine*, e.g., the Augsburg Confession round the tenet of Justification by Faith only. This is the second point of difference between the Continental Confessions and the English Articles: and it is capable of a simple explanation. As a rule the foreign formularies were each the work of one man. They bore inevitably the stamp of some one individuality. The formularies of Rome and England, on the other hand, have at least this in common, that they were on the anvil for a generation, bearing alike the marks of compromise, and of the touch of many hands. They were the work not of this or that eminent theologian, but of constitutional assemblies of the Catholic Church. They were not newly propounded systems of doctrine, but simply readjustments of traditional teaching. This is a direct consequence of

§ 3. **The place of the Articles in the English Reformation.**—The English Reformation, unlike the Continental, was in its origin a constitutional, not a doctrinal movement. It sprang too from above, and not from below. In its development, it followed the lines marked out from time to time by the Crown and the laity; and, though each decisive step was formally taken by divines, it was taken, as a rule, in the direction previously indicated by statesmen. This accounts for the moderate and conservative tone observable in what was done: as also for the anomalous and summary methods by which ends were often attained. The Convocations, or regular ecclesiastical assemblies of the Church, were required to lay down the formal justification for what was contemplated; but it was reserved for the Crown, either by Parliament or commissions of court divines, to carry through the details on the basis of the principles thus asserted.

It is as the exposition, or further application of these principles, that the various doctrinal formularies, the Articles included, find their true place and meaning in our history. When Henry VIII. found that the Pope would not meet his wishes in dissolving his union with Katharine, he laid before the spiritual assemblies of his realm two questions, challenging the claims of the Papal authority on which the reigning religious system rested. The Convocations, in reply decided, in 1533, that marriage with a deceased brother's wife was so repugnant to the divine law that the Pope could not dispense in such a case; and in 1534, that 'the Roman Pontiff has no greater jurisdiction in this realm of England conferred upon him by God in Holy Scripture than any other foreign bishop.' It was left to the Archbishop to pronounce the marriage of Henry and Katharine null and void in obedience to the first resolution, and to Parliament to put an end to the Papal jurisdiction on the basis of the second. But by such action a new principle had been silently affirmed: for both these decisions run up into the position that Scripture, and not the Pope, is of supreme authority in matters of faith and morals. So the constitutional reformation led on to the doctrinal; and the first series of Articles (the Ten Articles of 1536) made its appearance, significantly enough, in the year that the

Reformation Parliament (1529-1536) closed. That Parliament recorded its conviction more than once, that, in renouncing the usurpations of Rome, it was in no sense cutting itself off from the communion of the Catholic Church. Thus it said in 1532 (23 Henry VIII. c. 20), 'Albeit that our said sovereign the king, and all his natural subjects, as well spiritual as temporal, be as obedient, devout, catholic, and humble children of God and Holy Church, as any people be within any realm christened, etc.' And again in 1534 (25 Henry VIII. c. 21), 'Provided always, that this Act, nor any thing or things therein contained, shall be hereafter interpreted or expounded, that your grace, your nobles and subjects, intend, by the same, to decline or vary from the congregation of Christ's Church in any things concerning the very articles of the Catholic faith of Christendom, or in any other things declared, by Holy Scripture and the word of God, necessary for your and their salvations, etc.' The new standard of doctrine had, in one word, been accepted without any fear that the Catholicity of the realm was compromised: but it had now to be adjusted and developed.

This was the service rendered by the successive doctrinal formularies of which the Thirty-nine Articles are the last. These formularies differ widely in detail, according to the dominance of this or that tendency at the time of their composition. But it has not been sufficiently observed that what gives the whole series its unity and the English Church her general character of solidity and equilibrium during an exceptionally stormy period of her history, is that the doctrinal standard acted upon in the earlier constitutional changes was repeatedly re-affirmed in the later period of religious reconstruction, in such a way as to secure a progressive continuity from first to last. The form that the new appeal took was not to the authority of the Bible and the Bible only, but to that of the Scriptures and the undivided Church. Thus—

1. 1536. Tunstal, Bishop of Durham, writes in defence of the King's proceedings to Cardinal Pole. 'His full purpose and intent is, to see the laws of Almighty God

purely and sincerely preached and taught, and Christ's faith without blot kept and observed in his realm ; and not to separate himself, or his realm, anywise from the unity of Christ's catholic church, but inviolably, at all times, to keep and observe the same; to reduce his church of England out of all captivity of foreign powers, heretofore usurped therein, into the pristine estate, that all churches of all realms were in at the beginning. . . So that no man therein can justly find any fault at the King's so doing, seeing he reduceth all things to that estate, that is conformable to those ancient decrees of the Church, which the Bishop of Rome (at his creation) solemnly doth profess to observe himself, which be the eight universal councils.'

2. 1536. The Ten Articles :—' As touching the chief and principal articles of our faith, . . . they ought and must most constantly believe and defend all those things to be true, which be comprehended in the whole body and canon of the Bible, and also in the three Creeds . . . and that they ought and must take and interpret all the same things according to the selfsame sentence and interpretation, which the words of the selfsame creeds or symbols do purport, and the holy approved doctors of the Church do entreat and defend the same. . . .

'Item, That they ought and must utterly refuse and condemn all those opinions contrary to the said Articles, which were of long time past condemned in the four holy councils, that is to say, in the Council of Nice, Constantinople, Ephesus, and Chalcedonense, and all other sith that time in any point consonant to the same.'

3. 1537. The Bishop's Book ⎫ adopt almost the same
4. 1543. The King's Book ⎭ words.

5. 1559. Elizabeth's Act of Supremacy (1 Eliz. c. 1, § 36), provides that the Court of High Commission 'shall not in any wise have authority or power to order, determine, or adjudge any matter or cause to be heresy, but only such as heretofore have been determined, ordered, or adjudged to be heresy, by the authority of the canonical Scriptures, or by the first four general Councils, or any of them, or by any other general Council wherein the same was declared heresy by the express and plain words

of the said canonical Scriptures, or such as hereafter shall be ordered, judged, or determined to be heresy by the High Court of Parliament of this realm, with the assent of the clergy in their Convocation.

6. Canons of 1571.—'Inprimis vero videbunt [concionatores], ne quid unquam doceant pro concione, quod a populo religiose teneri et credi velint, nisi quod consentaneum sit doctrinae Veteris aut Novi Testamenti, quodque ex illa ipsa doctrina catholici patres, et veteres episcopi collegerint.'

Here then is the formative principle of the English Reformation considered in its doctrinal aspect. Worked on, perhaps unconsciously, by the Reformation Parliament, it was consciously worked out in the subsequent doctrinal formularies, such as the Articles. Its importance cannot be overrated. While it gives to the religious position of the English Church its peculiar prerogative of freedom combined with faithfulness to the past,

<blockquote>Non super antiquas stare sed ire vias,—</blockquote>

it furnishes the student of the Thirty-nine Articles with the right standpoint for their interpretation. Historically, their place in the course of the English Reformation indicates that they contain the final application of its cardinal principle. Doctrinally, they must be interpreted not by reference to the private opinions of their authors, but in subordination to the doctrinal standard which governed from the first all the changes, constitutional or religious, that were made.

CHAPTER II

THE DOCTRINAL FORMULARIES
OF THE REIGN OF HENRY VIII.

§ 1. **The religious confusion,** which had manifested itself by the close of the Reformation Parliament (1536), demanded the immediate attention of the government. Not that it was merely recent. On the contrary, it was of long standing. But in pursuing his policy of depressing the Church at home and repudiating the Pope abroad, at a time when doctrinal disorder was increasing, Henry had called out forces which it was now necessary to restrain. Even the bench of Bishops was, at this time, about equally divided between the partisans of the Old and the New Learning. Such was the phrase then in use; though it was felt to be, as indeed it is, open to some objection, because the Old Learning were the advocates of the more recent developments of mediævalism, while the New Learning at any rate professed themselves to be, not innovators, but renovators of primitive truth. To the New Learning belonged Archbishop Cranmer and some eight or nine of his suffragans, foremost among whom was Latimer, who preached at the opening of the Convocation (June 9, 1536) which accepted the first English doctrinal formulary. The other side, of about equal strength, was led by Gardiner; and while it contained stout champions of the mediæval order in men like Stokesley, Bishop of London, it also numbered in its ranks men of gentle temperament and wider sympathies such as Tunstal, Bishop of Durham. Unquestionably, it was the presence of learning and moderation on both sides that made it possible for the Episcopate as a whole to unite upon the basis of an appeal, in matters of doctrine, to the Bible, the Creeds, and the Undivided Church. But, if possible, there were reasons why a pronouncement was also desirable, at once on political and religious grounds.

1. Politically, 'the abolition of the Pope, the fall of the . . . monasteries . . . the generally hideous aspect which things had assumed, rendered it necessary to vindicate the realm by declaring that it still remained within the pale of Catholic Christendom.' Old and New Learning had this in common that both parties had loyally supported the Henrician proceedings. Now that they were about to be challenged both at home and abroad, by the Pilgrimage of Grace and by the Papal condemnation, it was essential to satisfy the English nation that the Catholic faith still remained, and other nations that the kingdom had not been led into schism by the king.

2. In religion, it was as necessary to secure unity as in politics to establish the claim to Catholicity. For the divisions of opinion, which were already apparent in the Episcopate, had been actively at work in lower ranks of life for a generation. (*a*) The ground was prepared by the early **Gospellers**, of whom Latimer himself had been one, armed with Wolsey's licence to preach throughout the kingdom. They left doctrine alone, and made 'war against abuses and superstitions, false miracles, worship of saints, too many pilgrimages, too much observance of the Pope's laws, and the mere mummeries which defaced religion.' (*b*) Then there were scholars of **Lutheran** sympathies, some of whom Wolsey had brought from Cambridge and planted in Cardinal's College at Oxford (1525), thinking, no doubt, at once to moderate their zeal and control their abilities in the interest of his own aims for a proper reformation. (*c*) About the same time sprang up the **Heretics**, as they were called in the language of the day, headed by William Tyndale. The debt which Englishmen owe to him as a translator of the Scriptures must not be allowed to obscure the other *rôle* which he played. His versions were put down partly because they were private and unauthorised ventures, but also because of the seditious and irreligious notes

with which they were adorned. In pamphlets and broadsheets also, publications of a more fugitive but therefore of a cheaper and more penetrating type, Tyndale and the Heretics attacked the received system both in Church and State. (*d*) To the questionings thus roused, a further contribution was made by John Frith and the **Sacramentaries**. Frith, though but a young man at his death in 1533, had had a part in all the earlier religious movements of his day. He first appears as a pupil of Gardiner at Cambridge. Then, for his parts and promise, he was included in the band of Lutheranising scholars transplanted by Wolsey to Oxford. Thence he went to Flanders, where he fell under the influence of Tyndale. Returning to England, he became a member of the secret society of the Christian Brethren, which existed to disseminate the prohibited books of the Heretics. Lodged at last in the Tower, he was betrayed into controversy with More, and produced, in his book on the Sacrament, a storehouse of learning from which Cranmer afterwards drew, but which led at once to Frith's death, and very shortly to the growth of the Sacramentaries as a school of religious opinion. They maintained the Zwinglian tenet that the Eucharist is merely the memorial of an absent Christ; and they derive their name from their unwillingness to acknowledge that the ordinances of the Gospel are more than *sacramenta*, or *mere signs*,[1] and not efficacious signs, or means of grace. (*e*) But it was the arrival, within two years after Frith's death, of 'Anabaptist strangers' from abroad, that carried the religious confusion to the point at which the English Spiritualty thought it imperative to intervene. They are first mentioned in these terms in a proclamation issued between May 25, 1535, when twenty-five of them, Hollanders by nation, were brought up for trial in St. Paul's, and the execution of fourteen of their number soon after. Their tenets will appear in connection with the Edwardian series of Articles, many of which were directed specially against them; but we can only account for the universal applause with which their cruel death was greeted, even by Latimer, on the supposition that

[1] *Cf.* Art. 29, 'the sign or sacrament of so great a thing.'

they brought with them those political principles of a communistic kind which, coupled with immoral excesses, had drawn down upon them in the Empire the wrath of Catholic and Protestant alike. There is a note, as of alarm, in the entry which Cromwell made in his famous pocket-book: 'First, as touching the Anabaptists, and what the king will do with them?' Henry set about a severe repression. Their religious tenets were condemned by the doctrinal formularies of 1537 and 1543. Their lives were threatened by a commission of 1538, by injunctions of 1539, and by Act of Parliament (32 Henry VIII. c. 49), § 11) of 1540. Thus they were effectually prevented, till Edward's reign, from adding to the religious confusion in England. But their arrival in 1535 had served to call attention both to the divergences that already existed, and to the possibility of further developments. On June 23, 1536, the Lower House of the Convocation of Canterbury presented to the Bishops a long list of doctrinal errors then prevalent. Only a short time elapsed before the answer appeared in the first authorised formulary of the Church of England, with the signatures of the King's Vicegerent, the two Archbishops, sixteen Bishops, besides Abbots, Priors, and other clergy.

§ 2. **The Ten Articles** thus came forth under full authority, as '*Articles devised . . . to stablish Christian quietness and unity among us, and to avoid contentious opinions.*' Such was their purpose.

Their contents fall into two parts:—
I. Five relating to doctrine:
1. The principal Articles concerning our Faith. 2. The Sacrament of Baptism. 3. The Sacrament of Penance. 4. The Sacrament of the Altar. 5. Justification.
II. Five 'concerning the laudable ceremonies used in the church.'
6. And first of Images. 7. Of honouring of Saints. 8. Of praying to Saints. 9. Of Rites and Ceremonies. 10. Of Purgatory.

In character, the Ten Articles bear the marks of compromise, with leanings (*a*) toward modes of statement acceptable to the King and the Old Learning, and (*b*) against the unqualified adoption of what was distinctively

Lutheran. They (c) directly exclude what savoured simply of Anabaptism or heresy. Thus the Rule of Faith is stated to be the Bible and the three Creeds, as interpreted by the holy approved doctors of the Church (Art. 1.). The Sacraments are fixed neither at two nor at seven, but three are explained, Baptism, Penance, and the Sacrament of the Altar, and the rest unmentioned (Arts. 2, 3, 4). The Anabaptist opinions against Infant Baptism are 'detestable heresies and utterly to be condemned' (Art. 2). Penance as a 'sacrament was institute of Christ' (Art. 3). As to the Eucharist, the term 'Transubstantiation' is not employed, nor is there any assertion of the desition of the natural substance of the elements; but yet it is said that 'under the form and figure of bread and wine . . . is verily, substantially, and really contained . . . the . . . body and blood of our Saviour Jesus Christ' (Art. 4). Justification—the point at which we should look for Lutheranism, if anywhere—is indeed defined in Melanchthon's words: but the ground of it, if not merit of ours, is not faith only, but 'contrition and faith joined with charity' (Art. 5). So far the Episcopate as a whole went in defining the necessaries of the Faith; and that doctrines, such as Transubstantiation, once counted as necessary, were now reduced to the level of the variable, shows that the Ten Articles stand at the opening of an era of doctrinal readjustment. They bear the marks not only of compromise, but of progress, and are transitional in character. It was exactly this, the distinction between the necessary and the variable, that was the real principle of the English Reformation. The distinction took a long time to work out; and the Ten Articles are mainly important as marking the beginning of the attempt, and standing at the head of a series of formularies by which the solution was finally reached. In the five remaining Articles concerning ceremonies, the line was drawn for regulating worship much as it lay at the end of Henry VIII.'s reign. The existing customs were defended on the whole, but with caveats, specially in the case of Purgatory, where the limits of our knowledge are carefully pointed out. Perhaps this attempt to draw the line in practice was, in policy no less than in theology, the weakest part of the document. The Ten Articles served their immediate purpose if not wholly to reassure Englishmen that the realm was still Catholic, at any rate to make it clear that the government was not minded, though negotiating (1535-6, winter) for a political union with the Lutherans, to accept their theological position. They remained the authoritative expression of doctrine till 1543, when they were superseded by the King's Book.

§ 3. **The Bishops' Book**, however, intervened. This was the name given to **The Institution of a Christian Man**, a formulary put out by the Episcopate in **1537**. Possibly the Bishops felt that the Ten Articles were not complete enough to remain the standard of faith, and determined to expand them into a sum of theology to be placed in the hands of the clergy. This, at least, is the character of their venture. It incorporates much of the language of the Ten Articles. It is 'pious rather than theological'; systematic, expository, popular. So it does not stand in the direct line of the development of our Articles; for they are theological, controversial, terse and technical. Nor did it acquire either authority or permanence. The Bishops' Book never received the sanction of Convocation or Parliament; while the King conceived a dislike to it, and, after submitting it to a careful revision, put it forth the same in substance and arrangement, but much improved in coherence and learning, under the title of **A Necessary Doctrine and Erudition for any Christian Man.** This was **The King's Book 1543**. Like its predecessor, it was conceived on a plan wholly different from Articles of Religion, and neither of these two Formularies of Faith put out in Henry's reign contributed to the language or arrangement of the later series of Articles. The *Necessary Doctrine* received the sanction of Convocation, Parliament, and the Crown, and was probably designed to have been the final confession of the Church of England. But it was displaced by formularies of another type, which owe their origin to a series of Articles drafted but never published, still less authorised, under Henry VIII., and known as

§ 4. **The Thirteen Articles, 1538.** If the Ten Articles mark the attempt to reduce the dangers feared from religious strife at home, the Thirteen Articles are an episode in Henry's attempt to meet the threatening aspect of affairs abroad by an alliance with the Lutheran Princes. The Papal Bull of Excommunication had been prepared against him since 1535, though it was not published till 1538. If the Emperor, who was now in fair accord with the Pope, should take advantage of it to avenge upon Henry the treatment which his aunt Katharine had received at the King's hands, things might become serious indeed for England. Henry stood in need of allies, and naturally sought them among the Emperor's opponents, the Protestant Princes of Germany. Since 1531 they had maintained a defensive alliance on the religious basis of the Augsburg Confession, and would have been glad to welcome Henry on those terms. But he only wanted political advantage; and the first mission which he despatched to Germany in the autumn of 1535, returned without success in the spring of 1536. In the Ten Articles of the following summer, the King made his protest against Protestantism; and it was clear that he would go no further at present. But early in 1538 negotiations were re-opened, and the Protestants sent three emissaries to create a concert with England. Politically, the mission was a failure, but it led to lasting results in the domain of religion. The King appointed a small committee of bishops and doctors to confer with the German envoys. Cranmer was president, but the Old Learning was effectively represented. They proceeded upon the plan of the Augsburg Confession; and upon its first part, which dealt with the fundamentals of the Faith, came to an agreement; but upon the 'Abuses' —for so the Confession described points of observance such as Communion in One Kind, Private Masses, and Clerical Celibacy—no such concord was attainable. The conference broke up in the autumn of 1538. In the next year the Statute of Six Articles (31 Henry VIII. c. 14) enforced under penalties the very doctrines and practices which the Germans had fastened upon as abuses: and from that time forward the danger of any religious union between the English Church and the Lutheran bodies of the Continent disappeared. But though the project was wrecked, to it may be traced the Lutheran complexion of our formularies, so far as they are Lutheran. There remains among Cranmer's papers, '*A Book containing divers Articles*,' which have been successfully identified with those upon which agreement was reached in the otherwise abortive discussion between the English and Lutheran divines. They are the **Thirteen Articles of 1538.** They have never had any authority; but they are of great interest as the connecting link between the English Articles and the Augsburg Confession. Where the language of that formulary filtered into the later Edwardian and Elizabethan Articles, it was not adopted indiscriminately, but only so far as it had secured the acceptance of a committee of English divines, on which the Old Learning was well represented.

The facts may be exhibited thus:—

I. The Thirteen Articles are: 1. De Unitate Dei et Trinitate Personarum. 2. De Peccato Originali. 3. De Duabus Christi Naturis. 4. De Justificatione. 5. De Ecclesia. 6. De Baptismo. 7. De Eucharistia. 8. De Penitentia. 9. De Sacramentorum Usu. 10. De Ministris Ecclesiae. 11. De Ritibus Ecclesiasticis. 12. De Rebus Civilibus. 13. De Corporum Resurrectione et Judicio Extremo.

II. Of these:—

1 is taken verbatim from Augsb. 1, and includes No. 1 of the Forty-two Articles.

2 corresponds with Augsb. 2, and transmits certain of its phrases to No. 8 of the Forty-two. But the two Articles of English birth state the extent of the Fall with less vehemence than the German.

3 is taken verbatim from Augsb. 3, and includes No. 2 of the Forty-two.

4 is condensed from Augsb. 4, 5, 6, and 20. It repeats Melanchthon's definition of Justification in the form in which it had been adopted and improved upon in No. 5 of the Ten Articles of 1536; but has apparently contributed nothing to the language of our later formularies upon the subject.

5 takes some expressions from Augsb. 7 and 8; and, though contributing nothing to No. 20 of the Forty-two (Of the Church), includes Nos. 33 and 27 of that series,

employing language, in both cases, which is *not* found in the Augsburg Confession.

6 is fuller than Augsb. 9, though stating the same doctrine. It has much in common with No. 2 of the Ten Articles; but has not contributed to No. 28 of the Forty-two.

7 is an expansion of Augsb. 10. The exact agreement of its terms with a form concerted at Wittenberg between the Lutheran and English divines during the politically fruitless mission of 1535-6, is one of the main reasons for identifying the series in which it stands as the net result of the conferences held in England in 1538. Its phraseology contains a slight reminiscence of No. 4 of the Ten Articles, but has nothing in common with No. 29 of the Forty-two.

8 deals with the subjects of Augsb. 11 and 12, but at greater length, and without contributing to our later formularies.

9 is a lengthier reproduction of Augsb. 13, and has been the means of transferring the language of the formulary, strengthened and safeguarded, to No. 26 of the Forty-two.

10 is based upon Augsb. 14, and is the link between its language and that of No. 24 of the Forty-two, but again with improvements.

11, 12, and 13, are long dissertations in the main agreeing with Augsb. 15, 16, 17, but with no parallels in the language of the later English Articles.

§ 5. In summary, then, it may be said, that the recognised doctrinal formularies of the reign of Henry VIII. contributed nothing directly to the form or language of the later English Articles. They were three in number, the Ten Articles of 1536, the Bishops' Book of 1537, and the King's Book of 1543. If the first of the series resembled the Edwardian and Elizabethan Articles to some degree both in form, as a set of Articles, and in purpose, to avoid strife, it was merged into the first, and, with it, superseded by the second, of the two books of doctrine which were conceived on a different plan and had a purpose quite distinct from Articles of Religion. These formularies proceeded by way of expounding the Creed, the Sacraments, the Ten Commandments, and the Lord's Prayer, with a few remarks appended on controverted points. They were positive and didactic in aim, in part resembling the later English Catechism, in part anticipating the theological expositions of the Council of Trent. They are characteristic products of the Henrician Reformation. For Henry and his bishops, save for the forcible suppression of a few obscure sectaries, never had to deal with projects of reform which were out of sympathy with the ancient system of the Catholic Church. They retained it intact; and even retained it, except for the abolition of the papal authority, in its mediæval form. It is assumed in the King's Book, inculcated as a whole, and defended only where necessary. But in the next reign it was not so easily taken for granted. The purely papal accretions in doctrine, which should have logically disappeared under Henry, dropped off without difficulty. But the Reformers, while honestly reaching after the restoration of primitive truth, had to defend a position, as yet hardly recovered, from the attacks both of the mediævalist Romanensian and the revolutionary Anabaptist. They did so by throwing up works to cover p int by point of the attack, in the type of formulary which we have inherited from their necessities, and which we call Articles—disjointed (*articula*), unsystematic, and occasional defences of a controversial and cautionary character. The Edwardian Reformers had one example ready to hand in the Thirteen Articles of 1538. It was the one formulary, alien to the wants of Henry's reign, but well fitted to serve in the changed circumstances under Edward. It accordingly survived, and gave birth to others. The doctrinal reformation of Henry's days was carried further; but the type of formulary in which its results were embodied disappeared.

CHAPTER III

THE FORTY-TWO ARTICLES OF THE REIGN OF EDWARD VI.

§ 1. The history of the origin of the Forty-two Articles appears to begin toward the end of the year 1549. On December 27 of that year Hooper, writing in a letter, says that Archbishop Cranmer 'has some articles of religion, to which all preachers and lecturers in divinity are required to subscribe.' This is the first hint of any new formulary of doctrine; and it would seem to show that measures of the kind, so far from being definitely planned, merely grew up in answer to special needs. Cranmer found it necessary to adopt some test of orthodoxy, and shaped articles for the purpose which may probably be regarded as 'an early draft of the great formulary afterwards issued as the Forty-two Articles.' He submitted them to other bishops; and they were thus beginning to enter upon a public career, when in 1552 they were laid before the Council at its request (May 2) and returned to the Archbishop. He added the titles, made other modifications, and then forwarded them, now forty-five in number (September 19), to Sir William Cecil and Sir John Cheke, 'patrons of the Reformation at the Court.' They were exhibited to the King, and presently referred (October 21) to the six royal chaplains 'to make report of their opinions touching the same.' A month later they were again in the Archbishop's hands for final revision (November 20-23). The next day (November 24) he returned the draft to the Council, with a prayer for subscription to be enforced and an expression of confidence in 'the concord and quietness in religion' that would follow. But a long delay ensued. At last they were signed by the King, now forty-two in number, on June 12, 1553, and a week later subscription was enforced by a royal mandate (June 19). But it cannot have been general, for in little more than a fortnight the King died (July 6), and the Reformation was in abeyance.

The Articles, however, had been **published** in May, and were thus in circulation a fortnight or three weeks before they were authorised. There were three editions of the summer of 1553, and a brief description of them is important, because it bears on the question of the authority of the Forty-two Articles, see § 2. They were printed:—

(1) Separately—by Grafton, in English, as *Articles agreed on by the Bishops and other learned men in the Synod at London, in the year of our Lord God 1552, for the avoiding of controversy in opinions, and the establishment of a godly concord, in certain matters of Religion. Published by the King's Majesty's commandment, in the Month of May A.D. 1553. (Richardus Graftonus typographus Regius excudebat. Londini, mense Junii, An. do.* MDLIII.)

(2) In company with a Catechism, which was probably the work of Poynet, Bishop of Winchester, and had been authorised by the King on May 20, 1553:—

(a) by Wolf, in Latin, under the title: *Catechismus Brevis Christianæ disciplinæ summam continens, omnibus Ludimagistris authoritate Regia commendatus. Huic Catechismo adjuncti sunt Articuli, de quibus in ultima Synodo Londinensi A.D. 1552 ad tollendum opinionum dissensionem, et consensum veræ religionis firmandum, inter Episcopos et alios eruditos atque pios viros convenerat: Regia similiter authoritate promulgati. (Excusum Londini apud Reginaldum Wolfium, Regiæ Majestatis in Latinis Typographum, A.D.* MDLIII.)

(b) by Day, in English, under the title: *A Short Catechism, or plain instruction, containing the sum of Christian learning, set forth by the King's Majesty's authority, for all Schoolmasters to teach. To this Catechism are adjoined the Articles agreed upon by the Bishops and other learned and godly men, in the last convocation at London, in the year of our Lord* MDLII, *for to root out the discord of opinions, and stablish the agreement of true religion: Likewise published by the King's Majesty's authority,* 1553. (*Imprinted at London by John Day.*)

§ 2. We are now in a position to approach the difficult question of the **authority of the Forty-two Articles**. Did they receive the sanction of Convocation, or not?

Convocation was sitting from March 22 to April 1, 1553. Its records were burned in the fire of London; but, according to historians who had access to them before that disaster, they were 'but one degree above blank;' and no evidence is forthcoming from them either way. There is, however, an antecedent improbability that the Articles would have figured in the minutes of the Synod at all. The 16th century was an age of religious uniformity, enforced by the State for political ends with weapons of its own; and the government of a strong but partisan minority, such as was the government of Edward vi., while it had something to fear from applying to Convocation, had nothing to gain. Nor did precedent, if it regarded any, point necessarily that way. 'The synodical authority that many good things had before the Reformation was often simply diocesan.' But now diocesan synods had been abolished, and the convocations, or provincial synods, had been reduced to the position of appendages to Parliament, which met only for the purposes of clerical taxation. Under such circumstances, the ecclesiastical measures of Tudor governments were carried through by the safer and simpler expedients of commissions of court bishops and conformable divines. Thus, so far as there is evidence for ascribing the authorship of the Forty-two Articles to Cranmer, it points to a commission of this kind appointed in 1551-2 to reform the Canon Law of the Church. There is a strong resemblance between the *Reformatio Legum Ecclesiasticarum* and the Edwardian Articles: and these two works were probably the joint production of at least the working members of one and the same commission, Cranmer in company with Peter Martyr and others.

To return however to the authority of the latter formulary. We are thrown back upon the titles to the Articles themselves; and, at first sight, they seem to be distinctly assigned to 'the Synod at London' of 1552-3. But in the next reign events happened which throw doubt upon the point. Six months after the supposed synodical authority had been given, Convocation met again, in October 1553. Weston, the prolocutor, complained that the Catechism 'bore the name of the honourable synod, although, as he understood, put forth without their consent.' It was admitted in reply that as to 'the Articles of the Catechism' (a curious but accurate phrase) the synod 'had no notice thereof before the promulgation': though it was argued that they might claim synodical authority indirectly, because the House had authorised persons to make ecclesiastical laws, and what was done by its delegates was done by itself. The allusion was probably to the commission just mentioned, but it was a lame defence. The next, made by Cranmer in the following spring, was lamer still. In April 1554, he was taxed by Weston at Oxford with having 'set forth a Catechism in the name of the Synod of London: and yet there be fifty, which, witnessing that they were of the number of the Convocation, never heard one word of this Catechism.' Now it is clear that by the 'Catechism' Weston here meant to refer to 'the Articles of,' or appended to, 'the Catechism,' as his opponent had phrased it in Convocation six months before. For the Catechism itself professes to rest on no authority but that of the King: nor does Cranmer reply, as we might have expected, by denying that the Catechism claimed sanction of the synod. His answer shows that the book as a whole was commonly known as the Catechism, and naturally enough, for the Catechism occupies thirty pages, and the Articles only eleven, out of a total of fifty-five. He confines himself to that part of it which claimed synodical authority, namely, the Articles alone, and admits their title to be misleading, while disowning all responsibility for it. 'I was ignorant,' he said, 'of the setting to of that title, and as soon as I had knowledge thereof I did not like it: therefore when I complained thereof to the Council, it was answered me of them that the Book was so entitled because it was set forth in the time of the Convocation.' But even that was untrue; for, as Parliament was dissolved in March, Convocation would not have been sitting when the Articles were published in May. It is true that two letters contemporary with their publication repeat the claim to synodical authority; and it seems to have been tacitly assumed in the year of their revival, 1563. But this was only in reliance upon the titles themselves, as they appeared in the three printed editions. When the King, in June 1553, issued letters to the bishops to compel subscription, he said nothing of the 'Synod at London,' but only declared the Articles to have been 'devised and gathered with great study, and by the learned and good advice of the greatest learned part of our bishops of the realm, and sundry others of our clergy.' The title of the earliest edition, that of Grafton, is consistent with this statement; though Wolf's and Day's insinuate more. The question is not settled; but with the facts of the case now before us, and having regard to the Tudor ways of doing things by select committees of court divines, it is probable that the Forty-two Articles had not synodical authority. In that case, the Church of England was not committed to them, even for the brief space of seven weeks which elapsed between their publication by the authority of Edward vi. and his death.

§ 3. The object of the Forty-two Articles is to be gathered from their contents and the circumstances of their compilation. (1) They look like an *unsystematic* collection with a *temporary* object in view. This is clear from their title. For, as dealing only with 'certain matters of Religion,' they do not profess to proceed on any plan: and, as meant merely 'for the avoiding of controversy in opinions,' they aim only at meeting a passing need. And this is quite in harmony with their history. Earlier in Edward's reign Cranmer had invited the continental reformers to join him in framing a common reformed confession: and his plan was to confine it to 'the several heads under dispute at the present day.' That project failed; but the national formulary which he took in hand instead followed the lines he had intended. This was also the method of the *Reformatio Legum Ecclesiasticarum*, a work, as we have seen, of nearly the same hands as the Forty-two Articles, and by consequence an excellent commentary on them. In its chapter on Heresies, it professes to deal exclusively with 'those of our own times.' But a comparison of the Forty-two Articles with the Thirty-nine gives the same impression. Beyond the general statement of the doctrine of the Trinity in Article 1, the earlier series omits any exposition of the Divinity of our Lord, and contains no article on the Holy Ghost. Article 5 asserts the sufficiency of Scripture, but says nothing of the Canon, and gives no list of the accepted books. There is not a word of Confirmation or Penance. On the other hand, Articles and clauses of the earlier series, apart from such as were felt in 1563 to proceed from a doctrinal standpoint then abandoned (*e.g.* Art. 29, § 3), were dropped in that year as obsolete or unnecessary, *e.g.*, the protest against *ex opere operato* (*cf.* Art. 26, § 2), a favourite phrase of the Mediævalists, which had been rendered innocuous before 1563; while several Articles and clauses, directed against Anabaptist errors which had died down in the interval, (*cf.* Art. 10, 16, 19, 39-42; and clauses in 8, etc.) also fell out. (2) What, then, it may be asked, was this temporary object? It was 'the establishment of a godly concord,' as the title says. In other words, the Forty-two Articles must be classed with the other measures of Edward's advisers. They were for the promotion of religious uniformity, and are *governmental* in object. No sooner had the Council learned (May 1552) that the Archbishop had a series of Articles at hand, than it demanded them for its own purposes. The remedy for religious division in our day is toleration. In those days it was uniformity. Not a government or a man in Europe but would have taken it for an axiom that the toleration of religious differences must be fatal to national security. So uniformity was enforced, by consent of Church and State, not simply because religious differences were as yet a new thing in the region of belief, but in the interest of public safety. When Cranmer returned his final draft of the Forty-two Articles to the Council, he urged that the clergy might be made 'to subscribe to the said Articles,' and anticipated as a result 'such a concord and quietness in religion . . . as else it is not to be looked for many years.' The Council took the same view, and regarded them as an admirable governmental engine. They were issued to secure a uniformity of doctrine; and there are traces of a twin series of fifty-four which were to have been published concurrently for a uniformity in ceremonies. This was not done in time: but no sooner were the Forty-two Articles put forth than they were made to serve the ends of governmental uniformity by the usual process of being offered for subscription under mandate from the King. This is the clue to a right estimate of

§ 4. **Their character.**—As a formulary adopted by the government to meet the needs of a temporary crisis, the Forty-two Articles are both *moderate* and *comprehensive*. 'The broad soft touch of Cranmer lay upon them' from the beginning, and the Council found in his work exactly what would serve their turn. Extremists were struck at, and the rest given scope. Who then were the extreme men?

(1) On the one side stood the **Mediævalists**, or supporters of 'the doctrine of the School authors,' various elements of which are expressly condemned in Arts. 12, 13, 23, 26, 29, 30. These tenets, it should be observed, are not necessarily to be identified with the official teaching of the Church of Rome, as settled at the Council of Trent, 1545-1563. That Council was proceeding concurrently with the formulation of our Articles. Where, then, there are statements relating to the same subject in the decisions of the two Churches, each case has to be taken on its merits; and, until it has been asked whether the English condemnation of any particular point in doctrine or discipline was uttered before or after the corresponding decision at Trent, it cannot be said that our Articles are aimed at the teaching of the Roman Church. In the main, it will be found that they deal rather with the current teaching of the later mediæval or pre-Tridentine period. Moreover, the Council of Trent was itself a reforming Council, and did not adopt the position of the Mediævalist without modification, either as found in the doctrine of the Schoolmen or in the current popular religion of the early 16th century. At the same time very little change took place at Trent with regard to the claims made for the Roman See, and the denial of independent action on the part of local churches. Where the English Articles take their own line upon such points, they came into conflict with the Church

of Rome from the first, as in Arts. 20, 21, 22, 25, 31, 33, 35, 36.

(2) **The Anabaptists** stood at the opposite extreme; and the condemnation of their errors occupies by far the larger part of the Forty-two Articles. No set of men earn such hatred as those who carry a revolution further than its accredited chiefs are willing to go. The Edwardian reformers had allied themselves with a political faction ready for revolution in doctrine for the sake of a revolution in property. The Anabaptists returned or revived after the death of Henry VIII., and were seen to be at once the enemies of social order and the subverters not of the outworks but of the citadel of the Christian faith. It was essential therefore for the leaders of the Reformation to save its credit by repudiating the teaching of these fanatics with especial vigour. Accordingly, from 1549 onwards, we find measures taken against them in rapid succession. The sect took root chiefly in the south-eastern counties, nearest the Continent. In 1549 a commission was appointed which condemned Joan of Kent; the Anabaptists were exempted from the general pardon, and engaged the attention of the Court-preacher Hooper. Early in 1550 many were forced to recant by a royal commission; and Ridley, now Bishop of London, sought out their conventicles, and put them down. They were thus the first separatists or dissenters from the Church of England. In September 1552 Cranmer was authorised, in another commission, to proceed against a sect which professed to have advanced further than hitherto, and was then known as Davidians, followers of a Dutchman named David George, but afterwards as the Family of Love. When the Forty-two Articles appeared in the following May 1553, it is not surprising that they were largely directed against these growing errors. To limit or to classify them is equally impossible. Some were mystical in tendency, some rationalist, some antinomian. The name Anabaptist represents but one error among many, namely their objection to Infant Baptism; perhaps the most offensive, perhaps the earliest, or perhaps the only one of their tenets common to all. But we may

best gather the character of their false teaching from two letters written at the time when the Forty-two Articles were in preparation:—

Hooper, writing on June 25, 1549, says:—'The Anabaptists flock to the place, and give me much trouble with their opinions respecting the Incarnation of our Lord; for they deny altogether that Christ was born of the Virgin Mary according to the flesh. They contend that a man who is reconciled to God is without sin, and free from all stain of concupiscence, and that nothing of the old Adam remains in his nature; and a man, they say, who is thus regenerate cannot sin. They add that all hope of pardon is taken away from those who, after having received the Holy Ghost, fall into sin. They maintain a fatal necessity, and that beyond and besides that will of His, which He has revealed to us in the Scriptures, God hath another will by which He altogether acts under some kind of necessity. Although I am unable to satisfy their obstinacy, yet the Lord by His Word shuts their mouths, and their heresies are more and more detested by the people. How dangerously our England is afflicted by heresies of this kind, God only knows; I am unable indeed from sorrow of heart to express to your piety. There are some who deny that a man is endued with a soul different from that of a beast, and subject to decay. Alas! not only are these heresies reviving among us which were formerly dead and buried, but new ones are springing up every day. There are such libertines and wretches who are daring enough, in their conventicles, not only to deny that Christ is the Messiah and Saviour of the world, but also to call that blessed Seed a mischievous fellow and deceiver of the world. On the other hand, a great portion of the kingdom so adheres to the popish faction as altogether to set at nought God and the lawful authority of the magistrates; so that I am greatly afraid of a rebellion and civil discord.'

Micronius writes on August 14, 1551, to the same effect:—'We have not only to contend with the papists who are almost everywhere ashamed of their errors, but much more with the sectaries, and Epicureans, and pseudo-evangelicals. In addition to the ancient errors respecting pædo-baptism, the Incarnation of Christ, the authority of the magistrate, the lawfulness of an oath, the property and community of goods, and the like, new ones are rising up every day, with which we have to contend. The chief opponents, however, of Christ's Divinity are the Arians who are now beginning to shake our Churches with greater violence than ever, as they deny the conception of Christ by the Virgin.'

It was then against the errors of the Anabaptists,

rather than against those of the Mediævalists, that the main attack of the Forty-two Articles, as a governmental and sedative formulary, was delivered. They are only mentioned by name in two, Arts. 8 and 37: but they are unquestionably the persons aimed at in 6, 14, 15, 18, 19, in each of which a definite set of persons is named: while tenets known to have been held among them are covered by the language of Arts. 24, 27, 28, 32, 33, 36, 38, 39, 40, 41, 42. Even those articles which look unpolemical, and contain restatement of the fundamentals of the Creed (Arts. 1-4) or an assertion of its authority (Art. 7), were inserted not to round off the formulary and give it the systematic air of a Confession, but because it was necessary to reaffirm the Church's adherence to essentials in view of the fact that some of the Anabaptists 'abandoned every semblance of belief in the doctrine of the Holy Trinity, and so passed over to the Arian and Socinian schools, then rising up in Switzerland, in Italy, and in Poland.'

(3.) But the tone of comprehensive moderation which the authors of the Forty-two Articles adopted in order to combat Mediævalists and Anabaptists, was not maintained in the doctrine of the Sacraments. Their sacramental standard was low, and they adopted several positions from which the Elizabethan series afterwards receded. This was due, in the main, to two causes (*a*) the downward course of Cranmer's beliefs about the Eucharist; and (*b*) the vehement disputes that had arisen between Cranmer and Ridley on the one side, and Hooper on the other as to the question, whether the sacraments confer grace (May 1550). According to Peter Martyr, a most competent witness, it was these disputes (and so not the desire, as has been supposed, for convocational sanction), that caused the long delay in the publication of the Articles, from November 1552 to May 1553. 'Whether grace be conferred by virtue of the sacraments,' he wrote at this time, 'is a sticking-place to many. Some would have it altogether affirmed: others see clearly the superstitions that such a sentence would bring with it. Many who are not unlearned or evil otherwise, will have it that children are not regenerate before baptism: and insist that grace is conferred by the sacraments.' It was this point, among others, that divided the Saxon from the Swiss reformers; and the two schools of their followers were now struggling for ascendency in England. It was agreed, on both sides, to reject the formula of the Schoolmen, who taught that the sacraments *contain* grace. That expression failed, as was thought, to insist with sufficient emphasis on the right disposition of the recipient as a necessary condition for the appropriation of the divine gifts. The Lutherans preferred to say that the sacraments *confer* grace; and, though that particular phrase did not find its way into the Forty-two Articles its substance appears in such assertions as that 'Sacraments be *effectual* signs of grace' (Art. 26) and 'Baptism a sign and seal of our new birth, whereby, *as by an instrument*, they that receive Baptism rightly are grafted in the Church' (Art. 28). This was the utmost concession which Peter Martyr and the Swiss faction could wring out of the 'many . . . not unlearned or evil otherwise,' among whom Cranmer stood first. He refrained from employing the objectionable phrase, but took care to emphasise the truth it was meant to guard, viz. : that the sacraments are means of grace, *i.e.* that God is responsible for human salvation. The Swiss, hampered by Calvin's theory that all men entered the world predestinated either to salvation or reprobation, could only look upon the sacraments as affecting the elect. They spoke of them not as *effectual* signs; but as signs *obsignatory* of a grace which was independently received.

But while the Forty-two Articles did not descend to this level upon the doctrine of the sacraments in general, they did sound the utmost depths in their doctrine of the Eucharist. This was again due to the influence of reformers of the Swiss type over the mind of their maker, Cranmer, specially of one John à Lasco. By the beginning of 1550, the Archbishop had been brought to abandon the doctrine of the Real Presence of Our Lord in the Sacrament, a belief as strongly held by Lutheran as by Mediævalist, and had become what is now called a Receptionist. Christ is present, according to this doctrine, not in the Sacrament, but in the worthy receiver: not by virtue of the act of Consecration, but by virtue of each act of Communion. Accordingly Art. 29 denies 'the real and bodily presence ... of Christ's flesh and blood, in the Sacrament of the Lord's supper.' Again, Art. 26 tacitly refuses a sacramental character to the five ordinances, other than Baptism and the Eucharist, which hitherto had enjoyed it, and denies that the sacraments are efficacious *ex opere operato*, in any sense. But all these negations were repudiated in 1563.

§ 5. One word as to the sources of the Forty-two Articles. They owe their origin to the controversies, and their character to the controversial exigencies, of the time. But they have their affinities with earlier documents, immediately with the Thirteen Articles of 1538 and through them with the Augsburg Confession of 1530. On comparing the Forty-two Articles with the Confession of Augsburg, it is clear at once that the English document is indebted to the German: but the debt is indirect. The clauses common to both are all found in the Thirteen Articles of 1538. Other language of the Forty-two Articles is traceable to this series, but not beyond it. There are but six in all which have drawn, through the Thirteen Articles, upon the Confession of Augsburg, viz.: Articles 1, 2, 24, 26, 27, 33, and, on examination of these, it appears that the debt of the Forty-two Articles to Lutheranism is a limited one. For the six deal only with the Holy Trinity, the Incarnation, the Ministry, the Sacraments, and the Traditions of the Church; not with the vexed questions of justification, etc., which Lutheranism brought to the front. The reason of this is to be sought, as has been already indicated, in the independent spirit which actuated the English divines who conducted the negotiations with the Lutherans under Henry VIII., and which never wholly forsook Cranmer. For instance, upon the burning question of justification, on which, in 1536, he had joined others in adopting a Lutheran definition, but in a strengthened form, he broke away from the Lutheran language altogether in 1553. Similarly, as he had in 1538 improved upon the Lutheran doctrine of the sacraments by adding that they are *effectual* signs of grace, so in 1553 by retaining this phrase, in spite of the Swiss protests, Cranmer manifests the chief debt of the Edwardian formulary to Lutheranism, namely its escape from the denial of sacramental grace, and, at the same time, he exhibits the freedom with which he treated his original. It thus appears that where Lutheranism had distinctive tenets of its own they were not reproduced in the Forty-two Articles, which are mainly indebted to it where its leading Confession repeats the language of Catholic theology. The declining influence of German Protestantism abroad after the Schmalkaldic War (1547), and its fall before the rising star of the Swiss faction in England about 1550, sufficiently account for the attenuated traces which it has left upon the Forty-two Articles. The brevity of statement and the comparative avoidance of controversy which they maintain are among the best proofs of independence. Where they resemble the *Reformatio Legum*, it is impossible to say which is the original, but only that both bear marks of a common workmanship.

CHAPTER IV

THE THIRTY-NINE ARTICLES OF THE REIGN OF ELIZABETH

§ 1. **The delay** that ensued between the accession of Elizabeth, November 17, 1558, and her revival of the doctrinal formulary of Edward's reign, must be put down to the situation of her government. Committed to a policy of watchful isolation abroad, it was her first care to secure religious peace at home. To this end the Queen at once proceeded to make provision for discipline and worship, and deferred the doctrinal settlement till a reconstituted hierarchy, with the powers of the Crown at its back, should have succeeded in re-imposing some measure of outward uniformity. By the 'Act restoring to the Crown the ancient jurisdiction over the State ecclesiastical and spiritual' (1 Eliz. c. 1), the Queen recovered the rights of the Crown over the Church, and also acquired new machinery to supplement the authority of the bishops, in restoring order. By the 'Act for the Uniformity of Common Prayer' (1 Eliz. c. 2), the new standard of worship to be enforced was set up. By the re-constitution of the hierarchy, which took place upon the consecration of Archbishop Parker, December 17, 1559, leaders were provided to see the settlement through. These measures had their effect. Only a small proportion of the clergy refused compliance. By 1563, when Convocation was invited to take in hand the revision of the Forty-two Articles in order to provide a permanent formulary of doctrine, it settled down quite congenially to the task.

The Archbishop, however, had found it necessary to put out on his own authority a temporary test, now

THE THIRTY-NINE ARTICLES 39

known as **The Eleven Articles**. It was compiled, under his own eye, about the time of his consecration, in 1559 or early in 1560. It had the sanction of the northern metropolitan and other bishops. It was the first tentative measure of the new reign designed 'for the uniformity of doctrine'; and the part which it played in the effort now set on foot for the restoration of Church order may be best inferred from the fact that it was appointed 'to be read by . . . parsons, vicars, and curates at their . . . first entry into their cures, and also after that, yearly at two several times . . . immediately after the Gospel.' Thus the Eleven Articles had real, but not formally binding, authority. They lacked the ratification of the Crown and the sanction of Convocation. But they served their turn in England; and after being legalised in 1566 for Ireland, remained the sole doctrinal formulary of the Irish Church till 1615. They are still of importance in the interpretation of the Thirty-nine Articles which superseded them, as an authentic record of the mind of the English Episcopate at the time.

§ 2. **The revision of 1563** took place in the Convocation which had been summoned by a writ of November 11, 1562, and met on January 12, 1563. In the interval the Archbishop had been at work on the Articles, with the aid, as it seems, of Guest, Bishop of Rochester. They adopted, as the basis of the revision, the Latin Articles of 1553: and there still exists, among the Parker MSS. at Corpus Christi College, Cambridge, a copy of the Articles in Latin as presented by the Primate to the Synod, with marks of corrections made there, and the signatures of bishops who subscribed it after they were made. We are thus enabled to trace exactly the changes made by the Archbishop, and then those made by the Synod :

(I.) *The formulary, as presented by the Archbishop to the Synod*, consisted like the Edwardian series of forty-two Articles ; for—
 (1) Four Articles had been added :—
  (*a*) Of the Holy Ghost (Art. 5), (*b*) Of Good Works (Art. 12), (*c*) Of the Wicked, etc. (Art. 29), (*d*) Of Both Kinds (Art. 30).

(2) Four Articles had been taken away:—
  (a) Of Grace (Art. 10), (b) Of Sin against the Holy Ghost (Art. 15), (c) Of the Law (Art. 19), (d) Of Hereticks called Millenarii (Art. 41).
(3) Seventeen others were modified either by way of amplification or curtailment.

Obs. It will be better to reserve comments on the changes made in the revision till we have traced out its course to the end. But this is the point for noticing *the second and last occasion on which our Articles were indebted to the influence of Lutheran formularies.* The Forty-two Articles borrowed indirectly from the Augsburg Confession through the medium of the Thirteen Articles of 1538. The Thirty-nine Articles have borrowed directly from the **Würtemberg Confession of 1552.** Parker and Guest were among the few reforming divines who had not consulted their safety by flight in the reign of Mary. The Archbishop disliked the Swiss theology and discipline which was found to have cast such a spell over the exiles on their return from Zurich and Geneva. Projects of political alliance with the Lutherans, which had been talked of in the first few months of the Queen's reign, had fallen through, or been dropped, with her growing security, as unnecessary: but Parker found material, in one of the later Lutheran formularies, upon which he might draw to supplement the deficiencies of the English Articles that he now had under review. This was the Confession of Würtemberg, a document drawn up, on the basis of that of Augsburg, for presentation by the ambassadors of the Lutheran State of Würtemberg at the Council of Trent in January 1552. From it the Archbishop borrowed:—

1. In Art. 2 the clause touching the eternal generation and consubstantiality of the Son.
2. Art. 5, Of the Holy Ghost.
3. In Art. 6 the statement that those books are to be taken as Canonical 'of whose authority was never any doubt in the Church.'
4. In Art. 10 the statement that man 'cannot turn and prepare himself by his own natural strength and good works, to faith and calling upon God.'
5. In Art. 11 the assertion that 'we are accounted righteous before God only for the merit of Our Lord and Saviour Jesus Christ, by faith.'
6. In Art. 12 the statement that good works 'cannot endure the severity of God's judgment.'
7. In Art. 20 (Of the Authority of the Church) a hint for its assertion that 'the Church hath authority in controversies of faith.'

Such was the extent of the obligation. Parker did not hesitate in Article 11 to make use of Lutheran language upon the point of Justification. But neither here, nor in the other phrases he borrowed which deal mainly with fundamentals, was there any departure from Catholic standards.

(II.) On January 19, 1563, it is on record that *the Synod began to consider the Articles*. They were signed by the bishops on the 29th : but by the erasure of Arts. 39, 40, and 42 of the Edwardian series, all dealing with tenets of Anabaptism now moribund, they had been reduced, for the first time, to the familiar number of **Thirty-nine Articles**. Other changes had also been introduced, to be noticed later ; but they were such as readily commended themselves to the Lower House where the amended draft arrived on February 5, and was generally signed by February 10. The Articles were then laid before the Queen in Council, published in Latin by Wolf, the Queen's printer, and ratified 'after having been carefully read and examined by the Queen herself.'

(III.) But as *published* the Articles were *only thirty-eight* in number : and Wolf's copy differs in two respects from the MS. as signed by the bishops on January 29 :

(1) It prefixes to Art. 20 the clause stating that 'The Church hath power to decree Rites or Ceremonies, and authority in controversies of faith.'

(2) It omits Art. 29, 'Of the wicked which do not eat the body of Christ in the use of the Lord's Supper.'

Both these changes were probably due to the Queen herself. The first was directed against the Puritan limitation of the right of the Church to legislate for herself in matters of ceremonies and doctrines : a limitation which would, if admitted, have rendered her common life impossible. The omission of Art. 29 was prompted by a desire to conciliate the Roman party and embrace them, if possible, within the limits of the English Church. It seems then, that neither of these alterations possessed synodical authority as yet. But the first clause of Art. 20 was successfully vindicated : and at the last revision Art. 29 was re-adopted by the bishops. It should be added also that, though the Parker MS.

contained the signatures of the Archbishop of York and his two suffragans of Durham and Chester, the Northern Convocation took no part in the revision of the Articles. Such concurrence as those signatures implied was only supplemented in 1605, when the Convocation of York formally accepted the Thirty-nine Articles.

§ 3. We may now proceed to a comparison of the **Thirty-nine with the Forty-two Articles.** Dr. Gibson illustrates it by 'the following conspectus of the principal changes introduced in 1563,' and says 'it will enable the reader to see without difficulty the importance of the revision, and the very real difference in tone and character that exists between the Elizabethan Articles and those of Edward's reign.'

> Obs. *Italics* denote the changes made by the Archbishop before the draft was submitted to the Synod. Ordinary type, those made by the bishops. **Heavy type**, the two changes mentioned as probably due to the Queen herself.

A. Additions.
  I. Four new Articles :—
   5. *Of the Holy Ghost.*
   12. *Of good works.*
   29. *Of the wicked*, etc.
      Omitted before publication; restored in 1571.
   30. *Of both kinds.*
  II. Clauses in other Articles :—
   2. '*Begotten from everlasting of the Father, the very and eternal God, of one substance with the Father.*'
   6. The clauses on the Canon of Scripture with the list of the canonical books of the Old Testament, and specimens of the Apocrypha.
   7. The clause on the Ceremonial and the Moral Law. ('Although the law . . . moral.' This clause was drawn from Article 19 of 1553.)
   8. '*And believed.*'
   10. 'The condition of man after the fall of Adam is such that he cannot turn and prepare himself by his own natural strength and good works to faith and calling upon God.'

17. *'In Christ.'*
20. **The Church hath power to decree Rites or Ceremonies, and authority in controversies of faith.'**
25. *The two clauses on the number of the Sacraments, and the five rites 'commonly called Sacraments.'*
28. *'Overthroweth the nature of a Sacrament.'*
- 31. *'The body of Christ is given, taken, and eaten in the Supper only after an heavenly and spiritual manner: and the mean whereby the body of Christ is received and eaten in the Supper is faith.'*
33. *'Every particular or national Church hath authority to ordain, change, and abolish ceremonies or rites of the Church, ordained only by man's authority, so that all things be done to edifying.'*
36. *The explanation of the Royal Supremacy ('Where we attribute . . . evil doers.')*

B. Omissions.
  I. Seven complete Articles :—
    10. *Of grace.*
    16. *Blasphemy against the Holy Ghost.*
    19. *All men are bound to keep the moral commandments of the Law.* (Omitted as a separate article : but part of it was embodied in Art. 7 of 1563. See above.)
    39. The resurrection of the dead is not yet brought to pass.
    40. The souls of them that depart this life do not die with the bodies nor sleep idly.
    41. *Heretics called Millenarii.*
    42. All men shall not be saved at the length.
  II. Clauses in other Articles :—
    3. 'For the body lay in the sepulchre until the resurrection : but his ghost departing from him was with the ghosts that were in prison, or in hell, and did preach to the same, as the place of S. Peter doth testify.'
    5. *'Although it be sometime received of the faithful as godly and profitable for an order and comeliness.'*
    8. *'Which also the Anabaptists do nowadays renew.'*

17. '*Although the decrees of predestination are unknown to us.*'
26. '*Our Lord Jesus Christ hath knit together a company of new people with Sacraments, most few in number, most easy to be kept, most excellent in signification, as is Baptism and the Lord's Supper.*'
   '*And yet not that of the work wrought* [ex opere operato] *as some men speak, which word, as it is strange and unknown to Holy Scripture, so it engendereth no godly but a very superstitious sense.*'
29. '*Forasmuch as the truth of man's nature requireth that the body of one and the self-same man cannot be at one time in divers places, but must needs be in some one certain place: therefore the body of Christ cannot be present at one time in many and divers places. And because (as holy Scripture doth teach) Christ was taken up into heaven, and there shall continue unto the end of the world, a faithful man ought not either to believe or openly to confess the real and bodily presence (as they term it) of Christ's flesh and blood in the Sacrament of the Lord's Supper.*'
36. '*The civil Magistrate is ordained and allowed of God: wherefore we must obey him, not only for fear of punishment, but also for conscience sake.*'

C. Substitutions and other changes.
   I. Articles rewritten:—
      11. *Of the justification of man.*
      24. *Of speaking in the congregation in such a tongue as the people understandeth.*
      32. *Of the marriage of priests.*
      35. *Of homilies.*
      36. *Of consecration of bishops and ministers.*
   II. Other changes:—
      22. '*The Romish doctrine*' was substituted for '*The doctrine of school authors.*'
      25. The order of the clauses was reversed.
      27. The clause on Infant Baptism was re-written.
      37. The first paragraph was rewritten ("The Queen's Majesty hath the chief power in this realm of

England and other her dominions, unto whom the chief government of all estates of this realm, whether they be ecclesiastical or civil, in all causes doth appertain, and is not, nor ought to be, subject to any foreign jurisdiction' was substituted for 'The King of England is supreme head in earth, next under Christ, of the Church of England and Ireland.')

Now the effect of these changes was to give to the Thirty-nine Articles, by contrast with the formularies that preceded them, an aspect of (1) **completeness**, (2) **Catholicity**, and (3) **independence**, or, in one word, something of a *final* and *permanent* character.

(1) It is plainly with a view to **completing** the teaching of the formulary upon fundamentals that the addition was made to Art. 2 of a statement upon the Divinity of the Son; and perhaps this was the motive for the introduction into Art. 10 of a more adequate definition on the freedom of the will and its forfeiture by Adam's fall. The insertion of Art. 5, on the Holy Spirit, can only have been prompted by a similar wish to round off the treatment of the doctrine of the Trinity. The desire for completeness was further associated with a desire for something permanent and comprehensive. Hence the omission of points likely to raise or revive unnecessary differences. Thus the disappearance of some types of Anabaptism accounts for the excision of a provocative allusion in Art. 9, for the dropping of a clause in Art. 36, and for the entire omission of Arts. 39-42. So too the Romanensian party, as they were called, a party still within the English Church, were to be conciliated by the temporary but politic withdrawal of Art. 29 on publication; and by omitting in Art. 25 to censure a phrase (*ex opere operato*) which, as recent controversy had proved, could be made use of without risk of confounding the efficacy of the Sacraments with their mechanical administration. It must be confessed, as will be shown presently, that the Thirty-nine Articles did not spare the feelings of that party on other points. But it was the mode of Christ's presence in the Mass that made most matter of difference for the time, and so their feelings were

consulted so long as the hope of a possible comprehension remained. In the same way care was taken to avoid points of theology, which might either be regarded as legitimately open to discussion, such as the meaning of Our Lord's descent into Hell (Art. 3) and the nature of Blasphemy against the Holy Ghost (Art. 16), or which were merely inscrutable, such as the supposed Divine Decrees (Art. 17), mentioned in that Article in 1553 and now rising into ominous prominence with the growth of Calvinism. All this points to a real desire for peace and permanence as the mark of the formulary now to be put forth. But a caution must be added. Complete it is not, nor was intended to be, in the sense of 'a full and systematic body of theology—reaching to all topics and sufficient for all times.' Many matters of faith are not dealt with by the Articles; nor are they the solitary formulary expressive of the Church's mind. Where they are affirmative they express it: but they are oftener content to censure error without expounding the corresponding truth. Then they have to be supplemented by the Prayer Book and other writings invested with a like authority. The Book of Articles, says Bishop Pearson, 'is not, nor is pretended to be, a complete body of divinity, or a comprehension and explication of all Christian doctrines necessary to be taught; but an enumeration of some truths, which upon and since the Reformation have been denied by some persons; who upon their denial are thought unfit to have any cure of souls in this Church or realm; because they might by their opinions either infect their flock with error, or else disturb the Church with schism, or the realm with sedition.'

(2) To assert **the Catholic position of the Church of England** as now nearing the end of her Reformation was, at least, as dear to the heart of the revisers of the Articles as the wish to fill up gaps in the work of their predecessors. It should be remembered that the last sessions of the Council of Trent were being held at the same time as the English Archbishop and Synod were busy with the Articles. It was these sessions that gave the air of finality to the new Romish system, and claimed for it a

monopoly of the title to Catholicity. But the two assemblies were watching each other: and our English divines, if less attracted by the prize of dogmatic precision than those of Trent, were equally bent on vindicating the right of the Church of England to be reckoned Catholic. Accordingly they re-wrote Art. 11 on Justification in terms at once more definite and scriptural, and added Art. 12 on Good Works to clear themselves of all association with Solifidianism.[1] With an eye to exclude the claim to election made on grounds of mere fatalism, they reverted to the scriptural phrase that the chosen of God are 'those whom he hath chosen *in Christ*' (Art. 17). But the sacramental articles of the Edwardian formulary were, as we have seen, those which most risked its credit for Catholicity. The Elizabethan revisers deliberately pulled up the tone of these to raise them above all suspicion. Thus in Art. 25, by making a distinction between the two 'Sacraments of the Gospel,' and 'those five commonly called Sacraments,' now for the first time enumerated, they assigned to Baptism and the Eucharist an assured pre-eminence, but at the same time recognised a sacramental character in the other rites. They also struck out from this place the protest against *ex opere operato*, and by so doing took away the appearance of exchanging the belief that 'Sacraments are effectual because of Christ's institution and promise' for the notion that would make them merely dependent on the faith of the recipient. They strengthened the language of Art. 27 on Infant Baptism; and, in Art. 28 dropped the paragraph which rejected 'the real and bodily presence (as they term it) of Christ's flesh and blood.' In its place they inserted a clause to the effect that 'the body of Christ is given, taken, and eaten in the Supper only after an heavenly and spiritual manner.' Bishop Guest, its author, has left it on record that it was intended 'not to deny the reality of the presence of the body of Christ in the Supper, but only the grossness and sensibleness in the receiving thereof.' Finally, Art. 37 by merely claiming for the Crown the 'chief government' of all its subjects, and expressly disclaiming for it any assumption of sacerdotal functions,

[1] See the comment on Art. 12 for an explanation of the term.

removed the offence which every Catholic would feel if any other than Christ Himself were called 'Supreme Head' of the Church, and any other than duly ordained ministers of His intruded into the ministering 'either of God's Word or of sacraments.'

(3) But to claim **the independence of the English Church** was the further purpose of those who framed the Articles. Papist and Puritan had not yet ranged themselves as religious parties outside the Church of the nation; and care had been taken, as we have seen, not to drive out the former. But, looking out for the moment over the wider field of European history, the Articles, it should be observed, took final shape at the end of the Reformation period. About the year 1563 every reforming movement had settled down on distinctive lines of its own. The day of conciliation was past, specially as between the Church of England and the Church of Rome. The Articles therefore took an independent line on matters still in dispute, and defined, even with some additional sharpness, several outstanding differences. Thus in Art. 6 a clause was 'dropped, as it would seem, upon the ground that toleration ought on no account to be conceded to ecclesiastical usages which stood at variance with express injunctions of the Word of God,' and the list of the Canonical Scriptures differed from that adopted by the Council of Trent seventeen years previously. The rejection of the claim of the five sacramental rites to be placed on a level with Baptism and the Eucharist in Art. 25, the contention that transubstantiation 'overthroweth the nature of a sacrament' in Art. 28, the original insertion of Art. 29 (on the wicked which eat not, etc.), the addition of the word 'blasphemous' in Art. 31, which looks like an answer to a challenge contained in one of the Canons of Trent; and the assignation of certain views as to Purgatory, etc., in Art. 22, no longer to the 'school authors,' but to the Romanensian or 'Romish' party, evince the independent spirit of watchful distrust with which the English divines pursued the current doctrine now in process of taking final form abroad. Discipline too was undergoing the same sort of crystallisation; and they spoke out with renewed emphasis upon such points as

service in the vulgar tongue (Art. 24), the marriage of priests (Art. 32), the rights of National Churches (Art. 34), and the validity of the English Ordinal (Art. 36), while they added an affirmation of Communion in Both Kinds (Art. 30). In all this they manifested a deliberate intention to take a line of their own, and to speak plainly in defence of it; where, as the doors were being shut upon each other by the different religious bodies of Christendom, there seemed some advantage in having the last word!

§ 4. **The dissatisfaction of the Puritans** with the Articles opened up at once a long struggle which forms the last chapter in their history. It led first to their final revision in 1571 and the enforcement of subscription: afterwards to a series of abortive attempts to amend or supplement them in the Puritan interest.

Considering the growth of Calvin's influence at the time when the Articles were in the making (1549-1563), it is remarkable how little interest the English formulary shows in the opinions which emanated from him, and became known in England as Puritan. The name Puritan dates from 1564, the year *after* the publication of the Elizabethan Articles; and this seems to show that the men who drew their ideals from Calvin were only just rising into recognition as a party. At any rate it is clear that the Thirty-nine Articles are in no sense a Calvinistic formulary. It is possible that Art. 10 of 1553 was dropped, and Art. 10 of 1563 improved, with a view to conciliate the growing school. But the Puritan leaders complained that 'the Article composed in the time of Edward VI. respecting the spiritual eating, which expressly oppugned and took away the real presence in the Eucharist, and contained a most clear explanation of the truth, is now set forth among us mutilated and imperfect' (Art. 28); and the claims to disciplinary authority made on behalf of the Church in Articles 20 and 33 were also distasteful to them.

It was on matters of discipline that the struggle with Puritanism began. On February 13, 1563, just three days after the Articles had been signed in the Lower House of the Convocation of Canterbury. the Puritans sought to measure their strength against the ceremonies, and were only defeated by a majority of one. It was a virtual victory, which taught them their strength, and encouraged them to try it outside. The Bishops, alarmed, sought to obtain from the Parliament of 1566 the power to enforce the Articles by subscription. But the Queen intervened, expressing her readiness to support the Articles by her prerogative, though 'not to have the same dealt in by Parliament.' The attempt dropped for a time.

But in 1571, when the Queen's position was exposed both to the assaults of the Papal Bull of Excommunication and to the dangers consequent upon Mary Stuart's presence in the realm, she allowed the project to be taken in hand by Parliament. By this time the Puritans were stronger, and tried to turn it to their own advantage. Elizabeth's third Parliament sat from April 2 to May 29, 1571. On April 7 the Puritan leaders re-introduced into the Commons the bill that had been summarily stopped five years before. Thence it was sent to the Lords on May 3, passed their House on May 21, and received the Royal Assent on the 29th. It thus became the statute 13 Eliz. c. 12, *An Act to reform certain disorders touching Ministers of the Church.* In view of the Anglo-Roman schism, the Act was undoubtedly aimed in the first instance at the Romanensian party in the Church. It enforced subscription upon all who had been ordained in the reign of Mary, *i.e.* by other than the reformed Ordinals of 1550, 1552, 1559. Every such person is required to 'declare his assent, and subscribe to all the articles of religion, which *only* concern the confession of the true Christian faith and the doctrine of the sacraments, comprised in a book imprinted, intituled : Articles whereupon it was agreed by the archbishops and bishops of both provinces, and the whole clergy in the Convocation holden at London in the year of our Lord God 1562 . . . for the avoiding of the diversities of opinions, and for the establishing of consent touching true religion put forth by the queen's authority.' But the Act goes on to say that every presentee to a benefice must 'first have subscribed the said Articles in presence of the ordinary, and publicly read the same in the parish church of that benefice, with declaration of his unfeigned assent to the same' : and similar assent was required from candidates for ordination. Thus the Act had a wider scope than to secure the acquiescence of the Romanensians : and two points in its draughtsmanship indicate that it was ingeniously designed to assist the Puritan cause. The word 'only' reads as if meant to be restrictive, and other measures of the session leave little doubt that its object was to limit the enforcement of subscription to such Articles as dealt with doctrine. Again, the edition referred to is the English edition printed by Jugge and Cawood in 1563, which, while it does not contain Art. 29, also omits the first clause of Art. 20, affirmative of the authority of the Church to decree rites and ceremonies.

§ 5. It was this attempt of Parliament to evade rather than override the settlement of 1563, that led to the **final revision of the Thirty-nine Articles in the Convocation of 1571.** The synod of the province of Canterbury sat from April 3 to May 30. Dr. Whitgift, who preached the opening sermon, made no reference to any revision ; and it probably arose in consequence of the proceedings in Parliament, which, so far from bringing to the Bishops the support they had once anticipated, looked as if they might lead to the destruction of discipline at one blow. Some countermove was necessary ; and on April 7th, the very day on which the bill for Religion was read the first time in the Commons, Archbishop Parker issued an order that all members of the Lower House of Convocation, who had not formerly subscribed the Articles, should do so at once, or be excluded from the House. Nothing further happened till the bill had reached the Lords on May 3. The next day, as it specified the edition of the Articles in English, the Bishops resolved upon a fresh revision of the whole series, which Jewel, Bishop of Salisbury, was to see through the press when it was 'fully agreed upon' (May 4). At their next session (May 11), they re-adopted Article 29 : and they made further minor alterations before the Convocation was dissolved on May 30. We can only *presume* that these changes were submitted to both Houses of the Southern Convocation before they were finally adopted : but from the precedent of 1563, as well as from the language of the Queen's Ratification, it is safe to do so. The Ratification appeared in both the new editions of the Articles which were issued from the press in this year of the last revision, 1571, the one in Latin by John Day, the other, in English by Jugge and Cawood. In its English form it states that 'This Book of Articles before rehearsed, is again approved and allowed to be holden and executed within the Realm by the assent and consent of our Sovereign Lady Elizabeth . . . Which Articles were deliberately read, and confirmed again by the subscription of the hands of the Archbishop and Bishops of the Upper House, and by the subscription of the whole Clergy in the Nether House in their Convocation in the year of our Lord God, 1571.' Thus the Articles, as finally revised, received synodical sanction.

As to Subscription, it will be noticed that the Crown and the Clergy ignored the distinction between doctrinal and disciplinary Articles set up by the Parliament. The same Synod, in its later sessions of this summer, expressly required that candidates for Holy Orders and all preachers should subscribe all the Articles without exception: and from that day to this the same rule has prevailed. No one form of subscription was at first put forth. But, in 1583, when the Puritan attack on ceremonies had now developed into an attempt to undermine the very organisation of the Church, Archbishop Whitgift set out a form, which was rigorously enforced and eventually adopted in the 36th Canon of 1604. Attempts were made, in the interests of comprehension in 1689, and of Latitudinarianism in 1772, to relax the rigour of subscription; but without effect. In 1865, however, after a Royal Commission had reported in favour of the substitution of a single form in place of the cumbrous forms till then in use, an Act of Parliament (28th and 29th Vict. c. 112) gave effect to their recommendations; and at the same time the Convocations of Canterbury and York obtained leave from the Crown to revise the Canons of 1604. They issued an amended version of Canon 36, which was confirmed by Royal Letters Patent; and the form of subscription now runs as follows:—

'I, A.B., do solemnly make the following declaration: I assent to the Thirty-nine Articles of Religion, and to the Book of Common Prayer, and of ordering of Bishops, Priests and Deacons; I believe the doctrine of the Church of England, as therein set forth, to be agreeable to the Word of God: and in public prayer and administration of the Sacraments, I will use the form in the said book prescribed, and none other, except so far as shall be ordered by lawful authority.'

It should be added that from *ecclesiastical persons only* has subscription been required by the Church of England.[1] The Crown and the Universities have at various times required it from laymen; but the requirement was made on their own authority and not by that of the Church. By the legislation of 1854 and 1871 it has been finally removed. The laity are simply required to abstain from impugning the Articles by Canon 5 of 1604.

It only remains to make two observations: (1) The changes made in the Articles at **the last revision** were of minor importance, and have left the character impressed upon them in 1563 entirely unaffected. Beside the restoration of Article 29, and the apparent ratification of the first clause of Article 20 by the Synod, there was but one positive addition in the completed list of the Apocryphal books now appended to Article 6. Other changes are merely 'emendations in the wording of thirteen titles, or corrections introduced into the English from the older Latin copy, or occasional explanations of phraseology believed to have been capable of misconstruction.' (2) The question which of the two final versions, Latin or English, should be regarded as of paramount authority, is best answered, by Waterland, thus, 'The Latin and English are both equally authentical. Thus much, however, I may certainly infer that if in any places the English version be ambiguous, where the Latin original is clear and determinate, the Latin ought to fix the more doubtful sense of the other (as also *vice versâ*), it being evident that the Convocation, Queen, and Parliament intended the same sense in both.'

[1] *i.e.* the clergy, and judges of the Courts Christian. *Cf.* Canon 127 of 1604.

§ 6. The Articles have thus maintained their position since 1571; but not without a struggle. There have been repeated but **abortive attempts to amend or supplement them in the Puritan interest**; and a brief account of these must now be given. It will at once complete the history of the Articles and afford a simple proof that they are *not a Calvinistic formulary*.

(1) **The Lambeth Articles of 1595**, so called because they were produced under the eye of the Primate himself, represent Calvinism at its zenith in the reign of Elizabeth. The Puritan leaders in the Parliament of 1571, demurred, as we have seen, to all the Articles dealing with questions of discipline and polity. But even their own Act (13 Eliz. c. 12) met with resistance. The Puritanic clergy in some instances refused to subscribe, as it required, to the doctrinal Articles, and were deprived. With the controversy about Church order which began with a rejection of the ceremonies and ripened into an organised attempt to substitute a presbyterian form of Church government for Episcopacy, we have nothing to do. It was boldly met by the repressive measures of Archbishop Whitgift (1583-1604); and its intellectual basis was successfully challenged by the school that rose into prominence with Hooker's *Ecclesiastical Polity*, 1594. But the same manifestoes which demanded changes in Church government, attacked the Articles on the ground that they were inconsistent with the Calvinistic doctrines of predestination and reprobation. 'Indeed,' says the Second Admonition to Parliament, 1572, 'the book of the Articles of Christian religion speaketh very dangerously of falling from grace, which is to be reformed, because it too much inclineth to their error.' Calvin's theories had taken root among clergy and people at large because of their influence in the Universities. There his *Institutes* had taken the place of the mediæval text-books swept away under Henry VIII.: and the chairs of theology were occupied by men who, while in exile at Geneva, had drawn their inspiration from the fountain-head. Oxford perhaps was less infected than Cambridge: but it was in Cambridge that the first voice was raised in protest against the

dominant opinions. On April 29, 1595, William Barrett, Fellow of Caius College, preached at the University Church against the indefectibility of grace, the received doctrine of assurance, and the idea of an irrespective reprobation. The sermon was denounced by the Cambridge doctors, headed by Whitaker, Regius Professor of Divinity. Both parties appealed to the Archbishop, who endeavoured to mediate. But as he himself had Calvinistic leanings, the result of his prolonged conferences with the Cambridge deputation, was a paper of propositions, known as **The Lambeth Articles**, November 1595, which, as the Lord Treasurer told Whitaker, when he showed them to him, ' were charging God with cruelty, and might make men to be desperate in their wickedness.' They run as follows :—

1. God from eternity hath predestinated some to life, some He hath reprobated to death.
2. The moving or efficient cause of predestination to life is not the prevision of faith, or of perseverance, or of good works, or of anything which may be in the persons predestinated, but only the will of the good pleasure of God.
3. Of the predestinated there is a fore-limited and certain number which can neither be diminished nor increased.
4. They who are not predestinated to salvation will be necessarily condemned on account of their sins.
5. A true, living, and justifying faith, and the Spirit of God sanctifying is not extinguished, does not fall away, does not vanish in the elect, either totally or finally.
6. A truly faithful man, that is, one endowed with justifying faith, is certain, by the full assurance of faith, of the remission of his sins and his eternal salvation through Christ.
7. Saving grace is not given, is not communicated, is not granted to all men, by which they might be saved if they would.
8. No man can come to Christ except it be given to him, and unless the Father draw him. All men are not drawn by the Father that they may come to the Son.
9. It is not placed in the will or power of every man to be saved.

The contrast of these awful doctrines with those of the Articles, and specially with the reticence of Article 17 which says nothing about predestination to reprobation, is at once apparent. The Queen, on hearing of them, at once ordered Lord Burghley to write to the Archbishop that 'she misliked much that any allowance had been given by his grace and the rest of any such points to be disputed.' Whitgift himself wrote to the University of Cambridge (November 24) that the Lambeth Articles 'must be so taken and used as the private judgments' of the compilers. They never received any further authority in England: and in a few months were forgotten until the party which had extorted them from Whitgift made a fresh attempt to engraft them on our Articles of Religion in the next reign.

(2) When the **Hampton Court Conference** met under James I. in **1604**, Calvinism as a religious power in England had seen its best days: though it afterwards gained a new lease of life and vigour because of its association with the struggle for political liberty. It had already been dethroned in both the Universities, in favour of the wider and more historical theology represented in Oxford by Hooker, Field, and Laud: and in Cambridge by Andrewes and Overall. The last mentioned had succeeded Whitaker, the draftsman of the Lambeth Articles, as Regius Professor of Divinity in 1595: and it was he who crowned the Catholic doctrines of the English Church by the addition to the Catechism of the questions and answers on the Sacraments. This was under the auspices of the Conference. The King himself did not shake off his suspicions of the movement against Calvinistic doctrine for some years: and then it was rather on political than on theological grounds that he drew towards the Church party. But from the first he looked upon the Puritans with disfavour: and it is not surprising that when they now urged the emendation and enlargement of the Articles in the interest of Calvinism, nothing was done. Reynolds, their spokesman at Hampton Court, 'moved His Majesty that the book of Articles of Religion, concluded 1562, might be explained in places obscure, and enlarged where some things were defective. For example, whereas, Art. 16, the words are these, "after we have received the Holy Ghost, we may depart from grace," notwithstanding the meaning be sound, yet he desired that, because they may seem to be contrary to the doctrine of God's predestination and election in the seventeenth

Article, both those words might be explained with this, or the like addition, "yet neither totally nor finally"; and also that the nine assertions orthodoxal, as he termed them, concluded upon at Lambeth, might be inserted into that book of Articles.' No concession was made; nor was any granted to certain Lincolnshire Nonconformists who, in December 1604, apologised for their refusal to subscribe the Prayer Book and Articles on the ground that 'they contain in them sundry things which are not agreeable but contrary to the Word of God.' The Puritans had in short to accept the fact that their Calvinistic tenets could not find a place within the four corners of the formularies of the Church.

(3) The controversy slept for a while; but, after a brief lull, it received a fresh impetus from a variety of causes, until in the next reign it was hardly checked by **His Majesty's Declaration, 1628.** James I. had a pedantic taste for theological controversy, and in 1618 he lent his patronage to the Calvinistic Synod of Dort in Holland. Its object was to secure the condemnation of the five points of 'The Remonstrance,' as it was called—a document in which the followers of one Arminius had challenged the reigning tenets on (1) predestination, (2) the extent of Christ's death, (3) free-will and human depravity, (4) the manner of our conversion to God, and (5) the perseverance of the saints. The revival of the controversy by this synod, at which a deputation of English divines was present by the King's command, re-awakened the strife in England; and opponents of Calvinism in this country became generally known as Arminians. But the name on English soil came to cover a political as well as a theological meaning. It was the name given to the party, now strong in reputation for learning, and rising, at last, in the royal favour, which, beside its advocacy of the Catholic principles of the English Reformation, gave in its adherence to the Crown, in the struggle for the Prerogative against Parliamentary Privilege. The English gentlemen who championed the cause of political liberty in Parliament naturally allied themselves with the Puritan Nonconformists whom otherwise they would have despised.

Calvinism thus regained an influence out of all proportion to its intellectual strength; but its claims to recognition were re-asserted in answer to a challenge from the opposite side. In 1622 Richard Montague published *A New Gag for an Old Goose*. It was a reply to a Roman attack upon the Church of England, called *The Gag for the New Gospel*, which took the line of assuming that the popular Calvinism of the day truly represented the principles of the Church, and then proceeded to demolish them. Montague contended that the doctrines in question were not those of the Church, but had been fastened upon her by the Puritans who persisted in interpreting her formularies in a non-natural sense. He was delated to Parliament, and reprimanded by the Archbishop. But he went home; and, with the King's approval, followed up his book by a second entitled *Appello Cæsarem*, 'in which he vindicated more fiercely than before his claim to be the true exponent of the doctrine of the Church.' Before its publication, however, James died, and it was issued with a dedication to his successor in 1625. The Commons immediately returned to the charge, and Montague for a while was committed to custody. But the storm was not allayed; and, partly to deliver Montague from his numerous assailants, Charles with the advice of Laud and other bishops put out a Proclamation in 1626 deploring the prevalent dissensions and imposing silence on both parties. It had some effect. But next year, when Cosin published his *Book of Devotions* based in the main on ancient forms, the Puritans made it the occasion of a definite challenge to the Church party. Their champion, Prynne, attacked it unsparingly in *A Brief Survey and Censure of Mr. Cosin's Cozening Devotions*, and prefixed to his work an address to Parliament praying that no man should be allowed to speak or write against the Calvinistic doctrines. The conclusions of the Synod of Dort were to be offered as a test to every clergyman in England. Those who refused to subscribe were to be at once excluded from holding any ecclesiastical office. The demand for tests at once aroused the opposition of Laud. He was the liberal theologian of his day, with a great dislike for requiring 'assent unto particulars.' The King shared it; and was thus persuaded to re-issue, in substance, the proclamation of 1626 with a view to quieting the whole controversy. It was now prefixed to a new edition of the Articles, as His Majesty's Declaration, 1628. 'We will,' said the King, 'that all further curious search be laid aside, and these disputes shut up in God's promises, as they be generally set forth to us in the holy Scriptures, and the general meaning of the Articles of the Church of England according to them. And that no man hereafter shall either print, or preach, to draw the Article aside any way, but shall submit to it in the plain and full meaning thereof: and shall not put his own sense or comment to be the meaning of the Article, but shall take it in the literal and grammatical sense.' As evidence of good faith, Montague's *Appello Cæsarem* was called in; and if any should continue the dispute, such order was to be taken with them that they 'should wish that they had never thought upon these needless controversies.' But the Commons would not let the matter rest. They resolved themselves into a theological debating society, and voted, January 1629, the following protestation: 'We, the Commons now in Parliament assembled, do claim, profess, and avow for truth the sense of the Articles of Religion which were established in Parliament in the reign of our late Queen Elizabeth, which by public acts of the Church of England, and by the general and concurrent exposition of the writers of our Church, have been delivered to us, and we do reject the sense of the Jesuits and Arminians.' No one would take such a pronouncement for the language of experts either in divinity or grammar: but it is clear that the House claimed to interpret the Articles by the rule of current popular ideas, and not 'in their literal and grammatical sense.' It was a confession that they could not be accommodated without violence to the Calvinistic theories: and once more the attempt to read them in that light failed.

(4) In 1643, when the Puritan party had now got the upper hand, Parliament took a bolder course. Instead of merely seeking to put its own interpretation

on the Articles, it authorised a revision of them: and as this was 'in order to render their sense more express and determinate in favour of Calvinism,' it is abundantly clear that as they stood they were not satisfactory from that point of view. On July 22, 1643, the **Westminster Assembly** of Divines appointed a committee 'to consider what amendments were proper to be made in the doctrinal articles of the Church of England, and report them to the assembly, who were ten weeks in debating upon the first fifteen.' They were 'very busy upon the sixteenth Article, and upon that clause of it which mentioneth departing from grace,' when the work was finally suspended by order of Parliament. The fifteen Articles of the revision have been printed by Neal, the Puritan historian: and a brief comparison of them with their originals is the best way to discover the points in which the Puritans would have wished our formulary other than it is.

Art. 1 is unchanged: and the changes in 4, 5, 12, 14, and 15 are of minor importance. But in Art. 2 the clause on the atonement, instead of asserting that Christ died 'to be a sacrifice, not only for original guilt, but also for *all* actual sins of men,' omits *all*, by way of making room for the tenet of 'particular redemption.' Art. 3 explains the descent into Hell as merely equivalent to 'continuing in the state of the dead, and under the power and dominion of death.' Art. 6 omits all mention of the testimony of the Church as the authority for what is canonical, so as to provide for the Calvinistic principle that the claim of a book to be scripture rests upon its harmony with the testimony of the Spirit in the believer's soul. It also eliminates the Apocrypha. It adds a list of the New Testament books: and, instead of laying stress upon the canonicity of sacred books, it rests their claim to deference upon the fact of their inspiration. Art. 7 clears the way for the Calvinistic resuscitation of Old Testament institutions; for one clause is added which implies that the civil precepts of the Mosaic Law are binding on the Christian, provided they be not 'such as were peculiarly fitted to the commonwealth of the Jews'; and another, by understanding 'the moral Law' as 'the ten commandments taken in their full extent,' provides for that perpetuation of the Jewish Sabbath in the Christian Sunday, which began first at this time, and has since been characteristic of English and Scotch Puritanism. Art. 8, respecting the Three Creeds, was accepted on condition that they should be re-translated and explained. Art. 9, on Original Sin, is made to bear the special impress of Geneva. It is asserted that original sin consists of the 'first sin imputed' as well as of inherent corruption; that man is not 'very far gone from original righteousness' but 'wholly deprived' of it; that he is 'of his own nature inclined *only* to evil'; they substitute 'regenerate' for 'baptized'; and affirm that concupiscence 'is truly and properly sin.' Art. 10 is weighted with an affirmation of the irresistibility of grace and a consequent denial of human freedom; for the grace of God is described as 'working so effectually in us, as that it determineth our will to that which is good.' Art. 11 elaborates the part of imputation and faith in the work of Justification. Art. 13 substitutes for 'works done before the grace of Christ' the words '.works done before justification,' the result of which was to indefinitely narrow down the range of God's goodwill to man. Such is the contrast between the Thirty-nine Articles and the spirit of Calvinism. But even so, when the Divines sent in their report to Parliament, they had to confess their dissatisfaction. Despite the alterations they had made, they regretted that very many things continued to be 'defective,' and 'other expressions also were fit to be changed.'

(5) **The Puritan objections were again restated after the Restoration.** At the Savoy Conference in 1661 the Puritans urged as one of their grievances that their preachers were obliged to accept the Articles as not contrary to the Word of God: and in 1689 Baxter recapitulated their complaints in his *English Nonconformity*. But, in so doing, he was obliged to add, by way of qualification, that 'the words of the Articles *in the obvious sense* are many times liable to exception, and there are many things in them that good men may scruple.' Again they did not lend themselves to the Puritan point of view.

The saying of Pitt that the Church of England has a popish Liturgy and a Calvinistic set of Articles has been often repeated and widely believed. There is this much of truth in any such attempt to mark a distinction between the Prayer Book and the Articles. The Prayer Book was drawn up on the ancient models; and, after Calvinism invaded the religious thought of this country, was twice revised on ancient lines in the seventeenth century. The Articles were the product of the middle of the sixteenth century. That was an age which had characteristics of its own, but neither Calvinism, nor indeed the adoption of any particular theological system, was then a characteristic of English thought. The Church was merely engaged in self-defence: and this imparted to the Articles a tentative and negative character. They are thus less definite than the liturgy; and so more susceptible of being taken in some other than their 'literal and grammatical sense.' After their completion, when Calvinism became the dominant theology for a generation, there was a long sustained effort to inoculate them with it. But they threw off the malady. This mere fact is enough to show that the once popular view of the Articles to which Pitt's dictum gave expression is an entire misconception. That interpretation of them to which Laud and his friends first recalled attention, is the one since vindicated as historically correct.

§7. It only remains to note the **arrangement of the Articles** as suggested by their subject-matter. They fall into four groups:—

    A. The Catholic Faith and where it may be found (Art. 1-8).
        1. The Faith (Art. 1-5).
        2. The Rule of Faith: Scripture and the Creeds (Art. 6-8).
    B. Personal Religion, or Man and his Salvation (Art. 9-18).
    C. Corporate Religion, or the Church, the Ministry, and the Sacraments (Art. 19-31).
    D. Miscellaneous Articles, relating to the discipline of the Church of England (Art. 32-39).

PART II.—EXPLANATION

NOTE

(1) Formulae composed in 1552-3 are printed in ordinary type: formulae, or parts thereof, common to the formularies of 1563, 1553, 1538, and 1530 in *italics*; additions of 1563, if from the Confession of Würtemberg, in **thick type**, between ☩ if from elsewhere; or, if then composed, between ☩.

(2) **The student is particularly advised to read the explanation of the Articles with a revised version of the Bible at his side, and to look out the references.** It has been found impossible to give them in full; and this part of the book will not be intelligible without study of the Scripture where referred to. It is however hoped that the explanation will suffice to make the passages of Scripture clear, so far as they bear upon the matter in hand.

(3) The text of the Articles here explained is that of the last revision in 1571. The Latin Articles of 1553 and 1563 will be found in the Appendix.

PART II.—EXPLANATION

Group A (Arts. 1-8), on **the Catholic Faith,** deal with

(i) *The Contents of the Faith,* including the doctrines of the Trinity (Art. 1), the Incarnate Son (Arts. 2-4), and the Holy Ghost (Art. 5).

(ii) *The Rule of Faith,* which is Scripture (Arts. 6, 7) and the Creeds (Art. 8).

ARTICLE I.

De fide in Sacrosanctam Trinitatem.	Of faith in the Holy Trinity.
(§ 1) Unus est vivus et verus *Deus, aeternus, incorporeus, impartibilis,* impassibilis, *immensae potentiae, sapientiae, ac bonitatis, creator et conservator omnium,* tum *visibilium* tum *invisibilium.* (§ 2) Et in unitate hujus divinae naturae *tres sunt Personae ejusdem essentiae, potentiae,* ac aeternitatis, *Pater, Filius, et Spiritus Sanctus.*	(§ 1) There is but one living and true God, everlasting, without body, parts, or passions; of infinite power, wisdom, and goodness; the maker and preserver of all things both visible and invisible. (§ 2) And in unity of this Godhead there be three Persons, of one substance, power, and eternity; the Father, the Son, and the Holy Ghost.

(i.) **Source.**—Art. 1 is derived from the Confession of Augsburg, through the medium of the Thirteen Articles. The words printed in italics are in all three formularies, and also appear in the *Reformatio Legum,* and the first of the Forty-two Articles. There has been no change in its terms since 1553.

(ii.) **Object.**—The Article excludes the older Sabellian and Arian heresies, but its object was to condemn those who were reviving them in the sixteenth century, *i.e.* the Anabaptists. These men, in their repudiation of the fundamentals of the Faith,[1] went so far as to abandon belief in the Holy Trinity. In 1555 Ridley alludes to 'the outrageous rule that Satan, our ghostly enemy, beareth abroad in the world, whereby he stirreth and raiseth so pestilent and heinous heresies, as some to deny the Blessed Trinity, some the divinity of our Saviour Christ, some the baptism of infants, etc.' Thus even these earlier Articles, which re-assert the elements of the Faith, were simply called forth by the necessities of the time.

(iii.) **Explanation.**—§ 1 begins (1) by assuming *the existence of God*. So does the Bible (Gen. i. 1); where it is taken for granted (Heb. xi. 6), and the 'proofs' of it assigned to the realm of Natural Religion (Rom. i. 19, 20). They belong to the preliminary study of 'evidences,' and concern us as Theists, not as Christians, still less as members of a particular Church. It would be out of place to set them forth here. Nor does (2) *the Unity of God*, which is the leading assertion of this section, require any comment but this, that monotheism is the first article, as of the Jewish (Deut. vi. 4), so also of the Christian, creed (1 Cor. viii. 4). But (3) some of *God's attributes*, as here stated, want explanation. He is called **the living and true God** by contrast with idols (1 Thess. i. 9); and the sense seems to be not only that God is self-existent (John v. 26), but that He perfectly comes up to our conception of what God ought to be (John xvii. 3). God also is **without body**, for 'God is a Spirit' (John iv. 24). To add that He is **without parts or passions** suggests, in English, a protest against anthropomorphism, or the ascription to God of human form and feelings; which is wrong (Isa. xl. 18), except in so far as it is either, (*a*) a legitimate consequence of our being made in the image of God (Gen. i. 26), or else (β) a necessary accommodation to the infirmity of human understanding (Gen. viii. 21; xi. 5, etc.). But the Latin has a different sense. **Impartibilis** means 'incapable of division,' and **impassibilis**, 'incapable of suffering.' (4) Then the Article treats of *God's relation to the universe*. He is **the maker of all things**

---

[1] See above, p. 33, for further evidence.

(Gen. i. 1; Rev. iv. 11); and this excludes both Gnosticism, which interposed a demiurge as the author of creation between God and His world, and Pantheism, which identifies Him with it. As **the Preserver of all things**, He is actively concerned in the maintenance of the universe that He made (John v. 17; Heb. i. 3); and so Deism, which holds that God made the world and then left it to go on by itself, is rejected as untrue.

§ 2 is a statement of the *doctrine of the Trinity*.

(1) This doctrine rests, of course, on a *Scriptural basis*. The mission of the Jewish Church was to guard the truth of the unity of God against the surrounding polytheism. So we do not expect to find in the Old Testament more than hints of personal distinctions within the Godhead. But such hints there are, recognisable by us, if not by contemporaries. There is (*a*) the threefold repetition of the Divine Name, both in blessing (Num. vi. 24) and praise (Isa. vi. 3). Again, (*b*) there are mysterious figures such as 'the Angel of the Lord,' who is in part identified with God (Gen. xviii. 1, 33, xix. 1) and in part distinguished from Him (Gen. xviii. 2); and 'the captain of the host of the LORD' (Josh. v. 14), who is also called 'the LORD' (Josh. vi. 2). Again, (*c*) the activity of God is ascribed throughout the Old Testament to the Spirit of God (Exod. xxxi. 3; Ps. civ. 30), or 'His Holy Spirit' (Ps. li. 11; Isa. lxiii. 10, 11); and in the Targums, or paraphrases of the Scriptures current among the later Jews, to 'the Word,' as in their reading of Gen. iii. 8, vii. 16; Exod. xix. 17; *cf.* John i. 1. In the New Testament these intimations give way to express revelation, as at Our Lord's Baptism (Matt. iii. 16, 17). Throughout His ministry Our Lord spoke much of His unique relation as Son to the Father (Matt. xi. 27; John v. 19-47); and towards its close, He spoke of the Holy Spirit in terms which only admit of His being taken for a Divine Person (John xiv.—xvi.). At last, in the final commission, He bade the Apostles 'go and make disciples of all the nations, baptizing them into the name of the Father, and of the Son, and of the Holy Ghost' (Matt. xxviii. 19); where (α) the use of 'name,' not 'names,' implies the unity of the Godhead; (β) the mention of the Son and the Holy

Ghost side by side with the Father indicates their Divinity; and (γ) the mention of the Holy Spirit along with the Father and the Son, which are clearly titles expressive of personal relationship, involves His Personality also. Thus we have in Our Lord's parting words the substance of the doctrine of the Trinity clearly revealed (*cf.* 2 Cor. xiii. 14).

(2) Its best *evidence* is to be found in the further revelation that 'God is love' (1 John iv. 8). Never was He a solitary God. Before creation was, He always had, within the circumference, so to say, of His own Being, the full satisfaction of His own needs. There was from eternity the Son to receive, and the Spirit to return, the Father's love.

(3) The truth of the Trinity is independent of the *technical terminology* in which it is expressed. That was a later growth, and one forced upon the Church in the effort to find intellectual justification for the two primary convictions of the earliest Christian consciousness. The first was that there is but one God. The next, that Christians must worship Jesus Christ. By the end of the fourth century the doctrine that in the **unity of the Godhead there be three Persons of one Substance** was finally accepted as the best security which human language could provide for combining faith in the unity of God with belief in the Divinity and Personality of God's Son and Spirit. This phraseology has never been superseded, though it must be remembered that all human language is inadequate to express the Divine realities. Its defence is that it has served its purpose of safeguarding 'the deep things of God'; for the doctrine of the Trinity, except for its repudiation by Anabaptists and Socinians, has been universally held by Christians, since the fourth century, in the form which it then received.

ARTICLE II

| De Verbo, sive Filio Dei, qui verus homo factus est. | Of the Word, or Son of God, which was made very man. |

(§1) *Filius, qui est Verbum Patris,* **ab aeterno a Patre genitus, verus et aeternus Deus, ac Patri consubstantialis** (§2) *in utero beatae Virginis* ex illius substantia *naturam humanam assumpsit:* ita *ut duae naturae, divina et humana,* integre atque perfecte *in unitate personae,* fuerint *inseparabiliter conjunctae:* ex quibus est *unus Christus, verus Deus et verus homo:* (§3) qui *vere passus* est, *crucifixus, mortuus, et sepultus, ut Patrem nobis reconciliaret, essetque hostia non tantum pro culpa originis* verum *etiam pro omnibus actualibus hominum peccatis.*

(§1) The Son, which is the Word of the Father, begotten from everlasting of the Father, the very and eternal God, and of one substance with the Father, (§2) took man's nature in the womb of the blessed Virgin, of her substance : so that two whole and perfect natures, that is to say, the Godhead and manhood, were joined together in one person, never to be divided, whereof is one Christ, very God and very man, (§3) who truly suffered, was crucified, dead, and buried, to reconcile His Father to us, and to be a sacrifice, not only for original guilt, but also for all actual sins of men.

(i.) **Source.**—Art. 2 is taken from the Confession of Augsburg, but mediately through the Thirteen Articles. The italics show what is common to all three formularies. The corresponding Article of 1553 was identical with our present one, except that it did not possess the clause in **thick type.** This was added in 1563 from the Confession of Würtemberg.

(ii.) **Object.**—The Article is framed in the language of the fourth and fifth centuries, which had then been adopted to bar out the older heresies about Our Lord's

Incarnate Person. But it is directed against the Anabaptists, who were reviving these errors. The fourteen who perished at the stake in 1535 met with their death for maintaining, among other things, that 'in Christ is not two natures, God and man; and that Christ took neither flesh nor blood of the Virgin Mary.' Similar denials of the Incarnation appear at intervals throughout the period of the Reformation.[1]

(iii.) **Explanation.**—§ 1 deals with the *Divinity of Our Lord*.

(1) *The terms* chosen to express it are two, both Scriptural. He is called **The Son**, not merely because of events, such as His miraculous Birth (Luke i. 35), Mission (John x. 34-36), Resurrection (Acts xiii. 33; Rom. i. 4), and Ascension (*cf.* Heb. i. 2-5 with Matt. xxviii. 18), all of which are said to have marked Him out, in time, as God's Son; but in the unique (John i. 14) sense of having the divine essence communicated to Him by the Father from all eternity. Such a sonship the Jews understood Him to claim when He 'called God His own Father' (John v. 18). Such St. Paul assigns to Him when he writes that 'God spared not His own Son' (Rom. viii. 32). The term 'Son,' however, might be open to misconstruction; and Arius, interpreting it by the analogy of human sonship, took it to mean that the Son is of more recent origin than the Father. It safeguards Our Lord's personality, but not His eternity. But this is secured by that other title of **the Word of the Father**; who, as 'in the beginning with God,' must be regarded as co-eternal with Him (John i. 1). The next phrase, **begotten from everlasting of the Father**, at once combines and explains these two supplementary terms. He is 'begotten,' else He would not be 'Son'; and this 'from everlasting,' otherwise He would not be 'the Word' which 'was God.' The communication of the divine essence which constitutes Him Son is thus not to be thought of as an event which once took place; for then the Father would not have been always Father, nor the Son always Son. It is to be thought of rather as an

[1] See above, pp. 17, 33, 66.

'eternal generation,' by which is meant an unchangeable relation or fact of the divine nature, the evidence of which is to be sought in what the Son has told us of the perfect intimacy between Himself and the Father (Matt. xi. 27). It follows from this that, if Son in such a sense, He is **Very** God; **and** if so 'begotten from everlasting,' **Eternal God**; and the statement of His Godhead concludes in the only formula which has been permanently equal to barring out its denial, whether by Arians or Anabaptists, viz. that He is **of one substance** (essence) **with the Father**.

(2) *The Scriptural evidence* for the Divinity of Our Lord is of that kind which produces moral certainty, not demonstration; and, when set forth, appears to be indirect in character. The growth of conviction as to Our Lord's Godhead is, as we should expect, traceable in the Gospels; its established hold is sufficiently, but yet inferentially, observable in the Epistles. Thus (*a*), in the Gospels, while Our Lord never speaks of Himself directly as divine, He makes claims which render it impossible to think of Him as less than God. He revises the law (Matt. v. 21, 22). He puts duty to Himself above the most sacred of human obligations (Matt. x. 37). He is able to satisfy the deepest wants of the soul (Matt. xi. 28). He assigns a mighty effect to His death (Matt. xx. 28); and, while a prisoner before Caiaphas, announces that He is to judge the world (Matt. xxvi. 64, *cf.* xxv. 31 *sqq.*). These claims are supported by miracles; and carried out in conduct, as in His acceptance of worship (Matt. viii. 2, ix. 18, etc.), and of conclusions drawn from His language, to the effect that He meant Himself to be taken as God (John v. 18, viii. 58, x. 30). Moreover, while making such claims, He successfully challenged His enemies to convict Him of sin (John viii. 46). Whatever the impression made on the crowd, it is clear that the Apostles, through the knowledge of His Humanity, so self-assertive and yet so sinless, came to the confession of His Divinity, not all at once, but gradually; Peter, in the first instance, to acknowledge His Messiahship (Matt. xvi. 16); Thomas, after the Resurrection, His Godhead (John xx. 28). In less than a generation, this belief of theirs is found, (*b*) in the Epistles, to be the accepted

creed of the Churches they established. We find, indeed, but few express statements of it, such as could be cited for proof texts (*e.g.* Phil. ii. 6-8; Col. i. 15-18; Heb. i. 2, 3). But proof texts are of less importance as evidence of the belief of the early Christians than indirect allusions. The Epistles are occasional writings, sent to Churches already instructed (2 Thess. ii. 15; 1 Cor. xv. 3) in the elements of the Faith. They deal with truths and practices that were in danger, not with such as were safe. The Divinity of Our Lord, then, is taken for granted; and if so, allusive hints are better evidence for it than direct assertion. But these abound, as in ascriptions of praise (Rom. ix. 5) or of titles (Tit. ii. 13; 2 Peter i. 1) to Our Lord. His name is coupled with the name of the Father in blessings (2 Cor. xiii. 14) and in hymns (Tit. iii. 4-7). He is to judge the world (2 Cor. v. 10); and exhortations to humility (Phil. ii. 6-8) and liberality (2 Cor. viii. 9) are enforced by an appeal to the example of His infinite condescension. When such language is introduced, quite incidentally, into letters addressed to whole Churches, it is indirect, but all the more conclusive, proof of their settled belief in Our Lord's Divinity.

§ 2 proceeds to a statement of *the Incarnation*.

(1) *Its terms* are an inheritance from the great controversies, which agitated the age of the first four Œcumenical Councils, as to the relation of the two Natures in the one Divine Person of Christ. In the struggle with Arius, the Council of Nicæa (325 A.D.) set its seal to the Church's belief that He is God. Thereupon the difficulty arose of combining this belief with a real acceptance of His true Humanity. On the one side there was a tendency, first with Apollinaris (c. 370 A.D.), and then, after the reaction of Nestorius (431 A.D.), with Eutyches (451 A.D.), to minimise His human Nature, with a view to securing the singleness of His Divine Person. Apollinaris proposed to solve the difficulty by depriving Him of a rational human soul, and so was led to compromise the *entirety* of Our Lord's human Nature. Eutyches, by maintaining that, after the Incarnation, there was but one Nature in Christ, endangered the *per-*

manence of our Lord's human Nature. Both errors were repudiated as equally fatal to our salvation ; for if Christ did not take our human nature complete in all its faculties, then it is but partially redeemed ; while, if He does not retain it now, the means, which the Incarnation set up, of conveying the Divine Life to us men (2 Peter i. 4), have broken down. On the other hand, an attempt was made by Nestorianism to secure the reality of Our Lord's human Nature, specially of His example, which Apollinaris, by denying Him a soul to be tempted, had imperilled. Nestorius held that for Mary's Son to have had a complete human experience, He must have had not only all human faculties, but a human personality also. Nestorius denied that Mary was Θεοτόκος, the Mother of God ; or, in other words, he denied that He who was born of her was, from the moment of His conception, no other Person than God the Eternal Son. This was to say in effect that the union between God and man was not essential, but temporary. It was not a union of two natures, divine and human, in the one Divine Person ; but a moral union only between two persons, God and a man, like in kind to that union of will which exists between God and a great saint, though closer in degree. In that case, only one man benefited by the 'Incarnation'; Christ's flesh, as not being the flesh of God, could not be life-giving (John vi. 54-57) ; or, in one word, the Incarnation and the Sacraments are impossible. Nestorianism was therefore rejected at the Council of Ephesus (431 A.D.) as fatal to the Unity of Christ's Person. In 451 A.D. Eutychianism was condemned at the Council of Chalcedon as destructive of the permanence of His humanity. The Article merely repeats the phraseology which was elaborated in the course of these controversies, not for the love of technicalities, but to bar out errors which then threatened the deepest spiritual interests of mankind. **The Son ... took man's nature** (not a human person) **in the womb of the blessed Virgin** (*i.e.* His humanity from the moment of its conception never belonged to any other person than that of the Divine Son) **of her substance : so that two whole and perfect natures, that is to say, the Godhead and the manhood, were joined together** in one Person, never to be divided, whereof is one Christ, very God and very man.

(2) *The Scriptural evidence* for this position can be but briefly set down. Two points are at stake—the unity of Christ's Person, and the permanent entirety of His human Nature. The first is implied in the directness with which, as in the Creed, successive activities, first in the divine and then in the human sphere, are ascribed to one and the same Person (John viii. 56-58, xvi. 28; 2 Cor. viii. 9; Gal. iv. 4; Phil. ii. 6-8), whose identity is thus represented as continuous before and after the Incarnation; or, again, in the boldness with which that is predicated of the one Person of Christ which is proper only to one of the Natures. For instance, Scripture affirms what is human of God—birth (John i. 14), a bodily organism (Acts xx. 28), capacity for suffering (1 Cor. ii. 8), and for being perceived by the senses (1 John i. 1); not, of course, of the Godhead, but of Christ's one Person in His manhood. Similarly it affirms what is divine of man, *e.g.* omnipresence (John iii. 13; 1 Cor. xv. 47), not of the manhood, but of Christ's one Person in His Godhead. The completeness of His human Nature is evident from its being subject to all affections properly incidental to man, whether physical, such as growth in stature (Luke ii. 52), hunger (Matt. iv. 2, xxi. 18), thirst (John xix. 28), weariness (John iv. 6), or mental, such as increase in wisdom (St. Luke ii. 52), grief (Mark viii. 12; John xi. 33), and indignation (Mark iii. 5). Its permanence is clear from the fact that, though rendered perfectly amenable to the laws of the spiritual order by the Resurrection (John xx. 19; Luke xxiv. 31; *cf.* 1 Cor. xv. 44), His Body retained an unmistakable identity (John xx. 16, 20, xxi. 7), and was not laid aside at the Ascension (Luke xxiv. 51; Acts i. 11). Finally, it is only in the belief that Our Lord united two whole and perfect natures in His one Person, that we can explain both sides of His being as portrayed in the Gospels. On the one hand, His power (John ii. 11) and knowledge (John i. 48, ii. 25, vi. 6, x. 15; *cf.* Matt. xi. 27) far exceed that of ordinary men; on the other, in asking for information (Mark vi. 38;

John xi. 34), showing surprise (Mark vi. 6; Luke vii. 9), waiting for the supply of His wants (John iv. 8), and admitting a measure of ignorance (Mark xiii. 32), He is seen under the limitations common to all men. The Epistles explain this double portraiture of Our Lord by saying that He deigned 'in all things to be made like unto His brethren' (Heb. ii. 17), sin only except (Heb. iv. 15); or that He 'emptied Himself' (Phil. ii. 7), not indeed of His Godhead, but of the unlimited enjoyment and exercise of its prerogatives.

§ 3 concludes with *the Atonement*. It is only such a Person as Jesus Christ who could atone; for, if not divine, His acts have no 'infinite worth;' and if not human, He cannot represent us. The Article therefore proceeds to assert that He **truly suffered** (this by way of repudiating the Anabaptist revival of Docetism, to the effect that Christ only suffered in appearance[1]), **was crucified, dead and buried** (all marks of the reality of His sufferings), with a twofold object.

It was (a) **to reconcile His Father to us**. This phrase has been objected to by Socinians and their sympathisers, who assert, truly enough, that it is not found in Scripture, which always speaks of man being reconciled to God (Rom. v. 10, 11; 2 Cor. v. 18-20; Eph. ii. 16; Col. i. 19-22). But neither are other phrases, which have been judged necessary to guard the sense of Scripture, *e.g.* 'Of one substance with the Father,' and it is this alone with which the Faith is concerned. The word 'reconcile' merely means the re-establishment of friendly relations, and decides nothing as to the side on which they may have been suspended. In Matt. v. 24, where we should expect the aggrieved brother to need reconciliation, it is the offending brother who is bidden to 'be reconciled.' In the second of the four passages above referred to, antagonism is implied as existing, and the reconciliation as effectual, on both sides,[2] for it removed

---

[1] Greek δόκησις.
[2] It is in this sense of setting 'at one,' or 'peace-making,' that 'atone' and 'Atonement' were used, and should now be understood.—*Cf.* Shakespeare's *Richard II*. I. i. 202; *Richard III*. I. iii. 37.

God's indignation (2 Cor. v. 19) as well as man's alienation (2 Cor. v. 20). Nor must it be overlooked that as here, so elsewhere, 'reconciliation is primarily associated by St. Paul with forgiveness of sins and deliverance from wrath (Rom. v. 8, 9), and only secondarily with man's change of heart.' It follows, therefore, that the Atonement removed a real barrier, or had an objective value, *i.e.* that

Christ came (*b*) **to be a Sacrifice, not only for original guilt, but also for all actual sins of men.** The Sin-Offering of the Old Covenant is the clue to what is meant in Christian theology by 'a sacrifice for sin' (*cf.* Lev. iv. and xvi. 11-15 with Rom. viii. 3; Heb. x. 6, 8, 12, etc.). Its aim was atonement or propitiation (*lit.* the covering of sin); and this was effected not by the death of the victim, but by the presentation of its blood (Lev. xvii. 11; *cf.* Lev. iv. 6 with Heb. xii. 24 and 1 Pet. i. 2). The sinner first identified himself with the victim by laying his hand upon its head (Lev. iv. 29), so that it might be regarded not as a substitute for, but as completely representative of, himself; and thereupon slew it. Then the priest at once caught and offered the blood, warm, quick, and living, at the altar (Lev. iv. 6), or, on the Day of Atonement, at the Mercy-seat itself (xvi. 14), so that it might be presented in God's sight as a covering for sin. Thus not death, but life through death, was the constitutive idea of the Sin-Offering; and the sacrifice is not completed by the blood shed at the slaying of the victim by the sinner, but only by the blood poured out in the sanctuary by the priest. Thus, when God 'set forth' His Son 'to be a Propitiation,' it was not the sufferings but the obedience (Phil. ii. 8), not the death endured but the life surrendered, which had the propitiatory effect. Scripture accordingly assigns our redemption to the Blood of Christ (Matt. xxvi. 28; Acts xx. 28; Rom. iii. 25, v. 9; Eph. i. 7; Heb. ix. 14, etc.; 1 John i. 7; Rev. i. 5, etc.); and so regards His 'sacrifice for sin' as indeed 'once finished in act' (John xix. 30; Heb. ix. 28, x. 10, etc.), 'but ever living in operation,' being pleaded perpetually in the heavenly sanctuary (Heb. ix. 24). Thus, Our Lord is described as 'a priest for ever' (Heb. v. 6); and if the worship of heaven centres round 'a Lamb standing, as though it *had been* slain' (Rev. v. 6), yet it is said that 'He *is* the Propitiation for our sins' (1 John ii. 2).

The importance of thus remembering that Our Lord is still active as 'a Sacrifice for sin' will appear in connection with Art. 31; where, moreover, the phrase describing the *universal efficacy* of His sacrifice, as good 'not only for original guilt, but also for all actual[1] sins of men,' is repeated. It was adopted to exclude a later mediæval error which held that Christ suffered on the Cross for original sin, and instituted the sacrifice of the altar for actual sins; but it also proved an effectual barrier to Calvinism,[2] the favourite tenet of which was that Our Lord died only for the elect. But see John iii. 16; 2 Cor. v. 15; 1 Tim. ii. 4-6; 1 John ii. 2.

In conclusion, it should be observed that the fact of the Atonement is quite independent of the various theories which have been propounded to explain it. Difficulties have mainly arisen from the theories; and they are due (*a*) to the one-sided pressure put upon the figures under which the Atonement is described in Holy Scripture, and (*b*) to ignoring the elementary truth that it does not stand alone in the divine plan of redemption.

Thus (*a*) there are three words used to describe it in the New Testament—Reconciliation or Atonement, Propitiation, Ransom. By pressing unduly the Scriptural phraseology of 'man being reconciled to God,' one school of theology has ended by emptying Our Lord's Death of any effect beyond that of recalling men to God by 'its power of impressive moral appeal; as if, by so dying, He was pleading not so much with God on behalf of men as with men on behalf of God.' But this is to forget that 'Christ died for our sins' (1 Cor. xv. 3), or 'put away sin by the sacrifice of Himself' (Heb. ix. 26), with the result that God ceased to 'reckon' it (2 Cor. v. 19); and so to bring the character of God into dishonour by representing His love as mere good-nature, which makes light of sin. On the contrary, it was a love which manifested

---

[1] See vol. ii., on Art. 9, for the meaning of these terms.
[2] See above, p. 60.

itself not by dispensing with propitiation, but by providing it (1 John iv. 10). A second school has come to lay undue stress upon this element of Propitiation, and to speak 'as if they thought that the Father had to be persuaded by the Son to lay aside a personal resentment against sinners, in consideration of the Son's voluntary sufferings and death; as if the Father's will pointed simply to justice, and the Son's simply to mercy.' The result has been to provoke indignation against the Atonement as morally offensive and injurious to the Divine character; but the offence lies with the theory. Its suggestion of two wills is contradictory to the doctrine of the 'one substance' in the Godhead. The will of the Son wrought in harmony with the will of the Father (Matt. xxvi. 39). Both were moved to action by the love of man (John iii. 16; Gal. ii. 20; Eph. v. 2). Both had a part in the great sacrifice; the Father in that He 'spared not' (Rom. viii. 32), but 'gave' (John iii. 16) or 'sent' (1 John iv. 9) His only Son; the Son in that He took it all upon Himself willingly (Heb. x. 5 sqq.). It is God the Father who 'commendeth His own love to us, in that while we were yet sinners Christ died for us' (Rom. v. 8; 1 John iv. 10). It was the 'wrath of the Lamb' (Rev. vi. 16) against sin that sustained Him in the conflict. A third school, starting from the Scriptural allusion to Our Lord's death as a Ransom (Matt. xx. 28; 1 Tim. ii. 6), developed a 'crude literalism that produced abhorrent results; they imagined that Christ's blood was an equivalent paid over to the devil in order to cancel his claim of dominion over mankind.' They forgot that 'ransom' means in Scripture no more than deliverance at a great expenditure, whether of God's power (Exod. vi. 6) or love (Isa. lxiii. 9); in this case, at the cost of Christ's blood (Acts xx. 28; Heb. ix. 12). But whether considered as Ransom, Reconciliation, or Propitiation, the Atonement is represented in Holy Scripture as finding its explanation in the efficacy of Christ's Blood (Eph. i. 7; Col. i. 20; Rom. iii. 25). The perfect life surrendered and accepted is thus the key to the mystery.

But there (*b*) remains the difficulty in what sense God can regard it as ours. Room has to be made not only for

EXPLANATION

the conception of substitution, but for that of representation. For, if Scripture speaks of Our Lord as doing for us what we could not do for ourselves (2 Cor. v. 21), and so in some sense making a vicarious offering for us (*cf.* Isa. liii. 5), this idea of substitution must not be pressed to mean that God could accept a bargain, legal fiction, or arbitrary exchange of innocent for guilty, but it must only be held in subordination to the idea of a real representation (2 Cor. v. 14). And so we arrive at the one safeguard of right thought about the Atonement. It came in the Divine plan between the Incarnation and the Sacraments. Without either, it is incomplete. For it was only as the Second Adam (1 Cor. xv. 45-47), or in virtue of His having taken our common human nature, that the Divine Victim was capable of actually representing all mankind upon the Cross; while it was only in view of His still closer and organic union with the Church which is His body (Eph. i. 23) that He could prospectively represent its members (1 Cor. xii. 27) there. Thus, on the one hand, He died 'for our sin; and not for ours only, but also for the whole world' (1 John ii. 2); on the other hand, 'God is the Saviour of all men, specially of them that believe' (1 Tim. iv. 10). Two conditions, in short, are required for dealing faithfully and reverently with the doctrine of the Atonement; first, to remember that human language is inadequate to describe not only the Divine Being,[1] but the Divine acts; and then, to be true to all the facts of Holy Scripture, not least to this, that in Scripture the Atonement remains a mystery neither to be explained away nor explained.

[1] See above, p. 68.

ARTICLE III

De descensu Christi ad inferos.

Quemadmodum Christus pro nobis mortuus est, et sepultus, ita est etiam credendus ad inferos descendisse.

Of the going down of Christ into Hell.

As Christ died for us, and was buried, so also is it to be believed that He went down into Hell.

(i.) **Source.**—Composed by the English Reformers, 1552-3.

(ii.) **Object.**—In the form in which it has stood since 1563, Art. 3 confines itself to stating the *fact* of Our Lord's Descent into Hell. In 1553 there was an additional clause referring to the *object* with which He went thither. Micronius, in a letter of May 20, 1550, writes that 'they are disputing about the descent of Christ into Hell'; and it is evident that Art. 3 of the Forty-two Articles was designed to close the controversies upon this point. It only served to embitter them. Alley, Bishop of Exeter (1560-70), drew the attention of the Synod of 1563 to the 'tragedies and dissensions' arising out of the subject of which he had had experience in his own diocese. The Article was accordingly reduced to its present limits. If the formulary of 1563 was to enjoy that character for completeness, which, at least in regard to the re-statement of essentials, was then intended, mention had to be made of the fact 'of the going down into Hell.' But in the interests of comprehension, where nothing was involved but the right interpretation of an isolated and difficult passage (1 Pet. iii. 18, 19, iv. 6), allusion to the object of this descent was dropped. This is a good instance of the way in which

EXPLANATION

the Articles, as Articles of Religion, not of Faith, sometimes 'avoid an issue rather than seek it.'[1]

(iii.) **Explanation.**—'Hell,' in the Authorised Version, is unfortunately used as the equivalent of Gehenna, the place of torment (Matt. v. 22, 29, 30), as well as for Sheol (Hebrew) or Hades (Greek), the place of departed spirits (Gen. xxxvii. 35; Matt. xi. 23). Like Sheol and Hades, 'Hell' should be regarded, both here and in the Creed, as a neutral term, deciding nothing as to whether the condition of the departed is happy or the reverse. In the Old Testament Sheol was merely 'the house appointed for all living' (Job xxx. 23), whether for saints like David (2 Sam. xii. 23), or for tyrants like Nebuchadnezzar (Isa. xiv. 9). But by our Lord's time Jewish belief about the future life had developed. The underworld was now held to be divided into two parts; the one a place of peace and rest for the souls of the faithful, called 'Abraham's bosom' (Luke xvi. 22), or 'Paradise' (Luke xxiii. 43); the other where the souls of sinners are described as 'being in torments,' though as yet in 'Hades' (Luke xvi. 23), not in Gehenna. By adopting this current language, Our Lord gave His sanction to the beliefs which it embodies. His promise to the dying robber, 'To-day shalt thou be with Me in Paradise' (Luke xxiii. 43), taken together with St. Peter's statement that His 'soul' was not 'left in Hades' (Acts ii. 24, 27; *cf.* Ps. xvi. 10), implies His descent thither; and this is the more probable meaning of Eph. iv. 9, 'He descended into the lower parts of the earth.'

These passages seem to suggest that the *object* 'of the going down of Christ into Hell' was to show how in death, as in life, He fulfilled every condition proper to man. And to judge from the point at which the subject is introduced into the Articles, between those which deal with the Incarnation and the Resurrection, as well as from the place which the clause 'He descended into Hell' occupies in the Western Creed, this might seem to have been regarded as the sole reason. It is significant that the clause began to establish itself in the Creed at

---

[1] See above, p. 7.

the time when Apollinarianism was making head, and this experience of Our Lord's human soul was appealed to in proof that He possessed our human nature in its entirety. But there was a further object. It is added in 1 Peter iii. 18 *sqq.* that 'being put to death in the flesh,' He was 'quickened in the spirit,' *i.e.* endowed with a new power of life in His human soul, 'in which also He went and preached to the spirits in prison' (iii. 19); and, further, that this preaching was a 'gospel' (iv. 6), in some way calculated to change their condition for the better. This much may be inferred from the passage; and the Church of England clearly interprets it of the Descent into Hell, for she appoints it to be read as the Epistle on Easter Even. What exactly the nature of this change for the better was, it is impossible to say; nor, inasmuch as Noah's generation only is specified as recipients of the preaching (iii. 20), can it be definitely asserted that others had a share in it too. It may have been only a special extension of mercy to them. They received exceptional treatment on earth. They occupy an exceptional place in Our Lord's teaching about the end (Matt. xxiv. 37; Luke xvii. 26), as in that of His Apostle here. On the other hand, there has been, from the earliest times, a strong tradition in the Church, which could not have arisen from any passage but this, to the effect that Our Lord's soul descended to the Old Testament saints and bettered their condition by the offer of the Gospel, so as to put them on the same footing with Christians at the Judgment. In that case, Noah's generation is to be regarded as one among the many others which had the offer of salvation preached unto them after death, because they had passed away before Christ came to proclaim it on earth. There is nothing to exclude such an interpretation in 1 Peter iii. 18—iv. 6; but, as thus interpreted, the passage lends no support to the notion that those who have had the offer in this life and refused it, will have another chance in the next.

ARTICLE IV

De Resurrectione Christi.

(§ 1) Christus vere a mortuis resurrexit, suumque corpus cum carne, ossibus, omnibusque ad integritatem humanae naturae pertinentibus, recepit, (§ 2) cum quibus in coelum ascendit, ibique residet, (§ 3) quoad extremo die ad judicandos homines reversurus sit.

Of the Resurrection of Christ.

(§ 1) Christ did truly rise again from death, and took again His body, with flesh, bones, and all things appertaining to the perfection of man's nature, (§ 2) wherewith He ascended into heaven, and there sitteth (§ 3) until He return to judge all men at the last day.

(i.) **Source.**—Composed by the English Reformers, 1552-3.

(ii.) **Object.**—The title suggests that Art. 4 follows, in the natural order, to supplement Arts. 2 and 3, which deal with what took place from the Incarnation to the Descent into Hell. But the structure of the Article is such as to lay stress on the fact of the Resurrection less for its own sake than with a view to asserting the reality of the manhood of Our Lord, now Risen and Ascended. There is evidence that much confusion of thought existed as to the nature of His glorified humanity. A section of the Anabaptists contended that the flesh of Christ had never been the flesh of a created being, and is now so deified as to retain no semblance of humanity. Lutherans, with an eye to their particular theory as to the mode of Christ's presence in the Eucharist, assigned to His glorified body the prerogative of omnipresence, which is inconsistent with the verity of His proper manhood.

(iii.) **Explanation.**—The Article falls into three sections.

§ 1 deals with *the Resurrection*; and (1), as to the *fact*, it states that **Christ did truly rise again from death**.

(*a*) The earliest evidence we possess is to be found in the *Epistles*, specially those of St. Paul. These were written all, or nearly all, before the Gospels; and the earliest of them carry the evidence back, on this point, to within living memory (1 Cor. xv. 6) of the time when the Resurrection took place. Thus, the Thessalonians are reminded (A.D. 52), within a few months of their conversion, how they had accepted the Risen Lord as the foundation of their hope (1 Thess. i. 9, 10). This was written from Corinth; and afterwards (A.D. 57) the Corinthians, in their turn, are reminded how, five years ago at their conversion, the fact of the Resurrection was preached and accepted as the corner-stone of their new creed (1 Cor. xv. 3 *sqq.*), and as a fact which rested on the indisputable witness not only of individuals (xv. 5, 7), St. Paul himself included (xv. 8), but of considerable numbers still alive (xv. 6). The Epistles never labour to prove, they assume, the fact (Rom. i. 4); and, more than this, they assign to it the supreme place in the religious consciousness of the Christian. For the faith by which he was justified or brought into relation with God and made a new man (Eph. iv. 24; 2 Cor. v. 17) is everywhere represented as centred not in the crucified, but in the Risen Lord, or in 'God who raised Him from the dead' (Rom. iv. 24, x. 9; Eph. i. 19, 20; Col. ii. 12; *cf.* 1 Peter i. 21). (*b*) We are thus prepared to find the fact of the Resurrection occupying the place of importance, as in the preaching of St. Paul (1 Cor. xv. 12), so in that of the Twelve. The Book of the Acts bears out the Epistles when it represents this to have been the burden of St. Peter's preaching from the day when Matthias was chosen to 'become a witness with' the Eleven 'of His resurrection' (Acts i. 22) up to the admission of the Gentiles with Cornelius (Acts x. 40; *cf.* ii. 24, iii. 15, iv. 2, 10, 33, v. 30). So (*c*) when the *Gospels* came to be written, the fact of the Resurrection is recorded in all four (Matt. xxviii. 6; Mark xvi. 6; Luke xxiv. 6; John xx.); and is made the culminating point of that one which criticism tends more and more to recognise as the earliest, and as in substance and range most nearly in accord with the Gospel message

EXPLANATION

as delivered by St. Peter (cf. Mark i. 4 and xvi. 6 with Acts x. 37-40). It was then unquestionably the belief of the first Christians that 'Christ did truly rise again from death.'

To go behind this historical evidence for the fact, and inquire into its possibility, would be to stray into the field of Christian Evidences. But when it is remembered that the Jews were not prepared for a resurrection except 'at the last day' (John xi. 24); that the disciples, so far from expecting their Lord to rise again (John xx. 9), actually derided the news as 'nonsense' (Luke xxiv. 11) when it came: but yet that, once convinced of its truth, they recognised its fitness (Acts ii. 24), and became, instead of runaways (Matt. xxvi. 56), bold in its defence (Acts iv. 13, 29, 31): then it is as impossible to hold that such a change was the result of hallucination, as it is, unless the Resurrection be a fact, to account for their success in founding the Church, whose very existence, with institutions of worship such as the weekly Eucharists (Acts xx. 7), and Sundays (1 Cor. xvi. 2), is a standing memorial to the Risen Christ. A complete reversal of human history would have to take place if the Resurrection were not a fact.

The Article next proceeds to (2) *the nature of the Resurrection body*; and states that **Christ took again His body, with flesh, bones, and all things appertaining to the perfection of man's nature.** Scripture makes it clear that He took again the same body, for it still bore marks of the Passion (Luke xxiv. 39; John xx. 20, 27); and was recognisable both in voice (John xx. 16) and bearing (xxi. 7). There was a reality and identity about it unmistakable; but also a difference. He appeared (John xx. 19) and vanished (Luke xxiv. 31) at will. Yet His body was not wholly spiritual, for He could be seen and touched (Luke xxiv. 39; John xx. 27); and He ate and drank with His disciples (Luke xxiv. 43; cf. Acts x. 41). It was thus a true human body, yet 'a spiritual body' (1 Cor. xv. 44) in the sense that it was 'glorified' (Phil. iii. 21), *i.e.* no longer bound by the laws and conditions of creaturely existence, but entirely amenable to those of the spiritual order. Probably this is the meaning of His saying that 'a spirit hath not flesh and bones as ye behold Me having' (Luke xxiv. 39). It is a phrase which suggests a real human bodily structure, without, however, that liability to corruption (1 Cor. xv. 50) which is incidental to ordinary human bodies here, and is expressed in the term 'flesh and blood' (Heb. ii. 14). The Article by adhering strictly to Our Lord's description of His risen body, asserts that, though changed, it retained every characteristic proper to a human body, *i.e.* that He retained at the Resurrection a true but glorified humanity.

§ 2. It was 'in,' not into, such a condition that He was 'received up' (1 Tim. iii. 16) at *the Ascension.* The **wherewith** marks the passage from the introductory to the cardinal statement of the Article,[1] which is that with such a glorified but true human body **He ascended into Heaven, and there sitteth.** The fact of the Ascension is rapidly passed over, as in the Scriptures. There is no account of it in SS. Matthew and John, though it is assumed by the latter as well known (John iii. 13, vi. 62, xx. 17). The last verses (xvi. 9-20) of St. Mark's Gospel in which it is just mentioned (xvi. 19) may not be his. St. Luke alone supplements the meagre allusion to it in his own Gospel (xxiv. 51) by a full account in the Acts (i. 6-11). St. Paul alludes to it but twice (Eph. iv. 8 and 1 Tim. iii. 16); St. Peter once (1 Pet. iii. 22). It is with the *Heavenly Session* that both Scripture and the Article are most concerned, and this as the purpose of the Ascension. The Ascended Lord is described in the New Testament under two figures. As in the Article, it is said that 'He there sitteth' (Rev. iii. 21); and again, as in the Creed, that 'He sitteth at the right hand of the Father' (Mark xvi. 19; Eph. i. 20; Col. iii. 1; Heb. i. 3, etc.). The latter figure carries with it the notion of power and dignity; the former suggests the ideas of rest after labour (Heb. xii. 2), along with those of expectation (Ps. cx. 1; Heb. x. 12, 13) and of authority as King and Judge (1 Pet. iii. 22 and iv. 5). But as with the Father rest is not inactivity (John v. 17), so the

---

[1] *Cf.* 'wherefore,' and the structure of Arts. 7, 10, 11, 16, 20, 31, 36.

EXPLANATION

Son is ever active both as King and High Priest. Twice it is said not that He sitteth but that He 'is at the right hand of God,' active first as Priest (Rom. viii. 34), and then as King (1 Pet. iii. 22; *cf.* John xiv. 2); and once His Priesthood is directly connected with the Session as if to show that, so far from the Session resulting in repose, it issues in the all-prevailing intercession of a royal priesthood (Heb. viii. 1). It is this activity, whether in ruling or interceding, which leads to His being described as 'standing' to succour Stephen (Acts vii. 56), or 'walking' in the midst of the seven golden candlesticks (Rev. ii. 1), and that habited as a priest in active service (Rev. i. 13). The present reality of His human interests adds the crowning proof to the present reality of His human nature.

There can be little doubt that the Article asserts this latter point with a view to setting up a barrier against a particular theory of the Eucharistic presence which had made some way abroad, and was bound up with the ascription of ubiquity to Our Lord's human nature. Zwingli denied the real presence of Our Lord in the Eucharist on the ground that 'He is gone into heaven, and therefore is not here,' it being against the truth of His human nature for His body to be in two places at once. Luther, anxious to maintain the real presence, used language which implied the later theory of his followers that the human nature was so permeated by the divine as to acquire the attributes of divinity, among them omnipresence. About 1550 the two schools of foreign Protestantism were struggling for supremacy in England, and the ubiquity of Christ's body became one of the foremost points in dispute. Swiss influences prevailed, and its ubiquity was denied in the clause of Art. 29 of 1553, since repudiated on other grounds. Article 4 had then been drafted to prepare the way for the denial. In 1563 it was retained as it stood, to keep the error out. It insists that Our Lord went into heaven, and 'there sitteth' in all respects very man, as in the entirety, so in the limitations of humanity. Among them must be reckoned relation to place; and omnipresence would be as destructive of His true humanity as omniscience. The fault of the controversy lay in its preference for *à priori* reasonings over the actual facts of Scripture, which are as decisive in respect to the appearances of His risen body in place (Luke xxiv. 15, etc.) and to His real withdrawal (Luke xxv. 51; John vi. 62, xiv. 28) as to His partial ignorance as man (Mark xiii. 32). The Lutheran theology on this point involved an Eutychian confusion of the two Natures. On the other hand, the presence of Our Lord's human nature, by virtue of its inseparable 'conjunction'[1] with His Divine Person, is part of the truth of the permanent union of the two Natures therein. Though not deified, it was glorified. With this the Article is in no way inconsistent. It is a truth essential to that 'infinitude in possibility of application' which belongs to the Body of Our Lord in the Sacraments, and is represented in Scripture as the direct result of the Ascension (John vi. 62, 63).

(§ 3) In concluding with **the Return to Judgment**, the Article merely affirms what is the characteristic addition made to Natural Religion by the faith of Christ. The universal conscience of mankind anticipates a final judgment (Rom. ii. 15, 16 *a*). The Gospel merely adds that all judgment is committed to Jesus Christ (Rom. ii. 16 *b*), the Son; and this because, as Son of Man (John v. 27; Acts xvii. 31), He is fitted to be as merciful and faithful in the office of Judge as in that of High Priest (Heb. ii. 17).

---

[1] For the 'omniscience,' see Hooker, E. P., V. liv. 7; and the 'omnipresence,' V. lv.

ARTICLE V

De Spiritu Sancto.	Of the Holy Ghost.
(§ 1) **Spiritus sanctus,** (§ 2) **a Patre et Filio procedens,** (§ 3) **ejusdem est cum Patre et Filio essentiae, majestatis, et gloriae, verus ac aeternus Deus.**	(§ 1) The Holy Ghost, (§ 2) proceeding from the Father and the Son, (§ 3) is of one substance, majesty, and glory with the Father and the Son, very and eternal God.

(i.) **Source.**—Added in 1563, from the Confession of Würtemberg.

(ii.) **Object.**—The Article was probably added with a view to giving the formulary a character of completeness, in regard, at least, to fundamentals. Traces remain in the Thirteen Articles of some who denied the Personality of the Holy Ghost, as in Ridley's letters and the Reformatio Legum of others who denied His Divinity. Archbishop Parker still found 'the realm full of Anabaptists, Arians, etc.'; and this would be a further reason for an explicit assertion of the true doctrine about the Holy Ghost.

(iii.) **Explanation.**—The Article, hardly touching upon § 1 the Personality, deals with § 2 the Double Procession and § 3 the Divinity, of the Holy Ghost.

§ 1. The *Personality* of the Holy Spirit is to some extent obscured by the use of the same term in the Greek of the New Testament for the Person (Rom. viii. 9) and for the spiritual gifts (1 Cor. xiv. 2, 12), and it is sometimes hard to decide which sense is meant; though, as a general rule, where the definite article is used with the Holy Spirit, stress is laid on His presence as a Divine Person (Matt. xxviii. 19; 2 Cor. xiii. 14), and where it is omitted, attention is called rather to the gift, operation, or communication of the Spirit (John vii. 39, xx. 22).

But the Epistles make a clear distinction between the Giver and His gifts. In 1 Cor. xii. 4-11, it is said that 'there are diversities of gifts, but the same Spirit,' and that He divides them to each man 'severally even as He will.' No influence or attribute, nothing short of a Person, can exercise the power of will. So He is constantly described either as acting upon, or being acted upon by, other persons; as leading (Gal. v. 18; Rom. viii. 14), witnessing (viii. 16), or interceding (viii. 27); and again, as being grieved (Eph. iv. 30), lied unto (Acts v. 3), resisted (vii. 51), and spoken against (Matt. xii. 32), like any other person. In the fourth of these passages, the argument implies that the Holy Spirit is a Person distinct, not merely from man, but from the Father; for He 'maketh intercession for us' to Him (Rom. viii. 26, 27). Our Lord's last discourses, as reported in the Gospel of St. John, confirm and amplify that belief in the distinct Personality of the Holy Spirit, which is thus seen to have been already traditional with the Apostolic Churches. There He is promised by Our Lord, not only as a 'Comforter' or 'Advocate' (xiv. 26)—itself a term implying personality—but as 'another Advocate' (xiv. 16), as true an Advocate (1 John ii. 1) and Person as Our Lord Himself. His duties, too, are those of a Person acting on other persons, to teach (xiv. 26), witness (xv. 26), convict (xvi. 8), and guide (xvi. 13); the masculine pronoun (xiv. 26, xvi. 13, 14) is, throughout these discourses of Christ, used of Him as the Agent in such work; and He is a Person distinct both from the Father and the Son as being 'the Holy Spirit whom the Father will send in My Name' (xiv. 26).

§ 2 affirms the *Double Procession* of the Holy Ghost when it describes Him as **proceeding from the Father and the Son.**

The word *proceeding* is a legacy from the controversies of the fourth century, and it has survived as the term best fitted to guard the truth that the Holy Spirit is a distinct Person. The distinct Personality of the Son from that of the Father was established by the acceptance of the phrase that, while the Father is 'unoriginate' or 'made of none,' the Son is 'begotten.' When Macedonius,

EXPLANATION

c. 360 A.D., denied the Divinity of the Holy Spirit and questioned the nature of His relation to the Father and the Son, the term 'Procession' was seized upon by the orthodox, and applied to the Spirit by way of securing a double truth. On the one side, as against the statement that He is but a creature, it asserted His eternal derivation from the Father; and, on the other, by contrast with the idea of generation, it maintained His distinction from the Son. What the word ultimately denotes, we cannot know. To us it simply serves to defend what is an eternal fact in the Divine Nature as revealed in Scripture, that the Spirit is a Divine Person—Divine, as owing His being, like the Son, to an eternal relation with the Father, and a Person, as possessing it, equally with the Son, in a mode of His own. The term was suggested by the language of John xv. 26, where the temporal mission of the Spirit as 'the Comforter whom I will send unto you from the Father,' *i.e.* at Pentecost, seems to be distinguished from the relation in which He eternally stands to the Father as 'the Spirit . . . which proceedeth from the Father.'

A further question afterwards arose, whether He is rightly described as *proceeding from the Father and the Son*. The clause 'and the Son' is unquestionably an excrescence upon the earlier Creeds, which was adopted, though without any intention of adding to or altering the Faith, by a local Spanish Council in 589 A.D., and in course of time established itself throughout Western Christendom, until it became one of the main points of difference with the East. The Articles are thus committed to it as a Western formulary. But the question remains, Can the phrase find support in Scripture? It is implied in the fact that the Holy Spirit is called not only 'the Spirit of God' (Matt. iii. 16; 1 Cor. ii. 11, 12), or 'the Spirit of your Father' (Matt. x. 20), but also 'the Spirit of His Son' (Gal. iv. 6), 'the Spirit of Jesus' (Acts xvi. 7), 'of Christ' (Rom. viii. 9), and 'of Jesus Christ' (Phil. i. 19). Passages which speak of Our Lord bestowing the Spirit (John xv. 26, xx. 22) thus receive their explanation in the thought that this temporal mission of the Spirit depends on the relation eternally subsisting between the Son and the Spirit, in that the Spirit is His to bestow (John xvi. 14). It would have been better if Western terminology had preserved the more accurate language of the East, and said that the Spirit proceeds *from* the Father *through* the Son; but so long as the 'Filioque' is used with the reservation that the Father alone is the Source or Fountain of Godhead, it may be accepted as expressive of a primary truth—the right of the Son in all that the Father has (John xvi. 15).

§ 3 concludes with an assertion of the *Divinity* of the Holy Ghost. He is **very and eternal God**. Nowadays He is often thought of as an attribute or influence; but few would regard Him as a creature. Scripture is decisive as to His Divinity. It ascribes Divine actions to Him, Creation (Gen. i. 2), the Incarnation (Luke i. 35), the re-creation (John iii. 5), and its own inspiration (2 Pet. i. 21). It directly calls Him God (*cf.* Acts v. 3 with 4; 1 Cor. iii. 16 with vi. 19), and places Him unhesitatingly on a level with the Father and the Son (Matt. xxviii. 19; 2 Cor. xiii. 14).

ARTICLE VI

De divinis Scripturis, quod sufficiant ad salutem.

(§ 1) Scriptura sacra continet omnia, quae ad salutem sunt necessaria, ita, ut quicquid in ea nec legitur, neque inde probari potest, non sit a quoquam exigendum, ut tanquam articulus fidei credatur, aut ad salutis necessitatem requiri putetur.

(§ 2) **Sacrae Scripturae nomine, eos Canonicos libros Veteris et Novi Testamenti intelligimus, de quorum authoritate in Ecclesia nunquam dubitatum est.**

‡ De nominibus et numero librorum sacrae Canonicae Scripturae veteris Testamenti.
Genesis.
Exodus.
Leviticus.
Numeri.
Deuteronomium.
Josuae.
Judicum.
Ruth.
Prior liber Samuelis.
Secundus liber Samuelis.
Prior liber Regum.
Secundus liber Regum.
Prior liber Paralipomenon.
Secundus liber Paralipomenon.
Primus liber Esdrae.

Of the Sufficiency of the Holy Scriptures for Salvation.

(§ 1) Holy Scripture containeth all things necessary to salvation : so that whatsoever is not read therein, nor may be proved thereby, is not to be required of any man, that it should be believed as an article of the faith, or be thought requisite or necessary to salvation.

(§ 2) In the name of Holy Scripture, we do understand those Canonical books of the Old and New Testament, of whose authority was never any doubt in the Church.

Of the names and number of the Canonical Books.

Genesis.
Exodus.
Leviticus.
Numbers.
Deuteronomy.
Joshua.
Judges.
Ruth.
The First Book of Samuel.
The Second Book of Samuel.
The First Book of Kings.
The Second Book of Kings.
The First Book of Chronicles.
The Second Book of Chronicles.
The First Book of Esdras.

Secundus liber Esdrae.	The Second Book of Esdras.
Liber Hester.	‘ The Book of Esther.
Liber Job.	The Book of Job.
Psalmi.	The Psalms.
Proverbia.	The Proverbs.
Ecclesiastes vel Concionator.	Ecclesiastes, or the Preacher.
Cantica Solomonis.	Cantica, or Songs of Solomon.
IV Prophetae majores.	Four Prophets the Greater.
XII Prophetae minores.‡	Twelve Prophets the Less.
‡ Novi Testamenti omnes libros (ut vulgo recepti sunt) recipimus, et habemus pro Canonicis. ‡	All the books of the New Testament, as they are commonly received, we do receive, and account them Canonical.
(§ 3) ‡ Alios autem libros (ut ait Hieronymus) legit quidem Ecclesia ad exempla vitae et formandos mores; illos tamen ad dogmata confirmanda non adhibet: ut sunt:	(§ 3) And the other books (as Hierome saith) the Church doth read for example of life and instruction of manners; but yet doth it not apply them to establish any doctrine. Such are these following:
Tertius liber Esdrae.	The Third Book of Esdras.
Quartus liber Esdrae.	The Fourth Book of Esdras.
Liber Tobiae.	The Book of Tobias.
Liber Judith.	The Book of Judith.
*Reliquum libri Hester.	*The rest of the Book of Esther.
Liber Sapientiae.	The Book of Wisdom.
Liber Jesu filii Sirach.	Jesus the Son of Sirach.
*Baruch Propheta.	*Baruch the Prophet.
*Canticum trium puerorum.	*The Song of the Three Children.
*Historia Susannae.	*The Story of Susanna.
*De Bel et Dracone.	*Of Bel and the Dragon.
*Oratio Manassis.	*The Prayer of Manasses.
Prior liber Machabaeorum.	The First Book of Maccabees.
Secundus liber Machabaeorum.‡	The Second Book of Maccabees.

* Added in 1571.

(i.) **Source.**—The Article repeats in § 1 the fifth of the Forty-two Articles, but with an omission. In 1553 the following clause stood after 'thereby': 'Although it be sometime received of the faithful, as godly and profitable for an order and comeliness.' It was dropped in 1563, probably with a view to simplification. The statement in § 1 of Art. 6, now related only to the basis of doctrine; Art. 20 being at the same time so improved as to provide a separate treatment of the basis on which institutions and ceremonies were to stand. But there were also large additions. § 2, in thick type, was supplied from the Confession of Würtemberg. The remainder, between ‡‡, was added by Archbishop Parker, except for the *complete* list of the books of the Apocrypha, which dates only from 1571.

(ii.) **Object.**—In § 1 the Article lays down the supreme authority of Scripture as the Rule of Faith, in opposition to two current errors: (*a*) that of the Mediævalist, deliberately adopted by the Council of Trent on April 8, 1546, which placed Tradition on a level with Scripture as a source of doctrine; and (*b*) that of an Anabaptist faction of 'Anti-book' religionists, who disparaged the authority of Scripture in favour of the immediate inspirations of which they claimed to be possessed, affirming that 'Scripture is given only to the weak' (*cf.* Art. 19 of 1553). The effect of both these errors is the same—to rob the Faith of that prerogative of immutability which belongs to it as 'the faith which was once for all delivered unto the saints' (Jude 3). On either of these principles of interpretation, there was an insecurity about the Faith which could only be provided against as in § 1, by asserting the sole sufficiency of Scripture in any 'article of the Faith.' But before 1563, a further note of insecurity had been sounded. The question now asked was not, What does Scripture mean? but, What is Scripture? and the Swiss were for deciding both points by reference to the judgment of the individual. The Article provided against the chaos that would have ensued if the limits of Scripture had thus been left open, by falling back upon the consent of the Church as the test of Canonicity in § 2, and then applying it in § 3.

(iii.) **Explanation.**—§ 1 in accepting *the sufficiency of the Holy Scriptures for salvation*, lays down the principle common to all the reforming movements of the time, which tested the system of the Mediæval Church by appeal to Scripture. But it is characteristic of the English Reformers that they asserted the principle as valid only (*a*) in a limited area, and (*b*) in a qualified form. Thus (*a*) the Article does not apply it to institutions or ceremonies, which are admissible so long as they 'be not repugnant to the Word of God' (Art. 34), but only to doctrine; and that, not all doctrine, but such only as concerns **things necessary to salvation**. Even for this, (*b*) the sanction required is not that it should be found in so many terms in Scripture, or **read therein**. Enough if it **may be proved thereby**. Moreover, if the further questions be raised, Who is to decide what is Scripture? or, again, Who is to decide what Scripture means, *i.e.* what 'may be proved thereby,' the answer to both is that this function rests not with the individual, but with the Church. Thus § 2, by contrast with Calvin's position that Scripture is 'self-authenticated,' affirms that its contents are such books as have been recognised by the Church; and Article 20 that, so far from its being clear enough for the individual to read its meaning for himself, as Luther held, 'the Church hath authority in controversies of faith.' It was by reserving so large an area to the authority of the Church that the Church of England parted company with the foreign reforming bodies, which, not content with making Scripture the basis of necessary doctrine, insisted also on the clearness of Scripture, and the right and competence of every individual to interpret for himself. Leaving this insecurity of mere individualism to be dealt with afterwards, § 1 provides against the uncertainty incident to the Roman position, as defined at Trent. The Roman Church then put Scripture and Tradition on a level with each other as *co-ordinate* sources of truth, saying that she 'receives and venerates' both 'with equal affection of piety and reverence.' This position the Article repudiates; but the very Convocation which accepted the Article in its final form evinced the high value put upon Tradition by the English Church as a *subordinate* guide to truth; a value never since obscured, and distinctive of her Reformation from first to last.[1] So far from being inconsistent with the assignation of such a high place to Tradition, Article 6, by its place in the series, requires it. In Protestant Confessions the Article asserting the sole sufficiency of Scripture stands first, taking the same place as is held in the definitions of

---

[1] See above, p. 14.

Trent by the decree co-ordinating Scripture and Tradition. In both systems everything is deduced from their respectively characteristic principles. In our formulary the Articles rehearsing the substance of the Faith stand first (Arts. 1-5); those dealing with the Rule of Faith second (Arts. 6-8); and in them is contained, along with a statement of the paramount authority of Scripture (Art. 6), a deferential recognition of the three Creeds (Art. 8). This is the logical order. The Church exists to teach, and the Bible to prove. It is also the order of fact. We receive religious, as we receive scientific, truth, on the testimony of others. We then verify the one by the study of the Scriptures, and the other by the study of nature; but in either case with an eye to formulated dogma; which, if religious, is to be found in the Creeds, and if scientific, in the established laws of nature.

The Scriptural evidence for this position is best appreciated by a glance (*a*) at Our Lord's method in teaching, and (*b*) at the place which the Scriptures themselves profess to occupy in the equipment of the Christian. Thus (*a*) He vividly emphasised the insecurity of mere tradition, by pointing to the moral confusion which resulted from setting it up as of co-ordinate authority with the fifth commandment (Mark vii. 13): and at the same time He established the sufficiency of Scripture in 'an article of the Faith' by showing, with equal directness, how the resurrection of the dead, instead of resting, as was then thought by its supporters the Pharisees, upon tradition, stood on a Scriptural basis, not indeed as a truth 'to be read therein,' but 'to be proved thereby' (Mark xii. 26, 27). This was but one instance of His constant habit of appealing to the Old Testament in proof of what He taught (Matt. iv. 4; John x. 34, etc.). The Apostles learned it from Him (Acts ii. 17-21, 25-28, 34, etc., xviii. 28). The inference is, now that the New Testament has been placed on the same level of authority (1 Thess. v. 27; Col. iv. 16; 2 Pet. iii. 16), that in things requisite as necessary to salvation, Holy Scripture is to be treated as the final court of appeal. But, in subordination to its claims, Our Lord also bade men pay heed to the official teaching of the constituted authority (Matt. xxiii. 2) which sat in Moses' seat. (*b*) The New Testament books maintain the same balance between Scripture as the only source of truth, and Tradition as the guide to its meaning. They were professedly written for converts previously instructed in the Faith (Luke i. 1; 1 Cor. xv. 2, 3; 1 John ii. 21, etc.), who were yet encouraged to search the Scriptures for themselves (Acts xvii. 11; 2 Tim. iii. 15), and to look upon them as written that they 'might know the certainty concerning the things wherein they were instructed' (Luke i. 4; John xx. 31). Thus, while, on the one hand, tradition by itself was unreliable, and had to be brought to the touchstone of the written Word, as the ultimate authority, still the duty of consulting Scripture was not to be undertaken independently of what the convert had learned from the Church. On the other hand, by adding that the Scripture was written 'for our learning' (Rom. xv. 4); or again, 'for teaching, for reproof, for correction, for instruction which is in righteousness; that the man of God may be complete, furnished completely unto every good work' (2 Tim. iii. 16, 17); St. Paul shows that, while it does not pretend to be imperative on questions of usage or ceremony, it is all-sufficient in the region of moral and spiritual truth.

§ 2 sets forth *the test of Canonicity*. In answer to the question, What is to be reckoned as Scripture, and upon what ground is it so reckoned? the Article replies: **In the name of Holy Scripture, we do understand those Canonical Books of the Old and New Testament, of whose authority was never any doubt in the Church.** The word *Canonical* was first applied to the Scriptures by Origen, c. 216 A.D. It is the adjective formed from the Greek 'Canon,' which means a rule or standard, serving to regulate other things (*cf.* 2 Cor. x. 13, 15, 16; Gal. vi. 16). The 'Canonical Books' then are such as have been admitted by reference to some rule. Such a rule or 'Canon' had been accepted for the writings of the Old Testament by the time of Our Lord (Luke xxiv. 44), though Canticles, Ecclesiastes, and Esther had not yet established their right to be included within its limits. But they were admitted before the century was out; and the Old Testament Canon thus completed was inherited from the Jewish by the Christian Church. Meanwhile the writings of the New Testament, as having been read from the first in liturgical worship[1] (1 Thess. v. 26, 27), were quickly placed on a level with 'the other [Old Testament] Scriptures' (2 Pet. iii. 16). By 200 A.D. a solid nucleus of four Gospels, the Acts, and thirteen Epistles of St. Paul had been accepted as Canonical. By 400 A.D. the limits of the Canon were practically the same as our own over the greater part of Christendom, the hitherto doubtful books, such as the Epistle to the Hebrews, having found admission. The question before us is, Who admitted? and, By reference to what Canon or rule? The most recent inquiries go to show that the admitting authority was that of the Church, Jewish or Christian, acting, however, less by formal decision, as in Councils, than by consent; and that the rule by conformity to which a book was admitted was that it should be traceable to, or at least bear the marks of, Prophetic, or, in the case of the Christian Scriptures, mainly Apostolic, origin. Any other test of Canonicity than this consent of the Church, so arrived at, breaks down just where it is most wanted. In modern times the organic function of a book has been suggested as a useful test. We are to find out the main drift of Holy Writ, and then ask, in reference to any particular book, whether its teaching is in harmony with that of Scripture as a whole. This was Luther's method; and it had disastrous results. It led him to disparage the Gospels by comparison with St. Paul's Epistles, and even to reject the Epistle of St. James, because it was not in harmony with the general drift of Scripture, which he held to be his doctrine of Justification by Faith only. Calvin proposed to test Canonicity by the concurrent witness of the Holy Spirit in the written Word and the believer's soul. But, however reassuring to the believer, this test also fails at

---

[1] The kiss was the Kiss of Peace, given after the reading of the Epistle, and later on, of the Gospels, at the beginning of the solemn part of the Eucharist then to follow.

the critical moment, *e.g.* when it is desired to convince others of the Canonicity of books whose claims have been disputed or might seem intrinsically disputable, such as Canticles, Ecclesiastes, and Esther. Protestantism, in short, but for the consent of the Church, would have no Bible; for on its own principles the Canon is an open question. This position the Article refused. It made the claim of a book to rank with the Canonical Scriptures to rest not with the individual, but with the Church; and the decision a matter not of doctrinal affinities, but of historic inquiry. The English Church thus rescued the basis of her Faith from insecurity, and planted herself firmly on Catholic ground.

§ 3 applies this test of Canonicity to **the other books**; which are commonly called the Apocrypha. The word is the neuter plural of a Greek adjective, whose equivalent in Hebrew or Aramaic means 'hidden.' The Apocrypha, as we call it, is a collection of apocryphal or 'hidden books.' As 'books,' or *the other books*, it should be noticed that they are reckoned as Scripture; and so, in fact, are frequently quoted not only by the ancient Fathers, but by the Reformers. Yet as 'hidden' it is implied that they do not stand on a level with the Canonical Scriptures. The term 'apocryphal' has now acquired a depreciatory tone, and means legendary, spurious, unworthy of credit. Such a bad sense may be traced back, in connection with it, as early as the second century A.D.; but as applied by the Jewish Church to certain books not included in the Hebrew Canon of the Scriptures, it simply meant 'hidden' in the sense of 'withdrawn from publicity.' The Jews rejected certain books as unsuitable for public reading, and so they became known as Apocrypha. Accordingly, they are not cited in the New Testament, though nearly every Canonical book of the Old Testament is there quoted. Nevertheless, they had a wide measure of popularity, and were included in the Septuagint and the old Latin version of the Scriptures made from it. Consequently, as the Fathers, with few exceptions, knew no Hebrew, and used these versions, the apocryphal books are frequently quoted as of like authority with the Old Testament

EXPLANATION

Scriptures, and particularly by St. Augustine (354-430 A.D.). Under his influence they were included in the list of Canonical Books framed at the Council of Carthage in 397 A.D., and came to be generally accepted in the West. The one Father, however, who, as a Hebrew scholar and critic, has a claim to be heard on the point is St. Jerome (346-420 A.D.). He gives a list of the Canonical Scriptures which coincides with our own, *i.e.* with the Hebrew Canon; and adds that 'whatsoever is without the number of these must be placed among the Apocrypha.' Elsewhere he observes, as the Article quotes him, that **the other books the Church doth read for example of life and instruction of manners, but yet doth it not apply them to establish any doctrine.** In the West even there was a succession of divines who noted this distinction between the apocryphal and the canonical writings, but the influence of St. Augustine was too strong for them; and the Council of Trent, in its session of April 8, 1546, after reciting a 'catalogue of the sacred books,' including those of the Apocrypha, decreed that 'if any one receive not, as sacred and canonical, these same books entire with all their parts, as they have been used to be read in the Catholic Church, and as they are contained in the old Latin Vulgate edition . . . let him be anathema.' To this the English Reformers in 1553 refrained from replying by enumerating the books of the Hebrew Canon only; though the distinction between its contents and the apocryphal books had been recognised in English Bibles of the reign of Henry VIII. The omission is not to be ascribed to hesitation, and may best be accounted for by supposing that the framers of the Forty-two Articles knew that they had dealt with the subject in their other work, the *Reformatio Legum*, where they devoted a section to it, and described the apocryphal books as 'sacred but not canonical.' That work remained a fiasco; but Archbishop Parker rescued its decisions on this point from obscurity, inserted the list of apocryphal books in Art. 6, and defined their position in the same sense. In their respective estimates of that position, the English Church is supported by scholarship, and Rome by mere adherence to tradition. But it must not be forgotten that the English Church, while refusing to credit the apocryphal books with any dogmatic authority, attaches to them a high value of their own. She reads them *for example of life and instruction of manners*; by permitting the use of Benedicite, by selecting from them both daily and Saints' Day Lessons in the choir offices, and by adopting Offertory Sentences from them at the Eucharist. She even quotes them in the Homilies, though under the loose influence of custom, as 'Scripture' and 'the Word of God.' For the light that they throw, not only on the heroic period of Hebrew history, which occurred between the close of the Old Testament Canon and the opening of the New Testament, but upon developments of beliefs and institutions during the interval, in accordance with which Our Lord largely shaped the doctrines and practices of His Church, the 'Apocrypha' are daily rising in the estimation of scholars. So far from being a mere collection of superstitious surplusage, as men think the name implies, they should be regarded as a sacred literature, a record of advance in spiritual truth, without which we should be at a loss to fully understand the New Testament itself.

ARTICLE VII

De Veteri Testamento.

(§ 1) Testamentum Vetus Novo contrarium non est, quandoquidem tam in Veteri quam in Novo per Christum, qui unicus est Mediator Dei et hominum, Deus et Homo, aeterna vita humano generi est proposita. (§ 2) Quare male sentiunt, qui veteres tantum in promissiones temporarias sperasse confingunt. (§ 3) † Quanquam lex a Deo data per Mosen, quoad ceremonias et ritus, Christianos non astringat, neque civilia ejus praecepta in aliqua republica necessario recipi debeant: nihilominus tamen ab obedientia mandatorum quae moralia vocantur nullus quantumvis Christianus est solutus. †

Of the Old Testament.

(§ 1) The Old Testament is not contrary to the New; for both in the Old and New Testament everlasting life is offered to mankind by Christ, who is the only Mediator between God and man, being both God and man. (§ 2) Wherefore they are not to be heard which feign that the old fathers did look only for transitory promises. (§ 3) Although the law given from God by Moses, as touching ceremonies and rites, do not bind Christian men, nor the civil precepts thereof ought of necessity to be received in any commonwealth; yet, notwithstanding, no Christian man whatsoever is free from the obedience of the commandments which are called moral.

(i.) **Source.**—This Article represents two of the series of 1553 thrown together. §§ 1 and 2 reproduce Art. 6 of the Edwardian formulary, and § 3 was taken from Art. 19 of that date, and appended here in 1563.

(ii.) **Object.**—It is aimed at two opposite errors, both current among the Anabaptist sectaries. Some of them rejected the Old Testament entirely, as we learn from Alley, Bishop of Exeter (1560-70). He notes 'the temerity, ignorance, and blasphemy of certain fantastical heads, which hold that the prophets do write only to the people of the Old Testament, and that their doctrine did pertain only to their time ; and would seclude all the fathers that lived under the Law from the hope of eternal salvation. And here is also a note to be gathered against them which utterly reject the Old Testament, as a book nothing necessary to the Christians which live under the Gospel.' This is the type of teaching repudiated in §§ 1 and 2. It denied the unity of the Old and New Testaments, and disparaged the former as a dispensation not merely preparatory, but contrary, to the age that was to come in Christ. Others, who are condemned in § 3, went to the opposite extreme, and insisted that the whole ceremonial and civil law of the Jews was a matter of divine obligation for Christians. We have already noticed the sympathy with which the Calvinists regarded such tenets at the Westminster Assembly.[1] The *Reformatio Legum* condemns in one paragraph both those who were for rejecting Judaism in its entirety, and those who would impose it upon Christians to the full. It thus bears witness to the prevalence of both the errors condemned in Article 7.

(iii.) **Explanation.**—The Article makes three principal assertions :—

§ 1 affirms that **the Old Testament is not contrary to the New.** This is not the same thing as saying that the Old Testament is not inferior to the New. No point has been brought into greater relief by the progress of Biblical scholarship than the imperfections of Old Testament religion. We have been taught, by a scientific study of the Old Testament, to find God stooping as low as mankind had fallen, in order to raise and restore them to His own image (Gen. i. 27). Many things, beside ' a bill of divorcement ' (Matt. xix. 7), God allowed for ' the hardness of men's heart' (*ib.* 8); not only the exterminating wars (Deut. xx. 16, 17), acts like that of Jael (Judges iv. 17 *sqq.*), and instruments of His purposes such as Jehu (2 Kings x. 30, 31), but a moral law which bound men by the harsh tones of external precept (Lev. xviii. 5 ; *cf.* Jer. xxxi. 33 ; Gal. iii. 11, 12 ; Rom. x. 5 *sqq.* ; Eph.

---

[1] See above, p. 60.

EXPLANATION

ii. 15), psalms of praise which sounded the jarring notes of vindictiveness (vii. xxxv. lxix. cix. cxxxvii.), and querulous self-righteousness (xliv. 17, lxxiv.), prophets and saints whose religion exhibits the same characteristics (Jer. xvii. 18, xx. 12 ; Neh. xiii. 14, 31). The Article does not shut the door upon a just criticism which endeavours to mark the stages of development in true religion or morals. Thus, in morals, it has no fault to find with the view that regards Old Testament imperfections as incidental to the gradual transition of the people of God to morality from crude morality ; it merely condemns those to whom the Old Testament is as *contrary* to the New Testament as immorality is to morality. Similarly in religion, the notion which it rejects is the notion that the Old Testament religion was not an earlier stage of development, but a phase of divine dealing organically disconnected with the present, and now past and gone. The Article maintains that the Old Testament and the New Testament are parts of one progress, not representatives of two distinct eras ; that the earlier was a preparation for the later, not contrary to it ; and that the whole is an orderly development, not a case of the supersession of one dispensation by another.

This unity the Article bases upon the hope of redemption through the Messiah which is common to both : **for both in the Old and New Testament everlasting life is offered to mankind by Christ.** But here we must be on our guard. We have no warrant for presuming that the old fathers had a detailed foreknowledge of the time and the way in which salvation was to come through Jesus Christ. On the contrary, Our Lord (Matt. xiii. 17) and His Apostles (1 Peter i. 10 *sqq.*)[1] speak of limitations in the prophetic vision. Times and seasons, in particular, were hidden from the Apostles (Acts i. 7) ; and, on one point, from the Son of Man Himself (Matt. xxiii. 36). *A fortiori*, we are not to test the Old Testament prophets by their power of consciously anticipating in detail the life and work of Jesus. Certainly there are wonderful correspondences observable in the event ; but, while

---

[1] *Cf.* 2 Pet. i. 20.

these indicate decisively a divine plan, they do not amount to presumption of prophetic acquaintance with it in each detail beforehand. Nor does the Article rest the unity of the Old Testament and New Testament upon any such minute parallelism between prediction and fulfilment, but merely upon the general position that the old fathers looked for salvation through Messiah. And, indeed, from the protevangelium (Gen. iii. 15) onwards, this is the unifying strand of the Scriptures. The fall of man was immediately followed by a promise of restoration, and that through suffering. Thereupon a race (Gen. ix. 26, 27), then a nation (Gen. xii. 1-3), then a tribe (xlix. 8-12), then a line of Kings (2 Sam. vii. 12-16), finally a personal Messiah (Isa. ix. 6), becomes the heir of the promise and the centre of Israel's expectation for its working out. At various points in the growth of this expectation, elements of prophetic (Deut. xviii. 15 *sqq.*), sacrificial (Isa. lii. 13, and liii.), and priestly (Zech. vi. 13) functions make their appearance, to be afterwards gathered up into the lineaments of the true Messiah. At last these lines of expectation converge upon Jesus. They may only have appeared parallel lines to those who preceded Him. But even so, the unique thing about Israel is that its prophets with their contemporaries, each at their several standpoints, kept their gaze steadily fixed on the future, and looked for a salvation to be *offered to mankind by Christ*. For this we have the explicit word of Our Lord and His disciples. 'Abraham,' He says, 'rejoiced to see My day: and he saw it, and was glad' (John viii. 56). And again, while the whole argument of the Epistle to the Hebrews emphasises the typical and anticipatory character of the Old Testament institutions (Heb. x. 1), it is distinctly asserted that the faith of the old fathers lay in their looking for their satisfaction in the Christ (Heb. xi. 26).

§ 2 It follows from this that **they are not to be heard which feign that the old fathers did look only for transitory promises.** But again we must distinguish. Old Testament scholarship has made it certain that early Hebrew religion was mainly concerned with this world. Thus its ideas of justice were based upon a doctrine of retribution in this life. It was held that right and wrong meet with their reward here (Exod. xx. 12, xxiii. 25-31; Deut. xxviii.); and, not to mention several of the Psalms (xxxvii. lxxiii. cxxviii.), the Book of Job is specially concerned with the working out of this theme. As the argument proceeds, the logic of facts becomes too strong for such a doctrine of retribution to survive; and belief in a future life dawns upon Job (*cf.* vii. 7-10, xiv. 7-15, xix. 25-27) as its true solution. But apart from the pressure of obstinate questionings, belief in continued existence after death was not altogether wanting even in the earliest times. Such an expression as 'gathered to his people,' which appears to mean more than 'buried in the family sepulchre,' is proof of this (Gen. xxv. 8, 17, xxxv. 29, xlix. 29, 33). Earth may have been pre-eminently the land of the living (Ps. lii. 5; Isa. xxxviii. 18, 19), and Sheol the realm of a shadowy existence (Ps. lxxxviii. 3 *sqq.*); yet it was not annihilation. From this point we find an upward though not uniform development of belief in a future life, rising from the thought of an underworld inhabited by those who have gone before (2 Sam. xii. 23), yet were but half their former selves (Isa. xiv. 9 *sqq.*); thence to a hope in a national resurrection (Hos. vi. 2; Isa. xxvi. 19; Ezek. xxxvii.); finally, through certainty that moral communion with God once sustained here cannot fail of continuance (Ps. xvi., xvii.) or vindication at God's hands (Job xix. 25-27) hereafter, to the conviction of a personal resurrection to reward or punishment for each individual soul (Dan. xii. 2, 3). Thus it is clear that, though the interest of the Old Testament writers is mainly centred in this life, the old fathers were forced to look beyond it. The Article rightly forbids us to say they *did look only for transitory promises*. It does not forbid us to show that their hold on the things eternal was slight and of gradual growth. In truth, Our Lord and His Apostles assert as much. He taught His hearers to see more in the Old Testament language about a future life than they had hitherto perceived, much more than can have been suspected by those who first uttered or heard it (Mark xii. 26, 27); and St. Paul says it was left for the Gospel to turn surmisings into certainties 'by bringing life and incorruption to light' (2 Tim. i. 10). Thus the Article leaves full room for the development of belief in a future life. All that it denies is that there ever was a period in which that belief was not, in some form, a factor in Israel's religious conceptions.

§ 3 maintains, in opposition to the school which would re-impose the Jewish Law in its entirety, that while the **ceremonial and civil law given from God by Moses do not bind Christian men, yet the commandments which are called moral do.** This hardly needs comment. The sacrifices were the types, of which Christ is the Antitype. The Old Testament institutions of worship stand to those of the New Testament as shadow to substance (Col. ii. 17). This is the whole argument of the Epistle to the Hebrews ; and St. Paul, in his Epistles to the Romans and Galatians, while recognising the function of the Law to have been preparatory (Gal. iii. 24), and to have served to intensify the sense of sin (Rom. v. 20) and condemnation (Rom. vii. 10), so as to make men feel the need of a Saviour (*ibid.* 24, 25), vindicates the liberty of Christians from the ceremonial requirements of the Law (*ibid.* viii. 1, 2). Thus the Apostles refrained from imposing them upon Gentile converts (Acts xv. 1, and 28, 29). They were of positive and temporary force only. Similarly the civil precepts of the Law, which were never imposed on any nation but the Jewish, lapsed when their national existence came to an end. But the moral law is eternal. This law Our Lord came 'not to destroy, but to fulfil' (Matt. v. 17). It is at once enforced and expanded; in the Sermon on the Mount (Matt. v.-vii.); in reply to the question about the great commandment (Matt. xxii. 37-40); and in the repeated reaffirmation of the great principles of conduct, in matters relating to society, the state, the family, and the individual which form the hortatory parts of St. Paul's Epistles, and are provided with fresh sanctions from the great armoury of Christian doctrine for this very purpose, in the previous argumentative introductions (*cf.* especially Rom. xii. xiii. ; Eph. iv. vi. ; Col. iii. iv.)

ARTICLE VIII

De Tribus Symbolis.

(§ 1) Symbola tria, Nicaenum, Athanasii, et quod vulgo Apostolorum appellatur omnino recipienda sunt et credenda ; (§ 2) nam firmissimis Scripturarum testimoniis probari possunt.

Of the Three Creeds.

(§ 1) The three Creeds, Nicene Creed, Athanasius' Creed, and that which is commonly called the Apostles' Creed, ought thoroughly to be received and believed ; (§ 2) for they may be proved by most certain warrants of Holy Scripture.

(i.) **Source.**—Composed by the English Reformers, 1552-3 : and in substance unchanged since.

(ii.) **Object.**—To assert the Catholic character of the English Reformation, especially against the Anabaptists who rejected both the substance of the Catholic Faith, and the Creeds which served as summaries of it.

(iii.) **Explanation.**—The Article makes two assertions :—

§ 1 asserts that **The three Creeds ought thoroughly to be received and believed.**

(*a*) In *origin*, the creed (for there was a creed before there were three creeds) probably owes its existence to the necessities, and its substance to the subject-matter, of Apostolic preaching. The earliest Christian missionaries taught and preached 'Jesus as the Christ' (Acts v. 42, ix. 20, 22), or 'Jesus as Lord' (Acts xi. 20 ; 1 Cor. xii. 3) : and this became a *symbolum* or watchword among Christians. But it speedily received expansion, so as to include the main facts of Our Lord's life (1 Cor. xv. 3-5) which were delivered as containing the core of the Gospel message ; and treasured as 'a form of sound words' (2 Tim. i. 13 ; Rom. vi. 17). Of such 'forms' there are abundant traces in the New Testament (Matt. xvi. 16; John vi. 69; 1 Cor. viii. 6; 1 Tim. iii. 16); so that it is clear that in substance the Creed is older than the Christian Scriptures, and took shape under the exigencies of missionary work.

(b) Its *form* is due to its connection with the Baptismal formula (Matt. xxviii. 19; *cf.* Tit. iii. 4-6). Baptism, of course, was the goal to which a missionary would lead his converts. They had to be taught what was meant by the Threefold Name, and before Baptism, were asked if they believed in it (*cf.* Acts viii. 37 [1]). They answered an interrogatory Creed, by rehearsing a declarative one: and the custom came to be known as the Traditio and Redditio Symboli, or the Delivery and Repetition of the Creed.

(c) In *number* the Creeds came to be reckoned as three, but none of them has a strict right to the name by which it is known. The *Nicene Creed*, which the Article places first, perhaps as alone enjoying universal authority, is so called because it was originally accepted as a test of orthodoxy at the Council of Nicæa, 325 A.D.; but as now recited it contains additional clauses, beginning at 'the Lord, and Giver of life,' which probably made their first appearance in the Church of Jerusalem about 350 A.D., and were afterwards generally adopted, with the approval of the Council of Constantinople in 381 A.D. This 'Nicene' Creed is thus specially associated with the Eastern Church, and was, in origin, a characteristically Conciliar Creed, intended for subscription by, and so binding on, the clergy (**We** believe). After a time it was introduced into Eucharistic worship, and now demands the loyal adhesion of the faithful laity. But to a layman of Western Christendom it does not stand quite on the same level of obligation as *that which is commonly called the Apostles' Creed*, to which, as the creed of his baptism, he has explicitly pledged himself by the most solemn of vows. The Apostles' Creed is the type of a Baptismal Creed. In substance earlier, in form, except for its retention of the individuality (**I** believe) and simplicity of the primitive creed, it is much later than

[1] An interpolation, but illustrative of a very early custom.

the 'Nicene' Creed. The form in which we now recite the Apostles' Creed appears for the first time in the middle of the eighth century; and is a version of Gallican extraction, which has superseded the older Roman Creed throughout the West. It is thus, by association, pre-eminently a Western Creed. How it came to be called the Apostles' Creed is disputed; possibly as emanating in its earlier form from Rome, the only Apostolic See of the West; possibly as in substance representing the teaching of the Apostles; ·but certainly not on the ground of its having been drawn up by the Apostles, as was supposed in the fourth century. There remains *Athanasius' Creed*, which can neither be ascribed to St. Athanasius (d. 373), nor, strictly speaking, be called a creed. Its structure is not that of a creed, but of a psalm, being admitted into ecclesiastical Psalters by the ninth century, and recited in conjunction with the psalms and canticles of the Daily Offices since the tenth; nor does it bear traces of the threefold division common to the older creeds; nor is it a summary of, but rather a prolonged meditation upon, the Christian Faith; nor was it meant for converts, but for instructed Christians. So it·is preferably spoken of by its older titles, such as ' the Psalm *Quicunque vult*,' ' *Expositio Fidei*.' It is only ' commonly called the creed of St. Athanasius.' Whatever its origin—whether it be the work of a single author of the fifth or sixth century, or, as some have recently and perhaps too readily thought, a composite document which attained its present form in the ninth century— it is admittedly a Latin formulary of Western origin emanating from the south of France, and powerfully affected by the language and theology of St. Augustine (d. 430 A.D.). This is not the place to discuss its difficulties; but it is only just to observe that they are due in no small measure to the mistranslations of the current English version; that they attach in less degree to the Latin original; and have been brought into prominence by the customary substitution of Mattins for the Holy Communion as the ordinary morning service for the laity on Sundays and Saints' Days. To such a custom the Prayer-Book lends no countenance.

§ 2 states the ground on which the three creeds are to be received. **They may be proved by most certain warrants of Holy Scripture.** Not that the creed is inferior in authority to the Scriptures; for, as we have seen, it is in substance older than the New Testament, and was in fact the kernel of the Apostolic preaching or 'Word of God'—a term then applied, not to the Scriptures, but to the oral utterances of Christian Apostles and Prophets (Acts iv. 29-31, etc.; 1 Thess. ii. 13; 2 Cor. ii. 17). The time came, however, when the Christian Prophets died, and inspiration, *i.e.* immediate revealed certainty as to the Faith, ceased with them. The Scriptures which they left behind them thus preserved the 'Word of God' in its final form. Since that date the Church has added to the Creed, not indeed in substance, but in explicit assertion. It follows, from the finality of Holy Scripture (*cf.* Art. 6), that the Creeds must be referred to it for acceptance. But it also follows, from the direct relation of the Creeds to the original 'Word of God,' that *they may be proved by most certain warrants of Holy Scripture.* Both Creeds and Scriptures emanated from the same inspired sources. They are related, in short, to each other as the key to the lock.

APPENDIX

NOTE.—(1) Blank spaces enclosed in [ ] indicate points at which new matter was afterwards inserted.
(2) Words between † † were subsequently dropped.

1553.

Articuli de quibus in Synodo Londinensi, Anno Dom. MDLII ad tollendam opinionum dissensionem et consensum verae religionis firmandum, inter Episcopos et alios eruditos viros convenerat.

1563.

Articuli, de quibus in Synodo Londinensi anno Domini, iuxta ecclesiae Anglicanae computationem, MDLXII ad tollendam opinionum dissensionem, et firmandum in vera Religione consensum, inter Archiepiscopos Episcoposque utriusque Provinciae, nec non etiam universum Clerum convenit.

I

De fide in Sacrosanctam Trinitatem.

Unus est vivus et verus Deus, aeternus, incorporeus, impartibilis, impassibilis, immensae potentiae, sapientiae, ac bonitatis, creator et conservator omnium, tum visibilium tum invisibilium. Et in unitate hujus divinae naturae tres sunt personae, ejusdem essentiae, potentiae, ac aeternitatis, Pater, Filius, et Spiritus Sanctus.

I

De fide in Sacrosanctam Trinitatem.

Unus est vivus et verus Deus, aeternus, incorporeus, impartibilis, impassibilis, immensae potentiae, sapientiae, ac bonitatis: creator et conservator omnium tum visibilium tum invisibilium. Et in unitate huius divinae naturae tres sunt personae, eiusdem essentiae, potentiae, ac aeternitatis, Pater, Filius, et Spiritus sanctus.

1553.

II

Verbum Dei verum hominem esse factum.

Filius qui est verbum Patris, [   ] in utero beatae Virginis, ex illius substantiâ naturam humanam assumpsit, ita ut duae naturae, divina et humana, integre atque perfecte in unitate personae fuerint inseparabiliter conjunctae, ex quibus est unus Christus, verus Deus et verus homo, qui vere passus est, crucifixus, mortuus et sepultus, ut patrem nobis reconciliaret, essetque hostia non tantum pro culpa originis, verum etiam pro omnibus actualibus hominum peccatis.

III

De descensu Christi ad Inferos.

Quemadmodum Christus pro nobis mortuus est et sepultus, ita est etiam credendus ad inferos descendisse. † Nam corpus usque ad resurrectionem in sepulchro jacuit, Spiritus ab illo emissus, cum spiritibus qui in carcere sive in inferno detinebantur, fuit, illisque praedicavit, quemadmodum testatur Petri locus. †

IV

Resurrectio Christi.

Christus vere a mortuis resurrexit, suumque corpus cum carne, ossibus, omnibusque ad integritatem humanae naturae pertinentibus, recepit, cum quibus in coelum ascendit, ibique residet, quoad extremo die ad judicandos homines revertatur.

1563.

II

Verbum Dei verum hominem esse factum.

Filius qui est verbum Patris, ab aeterno a Patre genitus verus et aeternus Deus, ac Patri consubstantialis, in utero beatae Virginis ex illius substantia naturam humanam assumpsit: ita ut duae naturae, divina et humana, integre atque perfecte in unitate personae, fuerint inseparabiliter conjunctae: ex quibus est unus Christus, verus Deus et verus homo: qui vere passus est, crucifixus, mortuus, et sepultus, ut Patrem nobis reconciliaret, essetque hostia non tantum pro culpa originis, verum etiam pro omnibus actualibus hominum peccatis.

III

De descensu Christi ad Inferos.

Quemadmodum Christus pro nobis mortuus est et sepultus, ita est etiam credendus ad inferos descendisse.

IV

Resurrectio Christi.

Christus vere a mortuis resurrexit, suumque corpus cum carne, ossibus, omnibusque ad integritatem humanae naturae pertinentibus, recepit, cum quibus in coelum ascendit, ibique residet, quoad extremo die ad judicandos homines reversurus sit.

1553.

[

]

V
Divinae Scripturae doctrina sufficit ad salutem.

Scriptura sacra continet omnia quae sunt ad salutem necessaria, ita ut quicquid in ea nec legitur necque inde probare potest, † licet interdum a fidelibus, ut pium et conducibile ad ordinem et decorum admittatur, attamen † a quoquam non exigendum est ut tanquam articulus fidei credatur, et ad salutis necessitatem requiri putetur.

[

1563.

V
De Spiritu sancto.

Spiritus sanctus, a Patre et Filio procedens eiusdem est cum Patre et Filio essentiae, maiestatis, et gloriae, verus, ac aeternus Deus.

VI
Divinae Scripturae doctrina sufficit ad salutem.

Scriptura sacra continet omnia quae sunt ad salutem necessaria, ita ut quicquid in ea nec legitur, neque inde probari potest, non sit a quoquam exigendum, ut tanquam articulus fidei credatur aut ad necessitatem salutis requiri putetur.

Sacrae Scripturae nomine eos Canonicos libros veteris et novi testamenti intelligimus, de quorum autoritate in Ecclesia nunquam dubitatum est.

Catalogus librorum sacrae Canonicae Scripturae veteris testamenti.

Genesis.	2 Samuelis.
Exodus.	Esdrae 2.
Leviticus.	Hester.
Numeri.	Iob.
Deuteronom.	Psalmi.
Iosue.	Proverbia.
Iudicum.	Ecclesiastes.
Ruth.	Cantica.
2 Regum.	Prophetae maiores.
Paralipom. 2.	Prophetae minores.

Alios autem libros (ut ait Hieronymus) legit quidem Ecclesia ad exempla vitae et formandos mores, illos tamen ad dogmata confirmanda non adhibet: ut sunt

1553.

1563.

Tertius et quartus Esdrae.
Sapientia.
Iesus filius Sirach.
Tobias.   Iudith.
Libri Machabaeorum 2.
[   ]
  Novi Testamenti libros omnes (ut vulgo recepti sunt) recipimus et habemus pro Canonicis.]

VI

Vetus Testamentum non est rejiciendum.

Testamentum vetus, quasi novo contrarium sit, non est repudiandum, sed retinendum, quandoquidem tam in veteri quam in novo per Christum qui unicus est Mediator Dei et hominum, Deus et homo, aeterna vita humano generi est proposita. Quare non sunt audiendi, qui veteres tantum in promissiones temporarias sperasse confingunt. [   ]

VII

De Veteri Testamento.

Testamentum vetus novo contrarium non est, quandoquidem tam in veteri quam novo, per Christum, qui unicus est mediator Dei et hominum, Deus et homo, aeterna vita humano generi est proposita. Quare male sentiunt, qui veteres tantum in promisiones temporarias sperasse confingunt. Quanquam lex a Deo data per Mosen, quoad ceremonias et ritus, Christianos non astringat, neque civilia eius praecepta in aliqua republica necessario recipi debeant: nihilominus tamen ab obedientia mandatorum, quae moralia vocantur, nullus quantumvis Christianus est solutus.

VII

Symbola tria.

Symbola tria, Nicenum, Athanasii, et quod vulgo Apostolicum appellatur, omnino recipienda sunt [   ]. Nam firmissimis divinarum Scripturarum testimoniis probari possunt.

VIII

Symbola tria.

Symbola tria, Nicenum, Athanasii, et quod vulgo Apostolicum appellatur, omnino recipienda sunt et credenda. Nam firmissimis Scripturarum testimoniis probari possunt.

INDEX

Admonition, The Second, 54.
Alley, Bishop, 80, 103.
Anabaptists, 17, 19, 32 ff, 41, 45, 65, 75, 89, 95, 103, 109.
Andrewes, Bishop, 56.
Apocrypha, the, 100.
Apollinaris, 72.
Apostles' Creed, the, 5 ff, 110.
Appello Cæsarem, 58.
Arianism, 3.
Arians, 1, 33.
Arius, 2, 70.
Arminius, 57.
Articles, authority of, 5; character of, 4, 24; and Confessions, contrast of, 10; purpose of, 5.
—— (1536), the Ten, 11 f, 18 ff.
—— (1538), the Thirteen, 8, 21 ff, 36, 65, 69.
—— (1552), the Forty-five, 25.
—— (1553), the Forty-two, 25; authority of, 26; authorship of, 27; character of, 31; object of, 29, 34; origin of, 25; revision of, 38; sources of, 36.
—— (1559), the Eleven, 39.
—— (1563), the Thirty-eight, 41.
—— (1563), the Thirty-nine, 38; arrangement of, 62; attempted revision of (1643), 60; character of, 45 ff; comparison of, with the Forty-two, 42; not Calvinistic, 49, 54, 59; origin of, 41; revision of (1571), 51.
Articles (1595), the Lambeth, 9, 54 f.
Ascension, the, 86.
Athanasian Creed, the, 111.
Atonement, the, 75 ff.

BARRETT, WILLIAM, 55.
Baxter, 61.
Bishops' Book, The, 20.
Burghley, Lord, 55.

CALVIN, 7, 35, 49.
Calvinism, 56 ff.
Canon, the, 98.
Canonical, 98.
Canonicity, 98.
Catechism, the, 56.
Charles I., 58.
Confessions, 8; Protestant, 96 f; Augsburg, 7 f, 21, 36; Consensus Tigurinus, 9; Formula of Concord, 8; Scottish, 9; Second Helvetic, 9; Westminster, 9; Würtemberg, 9, 40, 69, 89, 95.

Cosin, 58.
Cranmer, Archbishop, 15, 17, 21 f, 25, 27 ff, 34.
Creed, origin of, 3, 108.
Creeds, 108 ff.
Creeds and Articles, 1 ff; authority of, 5; character of, 4; purpose of, 6.

DECLARATION, His Majesty's, 57 ff.
Descent into Hell, the, 80 ff.
Divine Decrees, the, 46.
Divinity of Our Lord, the, 70 ff.
Docetism, 75.
Dort, Synod of, 57.

ELECTION, 7.
Elizabeth, Queen, 38.
English Church, Catholicity of the, 46; Doctrinal Continuity of, 12 ff.
Ex opere operato, 36, 44, 45, 47.
Eucharist, Doctrine of the, 35, 47, 83, 87.
Eutyches, 72 ff.

Fidei Ratio, 7.
Field, 56.
Formularies, Lutheran, 8; Roman Catholic, 9; Swiss, 9.
Frith, 17.
Future Life, Doctrine of the, 107.

GARDINER, Bishop, 15, 17.
Gibson, Dr., 42.
Gnosticism, 67.
Gospellers, the, 16.
Guest, Bishop, 39 f, 47.

HAMPTON COURT CONFERENCE, the, 56.
Hell, meaning of, 81.
Heretics, the, 16,
Holy Spirit, Doctrine of the, 89 ff.
Hooker, 54, 56.
Hooper, Bishop, 32-34.

INCARNATION, the, 69 ff.
Institutes, Calvin's, 7, 54.
Institution of a Christian Man, The, 20.

JAMES I., 56 ff.
Jewel, Bishop, 51.
Justification, 7, 19, 61.

King's Book, The, 20.
Kiss of Peace, the, 99.

LAUD, Archbishop, 56, 58.
Luther, 7.
Lutheranism, 19; our debt to, 22, 35, 40.
Lutherans, 16, 20, 35, 83.

MEDIÆVALISTS, the, 31.
Melanchthon, 8.
Messianic Prophecy, 106.
Micronius, 33.
Montague, 58.

Necessary Doctrine, The, 20.
Nestorius, 72 f.
New Learning, the, 15.
Nicæa, Council of, 3, 72.
Nicene Creed, the, 110.

ŒCUMENICAL COUNCILS, the, 72 f.

INDEX

Old Learning, the, 15.
Old Testament, the, 103 ff.
Overall, Bishop, 56.

PANTHEISM, 67.
Parker, Archbishop, 8, 38, 46, 51, 89, 95.
Pearson, Bishop, 46.
Peter, Martyr, 27, 34 ff.
Pitt, 62.
Priesthood, Our Lord's, 87.
Propitiation, 77 ff.
Protestants, the, 21.
Prynne, 58.
Purgatory, 19.
Puritans, dissatisfaction of the, 49 ff.

RANSOM, 77 ff.
Real Presence, the, 35, 45, 47, 49, 87.
Receptionism, 35.
Reconciliation, 77 ff.
Redditio Symboli, 110.
Reformatio Legum, the, 29, 37, 65.
Reformation, the, 7; principles of the, 7; the English, 10; principle of, 14, 19.
Resurrection, the, 83 ff.
Reynolds, 56.
Ridley, Bishop, 32, 34, 66, 89.
Risen Body, nature of Our Lord's, 85 ff.
Romanensians, the, 45, 48, 50.

Rome, Church of, 48.

SABELLIANISM, 65.
Sacramentaries, the, 2, 17.
Sacraments, doctrine of the, 2, 34 f, 47, 73; number of the, 19, 36.
Sacrifice, Christ's, 76.
School authors, the, 31.
Schoolmen, the, 35.
Scripture, authority of, 95 ff.
Six Articles, Statute of, 21.
Statute 13 Eliz. c. 12, 50.
Subscription, 52 f.
Supremacy, Act of (1 Eliz. c. 1), 38.
Swiss faction, the, 35, 37.

TOLERATION, 30.
Traditio Symboli, 110.
Tradition, Scripture and, 95 ff.
Transubstantiation, 48.
Trent, Council of, 9, 31, 46, 95 f.
Trinity, the Holy, 65 ff.
Tyndale, 16 f.

UBIQUITARIANISM, 87.
Uniformity, 30, 39; Act of (1 Eliz. c. 2), 38.

WESTMINSTER ASSEMBLY, the, 60.
Weston, 27 f.
Whitaker, Dr., 55 f.
Whitgift, Archbishop, 51 ff.

ZWINGLI, 7, 87.

Oxford Church Text Books

The Thirty-nine Articles

THEIR HISTORY AND EXPLANATION

BY

THE REV. B. J. KIDD, B.D.

KEBLE COLLEGE

TUTOR OF NON-COLLEGIATE STUDENTS, OXFORD

IN TWO VOLUMES

VOL. II

ARTICLES IX-XXXIX

RIVINGTONS

34 *KING STREET, COVENT GARDEN*

LONDON

1899

INTRODUCTORY NOTE

THE author wishes to express his obligations to the works of Archdeacon Hardwick, Dr. Maclear, and Dr. Gibson, on the Articles, obligations which it is impossible, in so short a compass, to acknowledge in detail.

CONTENTS

Part II.—Explanation

		PAGE
Article IX.,	. . . . . .	121
,, X.,	. . . . . .	128
,, XI.,	. . . . . .	131
,, XII.,	. . . . . .	138
,, XIII.,	. . . . . .	140
,, XIV.,	. . . . . .	143
,, XV.,	. . . . . .	147
,, XVI.,	. . . . . .	149
,, XVII.,	. . . .	153
,, XVIII.,	. . . . . .	159
,, XIX.,	. . . .	161
,, XX.,	. . .	174
,, XXI.,	. . . . . .	183
,, XXII.,	. . . .	189
,, XXIII.,	. . . .	203
,, XXIV.,	. . . . . .	207
,, XXV.,	. . . . . .	209
,, XXVI.,	, ...	217
,, XXVII.,	. . . .	221
,, XXVIII.,	. . . .	226
,, XXIX.,	. . . . .	236
,, XXX.,	. . . , .	239
,, XXXI.,	. . . . . .	241

Article XXXII.,	247
,, XXXIII.,	249
,, XXXIV.,	251
,, XXXV.,	255
,, XXXVI.,	257
,, XXXVII.,	263
,, XXXVIII.,	268
,, XXXIX.,	270
THE RATIFICATION,	272
HIS MAJESTY'S DECLARATION,	273
APPENDIX—The Latin Articles of 1553 and 1563 (VIII.-XLII.),	275
INDEX,	292

PART II.—EXPLANATION

NOTE

(1) Formulae composed in 1552-3 are printed in ordinary type: formulae, or parts thereof, common to the formularies of 1563, 1553, 1538, and 1530 in *italics*; additions of 1563, if from the Confession of Würtemberg, in **thick type**, between †† if from elsewhere; or, if then composed, between ‡‡.

(2) **The student is particularly advised to read the explanation of the Articles with a revised version of the Bible at his side, and to look out the references.** It has been found impossible to give them in full; and the explanation will not be intelligible without study of the Scripture where referred to. It is however hoped that the explanation will suffice to make the passages of Scripture clear, so far as they bear upon the matter in hand.

(3) The text of the Articles here explained is that of the last revision in 1571. The Latin Articles of 1553 and 1563 will be found in the Appendix.

THE THIRTY-NINE ARTICLES

Group B. Articles dealing with **Personal Religion, or Man and his Salvation (Arts. 9-18).**—They fall into two sections, such as concern:—

(i) *Justification*—The subject brought into prominence by **Luther** (Arts. 9-16). Thus, after stating the nature of Original Sin (9), and its effect on the will, or the need of Grace (10), the formulary treats of the ground of Justification (11), and the true value of Good Works, whether following (12) or preceding (13) it. Works of Supererogation are repudiated (14) as impossible, for Christ alone is without sin (15), and men sin after Baptism (16).

(ii) *Predestination or Election*—The subject brought into prominence by **Calvin** (Arts. 17, 18). Predestination to life is God's purpose for men (17), but He wills to effect it only by the name of Christ (18).

ARTICLE IX

De Peccato Originali.

(§ 1) Peccatum originis non est (ut fabulantur Pelagiani) in imitatione Adami situm, sed est *vitium* et depravatio naturae cujuslibet hominis ex Adamo naturaliter *propagati*, qua fit ut ab originali justitia quam longissime distet, ad malum sua natura propendeat, et caro semper adversus spiritum concupiscat; unde in unoquoque nascentium iram Dei atque damnationem meretur. (§ 2) Manet etiam in renatis haec naturae depravatio, qua fit ut affectus carnis, Graece φρόνημα σαρκός (quod alii sapientiam,

Of Original or Birth Sin.

(§ 1) Original sin standeth not in the following of Adam (as the Pelagians do vainly talk), but it is the fault and corruption of the nature of every man that naturally is engendered of the offspring of Adam, whereby man is very far gone from original righteousness, and is of his own nature inclined to evil, so that the flesh lusteth always contrary to the spirit; and therefore in every person born into this world, it deserveth God's wrath and damnation. (§ 2) And this infection of nature doth remain, yea, in them

alii sensum, alii affectum, alii studium carnis interpretantur), legi Dei non subjiciatur. Et quanquam renatis et credentibus, nulla propter Christum est condemnatio, (§ 3) peccati tamen in sese rationem habere concupiscentiam fatetur Apostolus.

that are regenerated, whereby the lust of the flesh, called in Greek φρόνημα σαρκός (which some do expound the wisdom, some sensuality, some the affection, some the desire of the flesh), is not subject to the law of God. And although there is no condemnation for them that believe and are baptized, (§ 3) yet the Apostle doth confess that concupiscence and lust hath of itself the nature of sin.

(i) **Source.**—Composed by the English Reformers, 1552-3, with slight verbal reminiscences of previous formularies. Thus *originalis justitia* is borrowed from No. 2 of the XIII. Articles, though it does not occur in the Confession of Augsburg. The Pelagians, however, and that which they denied (the *vitium* characteristic of every one *secundum naturam propagati*), are mentioned for condemnation in all three. But our Article shows marked independence both in its general wording and in its rejection of the statement, common to both the preceding series, that concupiscence is 'vere peccatum.'

(ii) **Object.**—To exclude Pelagianism, 'which, also,' as the Article itself said in 1553, 'the Anabaptists do nowadays renew.' Similar testimony to their revival of the old error is borne by the *Reformatio Legum*.

(iii) **Explanation.**—§ 1 deals with **Original sin.** (1) The phrase itself is not scriptural, and is due to S. Augustine, who made the expression 'Peccatum originale' (*cf.* title), or 'Peccatum originis' (*cf.* text), current coin in Western theology. In its English dress, *Original sin* is open to misconception, as if it referred to sin done originally in some former state of existence. But 'origo' means 'birth,' and 'peccatum,' here, 'sinfulness' rather than 'sin'; and 'peccatum originale' is best represented, as in the title, by *Birth Sin*, though even that expression does not quite convey the notion of 'a sinful tendency accompanying the very origin of our human existence,'[1] which is the meaning of the Latin phrase, as employed

[1] Bright, *Waymarks in Church History*, p. 190.

by S. Augustine. This meaning it acquired in the Pelagian controversy of the early fifth century; and (2) the Article proceeds to condemn the Pelagian heresy by way of shewing *what Original sin is not*. It **standeth not in the following of Adam, as the Pelagians do vainly talk.** This expression is much clearer in the Latin, which, in modern English, would be rendered, 'does not consist in imitating Adam.'[1] Pelagius (?370-?440) was a monk of British extraction who went to Rome, and was looked up to in his day as both devout and learned. Roused to indignation by the moral slackness of easy-going Christians, he preached exertion to the indolent, and told them that they could do better if they would. He was shocked at hearing of Augustine's prayer, 'Give me the power to do what Thou commandest, and then command what Thou wilt.' 'Give the power?' he would say; 'why, you *have* the power.' With excellent motives, he was thus led to his first heretical proposition; for, over-confident in the unaided efficacy of the human will, he proceeded (*a*) to a *denial of the necessity of supernatural and directly assisting grace*—'grace' being here taken in the then, as now, received sense, in which it is 'merely a convenient theological expression for the personal action of the Divine Paraclete,'[2] or 'the power that worketh in us' (Eph. iii. 20). But then followed a second proposition. The denial of the need of real grace was justified by (*b*) a *denial of the reality of Original sin*: for Pelagius would not admit the presence of that sinful tendency which accompanies us from our birth. When confronted with the fact of universal depravity, rather than account for it thus, all he would say was that it followed from the universal imitation of Adam's example. The Article characterises this as 'vain talk': for a universal effect must have a common cause. Moreover, 'death,' the penalty of sin, 'reigned from Adam until Moses, even over them that had not sinned after

---

[1] For 'standeth'='consisteth'; *cf.* second collect at Mattins, 'in knowledge of whom standeth our eternal life' (*Quem nosse vivere*).
[2] Bright, *Lessons from the Lives of Three Great Fathers*, p. 162, n. 3.

the likeness of Adam's transgression' (Rom. v. 14). This points to a congenital sinfulness, or an inherited tendency to sin; and supports the next statement of this section, upon (3) *what Original sin is*. **It is the fault and corruption of the nature of every man.** (*a*) In *extent* it is described as universal, reaching to every man **that naturally is engendered of the offspring of Adam,** our Lord, of course, excluded, for He was supernaturally engendered (Matt. i. 18, 20, 23). (*b*) In *effect* it is (α) *privative*, for it is that **whereby man is very far gone from original righteousness**; (β) *positive*, for, in consequence of it, **he is of his own nature inclined to evil;** and (γ) *punitive*, for **the flesh lusteth always contrary to the spirit, and therefore in every person born into this world, it deserveth God's wrath and damnation.**

Now the meaning of this definition depends upon close attention both to what it asserts and to what it refrains from asserting. Man, as he left the Creator's hands, was formed in *original righteousness*. By this, it is not meant that he was either morally or intellectually a perfect being. Before he sinned (Gen. ii. 25), as after (iii. 7 and 21), his knowledge of the arts of civilisation was elementary. They are represented as an aftergrowth (iv. 20-22). His knowledge of moral distinctions was equally rudimentary (ii. 17, 25; iii. 5). He was, in fact, in a state of childlike innocence, not created perfect, but on the way to become so; and so was in this sense 'very good,' as 'made in the image of God' (i. 27, 31), and capable of enjoying communion with Him (iii. 8). Thus he could not have had concupiscence or lust, but he had a power of choice: otherwise the temptation (iii. 1) would have been an impossibility. Yet it was resisted (iii. 2-5): and divines have therefore held that our first parents' freedom to choose was not wholly unconditioned, but aided by a bias toward good. This state of man before the Fall they call *original righteousness*: but while some have looked upon it as a supernatural condition, others have regarded it as a natural one. What happened then at the Fall? On the first view, man lost the supernatural gift, and descended to the natural level. The Fall was a loss, and left man by

EXPLANATION 125

nature good but weak. On the second, he fell below the natural level, and was left by nature inclined to evil, more than weak, but not wholly bad. The Fall was a *privatio* but a *depravatio* too. Thus physical corruption or death, which in itself is a purely natural phenomenon, re-asserted its sway over his body: and was now further associated with sin as its penalty (Rom. v. 12, 21). But moral corruption also laid hold of his spiritual being: so that he was not only *deprived* of his bias toward good but *depraved* by a bias toward evil, not merely *very far gone from original righteousness* but *of his own nature inclined to evil*. In thus making the effect of the Fall positive as well as privative, the Article ranges itself with S. Augustine in opposition to the Greek and earlier Latin Fathers. They looked upon Original sin as involving the loss of the supernatural bias toward good and nothing more. So did the Scotists. But, in regarding it as a positive taint transmitted at birth from one generation to the next, the Western theology of S. Augustine and the Thomists is more in accordance both with experience and with Holy Scripture. Heredity is now an accepted scientific fact; and that direct bias towards evil, of which all men are conscious in themselves, demands no other explanation. The Scriptures, not content with insisting on the universality of sin (Gen. vi. 12; Mark x. 18), regard it as engrained 'within,' in the very hearts of men (Gen. vi. 5; viii. 21; Deut. x. 16; Jer. xvii. 9; Mark vii. 21-23; Rom. vii. 18; viii. 7). Our Lord even speaks of men as 'being evil' (Matt. vii. 11) and as 'lost' (Luke xix. 10), and 'He knew what was in man' (John ii. 24). But it is reserved for S. Paul to supply the key to such comprehensive language, by calling attention to the solidarity of the race in Adam, as alone accounting for this universal presence of sin and its penalty, death, by transmission from him (1 Cor. xv. 22; Rom. v. 12-21).

But the self-restraint of the Article is as remarkable as its assertions. On June 17, 1546, the Council of Trent had committed itself merely to the view that original sin is 'a loss of holiness and righteousness.'[1] It

---

[1] Sess. v. c. 2.

was but a *privatio naturae*. The Article goes further, and asserts that it is a *depravatio naturae*. But it stops short of saying that it is a *tota depravatio*, or that 'man is wholly deprived of original righteousness, and is of his own nature inclined only to evil.'[1] Expressions such as this are characteristic of the Lutheran and Calvinist confessions, and are neither Scriptural nor true. If true, man would have been left by the Fall incapable of redemption: and in the Bible, not only are 'the lost' made the very subjects of redemption (Luke xix. 10; *cf.* Eph. ii. 1), but the possibility of this is hinted in the fact that even fallen man is still spoken of as retaining his likeness to the image of God (Gen. ix. 6; 1 Cor. xi. 7; Jas. iii. 9). Thus he 'knows how to give good gifts' to his children (Matt. vii. 11), and both the conscience (Rom. ii. 14, 15) of the heathen and the principles on which the judgment in store for them (Matt. xxv. 31-46; Rom. ii. 12, 16) will be conducted witness to the truth that the heart of man, even when as yet untouched by redemption, so far from being totally depraved is 'naturally Christian.'[2] A further limitation is acknowledged in the extent of the punishment due to Original sin. We 'were by nature children of wrath' (Eph. ii. 3), and so *it deserveth God's wrath and damnation*: but it is not said that it invariably meets with the treatment which, as a positive taint or disorder defacing God's handiwork, it deserves. For instance, the Church of England says, 'It is certain by God's word that children which are baptized, dying before they commit actual sin, are undoubtedly saved.'[3] She pointedly omits to add, as the Bishops' Book added, 'and else not.'

§ 2 describes *the effect of Baptism in the removal of Original sin*. Baptism is credited, as in the Catechism, with a double effect. **There is no condemnation to them that believe and are baptized** (Rom. viii. 1). It is a remission of sin. It is also a regeneration; for *renati* is translated first by *regenerated* and then by *baptized*.

[1] The Article as revised by the Westminster Assembly, 1643. *Cf.* vol. i. p. 61.
[2] Tertullian, *Apol.*, c. 17.
[3] Rubric at the end of the Baptismal Service.

EXPLANATION

Now deliverance from sin means rescue both from its guilt and power. That Baptism procures forgiveness and so removes guilt is clear from such passages as Acts ii. 38; xxii. 16, etc.: but the power of sin lies in the hold which it has on us through that **infection of nature**, or appetite for corrupt pleasure, against which Apostles had both to warn their converts (Gal. v. 16; Col. iii. 5; 1 Pet. ii. 11; 1 John i. 8) and struggle themselves (1 Cor. ix. 27; Rom. vii. 18, 19). Our personal experience is sufficient proof that it **doth remain, yea, in them that are regenerate**: and that the instincts and interests of our lower nature, which are what is meant by 'the mind of the flesh' (Rom. viii. 6, 7) are not eradicated by Baptism.

§ 3 addresses itself to the question, much debated at the time, whether this *concupiscence* is of itself sin. The Council of Trent had already decided that it 'is not called sin as being truly and properly sin in the regenerate, but because it is of sin and inclines to sin.'[1] The Lutheran and 'Reformed' bodies held, as in the Westminster Confession, that 'both itself and all the motions thereof are truly and properly sin.'[2] The Article is content to steer midway between these extremes. **The Apostle doth confess that concupiscence and lust hath of itself the nature of sin.** It recognises the dangerous tendency of concupiscence, but holds that 'lust' only 'when it hath conceived, beareth sin' (Jas. i. 15). Sin lies not in the motions of the flesh but in the consent given to them by the will. S. James, however, is not *the Apostle* but S. Paul: though it may be doubted what passages of S. Paul the author of the Article had in mind. Possibly Rom. vi. 12; vii. 8; Gal. v. 16-24, in all of which lust is spoken of as closely connected with sin.

---

[1] Sess. v. c. 5.   [2] vi. 5.

ARTICLE X

De Libero Arbitrio.

(§ 1) Ea est hominis post lapsum Adae conditio, **ut sese, naturalibus suis viribus et bonis operibus, ad fidem et invocationem Dei convertere ac praeparare non possit.** (§ 2) Quare absque gratia Dei, quae per Christum est, nos praeveniente ut velimus, et co-operante dum volumus, ad pietatis opera facienda, quae Deo grata sint et accepta, nihil valemus.

Of Free Will.

(§ 1) The condition of man after the fall of Adam is such, that he cannot turn and prepare himself, by his own natural strength and good works, to faith and calling upon God. (§ 2) Wherefore we have no power to do good works pleasant and acceptable to God, without the grace of God by Christ preventing us that we may have a good will, and working with us when we have that good will.

(i) **Source.**—§ 1, in **thick type**, was introduced in 1563 from the Confession of Würtemberg, by way of preface to § 2, which stood as it is in 1553.

(ii) **Object.**—The structure of the Article resembles that of other Articles, in which the last is meant to be the emphatic clause, the object of the earlier clauses being merely to lead up to, and serve as a basis for, the cardinal statement in conclusion.[1] The Article would therefore have been better entitled,[2] 'Of the need of grace,' its object being to supplement the last by disavowing all sympathy with the Anabaptists who denied such need. Of Free Will itself nothing is directly said. What is denied is the power of man to turn to God and serve Him unaided. What is asserted is the need of grace, both preventing and co-operating.

(iii) **Explanation.**—§ 1 deals with *man's incapacity for good since the Fall*, which follows directly from the view

---

[1] *Cf.* Arts. 7, 11, 16, 20, 21, 31, 32, 36.
[2] For inexact titles, *cf.* Arts. 13, 31.

taken of Original sin in Art. 9. It is not only a *privatio* or loss of higher goodness, but a *depravatio naturae*, a real corruption of our nature. It follows that, if this be **the condition of man after the fall of Adam** ... **that he cannot turn and prepare himself by his own natural strength and good works to faith and calling upon God.** His condition is one of slavery to sin (Rom. vii. 14; viii. 8).

§ 2 states that, in consequence, **to do good works pleasant and acceptable to God** we want **grace** both **preventing** and **working with us.** These expressions require notice. The clause in which they occur is quoted almost verbatim from S. Augustine,[1] whose controversy with Pelagius had reference to God's treatment not of those who lived and died without ever having heard the Gospel, but of Christians. Thus (*a*) *good works pleasant and acceptable to God* is a technical phrase for the works of Christians done in a Christian spirit and from Christian motives. In Art. 10 it is stated that they are impossible apart from Christ: in Art. 12 that 'they are the fruits of faith and follow after Justification': in Art. 13 that 'works done before the grace of Christ are not pleasant to God,' the reason being added that 'they spring not of faith.' Nothing is said as to the good works of the heathen, and the way in which God regards them. The question is not raised. (*b*) *Grace* is a word that has different senses in Biblical and Ecclesiastical usage. In Scripture, it is used as the equivalent of (*a*) 'attractiveness' (Luke iv. 22); (β) 'favour,' specially as shewn by a superior towards an inferior (Gen. vi. 8); then, with S. Paul in particular, it is used of (γ) 'God's unmerited favour,' specially in opposition to 'debt' (Rom. iv. 4) or 'works' implying merit (Rom. xi. 6). It is in this sense that the word takes a prominent place in the vocabulary of Justification (Eph. ii. 8, 9). Finally, the cause being put for the effect, 'grace' denotes (δ) the 'favour' in which the Christian stands (Rom. v. 2) or any particular gift which, by the divine favour, he enjoys (Acts vi. 8). But the New Testament stops short of the sense ascribed to 'grace' in ecclesiastical usage

---

[1] *De Gratia et Libero Arbitrio*, § 33.

from the time of S. Augustine, according to which it means not simply kindly feeling on the part of God, but His actual help. Grace is power. That power whereby God works in nature is called force. That power whereby He works on the will of His reasonable creatures is called grace[1] in theology. It is freely recognised in the New Testament (Eph. iii. 20), but not under this name except in 1 Cor. xv. 10: and the key to the passage from the Biblical sense of 'grace' as 'favour' to the Ecclesiastical sense of 'grace' as 'help' lies in the fact that with God to favour is at once to bless. But the distinction is important, as will appear in Art. 11. (c) *Prevenient* and *co-operating* grace are again Augustinian terms. The first is needed to incline the will to choose the good (John vi. 44; Acts xvi. 14); the second to assist us in doing it (John xv. 4, 5; 1 Cor. xv. 10; Gal. ii. 20). In Phil. ii. 13 S. Paul insists that we need both the one and the other, and yet (ii. 12) that grace dispenses neither with human effort nor responsibility. The Collects of the Prayer Book,[2] many of which go back to the time when Pelagianism was still an enemy to be reckoned with, are the best summaries of the teaching of Scripture on the need both of prevenient and co-operating grace.

[1] *Cf.* Liddon, *University Sermons*, i. pp. 44, 66; ii. pp. 34, 188; *Advent Sermons*, i. p. 234; *Christmastide Sermons*, p. 217: and note 'full of grace and power,' Acts vi. 8.
[2] See 1st Sunday after Epiphany; Easter Day; 1st, 9th, 17th Sunday after Trinity; and 'Prevent (=start) us, O Lord,' etc.

ARTICLE XI

De Hominis Justificatione.

(§ 2) **Tantum propter meritum Domini ac Servatoris nostri Jesu Christi, per fidem, non propter opera et merita nostra, (§ 1) justi coram Deo reputamur.** (§ 3) Quare sola fide nos justificari, doctrina est saluberrima, ac consolationis plenissima; ut in Homilia de Justificatione hominis fusius explicatur.

Of the Justification of Man.

(§ 1) We are accounted righteous before God, (§ 2) only for the merit of our Lord and Saviour Jesus Christ by faith, and not for our own works or deservings. (§ 3) Wherefore that we are justified by faith only is a most wholesome doctrine, and very full of comfort; as more largely is expressed in the Homily of Justification.

(i) **Source.** — The Article is an improved version of that on Justification in the series of 1553, prefixed in 1563 by the clause in **heavy type**, which is based upon the language of the Confession of Würtemberg.

(ii) **Object.** — It is directed against ideas of human merit, so long prevalent throughout the Western Church before the Reformation, and then shared by the Anabaptists. But while it so far sides with Luther on Justification, it carefully avoids the distinctively Lutheran phraseology: *e.g.* that a man is justified when he believes himself to be justified; or that his faith is the cause, rather than the condition, of his justification; or that Christ's righteousness is imputed to the sinner for his justification. Further, it silently corrects the Council of Trent, which, in its session of January 13, 1547, had decreed that 'justification is not merely the remission of sins, but also the sanctification and renewal of the inner man.'[1] The Article follows S. Paul in distinguishing between Justification and Sanctification.

[1] Sess. vi. c. 7.

(iii) **Explanation.** — § 1, opening with the statement that **We are accounted righteous**, raises two questions. There is (*a*) the *linguistic* question, What is the meaning of 'justify'? The Article uses the phrases *We are accounted righteous by faith* and *We are justified by faith* synonymously, thus clearly taking 'justify' to mean 'make out righteous' rather than 'make righteous.' In this it has the support of Scripture. The Greek word δικαιόω, by analogy with other words of the same form,[1] except such as are derived from adjectives having a physical meaning,[2] *e.g.* 'blind,' means invariably to 'account' or 'treat as righteous.' In the New Testament it occurs but eleven times outside the epistles of S. Paul. Thus the divine 'Wisdom is' said to be 'justified' *i.e.* vindicated or proved righteous, 'by her works' (Matt. xi. 19 = Luke vii. 35): and the word is used in the forensic sense of acquittal as opposed to condemnation before a judge (Matt. xii. 37). In S. Paul's epistles the word occurs twenty-seven times. In some cases it is unambiguous, and must mean 'treat as righteous,' *i.e.* 'acquit': in none can the meaning 'make righteous' be established for it. For, with S. Paul, as in the Gospels, the decisive passages are such as connect it with a verdict of acquittal in court, and speak of God as being pronounced righteous by the judgment of mankind (Rom. iii. 4); or of man as unable to 'condemn' His 'elect' where He 'justifieth' (Rom. viii. 33); or of the Apostle himself as not being acquitted even by the verdict of his own conscience, clear as it is, but only by the last Judgment of all (1 Cor. iv. 4). Thus on linguistic grounds of New Testament interpretation, the Article would be in the wrong if it took 'we are justified' to mean anything else but 'we are accounted righteous.' But this raises (*b*) the *theological* question, What is the relation, in time, of Justification to Sanctification? Is a man accounted righteous (justified) before he is made righteous (sanctified)? Considerations of an *à priori* kind appear to require that he should be

---

[1] *c.g.* ἀξιόω = deem worthy.
[2] *c.g.* τυφλόω = make blind.

EXPLANATION

made righteous first, for otherwise there would seem to be an element of unreality, and therefore of immorality, in God's dealings with mankind if He be represented as accounting the sinner righteous when as yet he is not really so. Such considerations, coupled with an imperfect knowledge of Greek, may have led Western theologians to take *Justificare* in the sense of 'make righteous,' and to hold that before God justifies a man He imparts to him an infused righteousness. Accordingly the Council of Trent made Justification to include Sanctification. But the facts of language do not permit of this, nor does New Testament usage. Further, in Rom. iv. 5 the person treated as righteous is assumed to be not actually righteous but 'ungodly.' We must therefore conclude (a) that S. Paul regards Justification simply as the bestowal of forgiveness for the past, and so separates it in thought from God's other gift of Sanctification or growth in grace afterwards. Both are connected with Baptism (1 Cor. vi. 11). But while Justification is no more than the initial act of the Christian life, when we are forgiven (*cf.* Rom. iii. 24, 25 with Eph. i. 7) and received into favour (Rom. v. 1, 2), Sanctification is its gradual perfecting (Rom. vi. 19, 22), and while the one represents the work of God the Son for us 'who redeemed me and all mankind' (Rom. iii. 22-26; Gal. ii. 16, 17), the other is the work of God the Holy Ghost within us, who 'sanctifieth me and all the elect people of God' (1 Thess. iv. 3, 8; 2 Thess. ii. 13; *cf.* 1 Pet. i. 2); (β) that thus Justification precedes Sanctification, and so God *justifies by anticipation*, treating the sinner as the Prodigal Son was treated by his father (Luke xv. 20-22), not by reference to what he is at the moment when he is received into favour, but to what he gives promise of becoming through his faith; but yet (γ) that Justification and Sanctification, distinguishable as they are in thought, are inseparable in actual life because of its organic unity. The former is the subject of Rom. i.-v., the latter of vi.-viii.; but they are one whole. 'Being now made free from sin'—that is Justification—'ye have your fruit unto Sanctification, and the end eternal life' (Rom. vi. 22). These are the three stages in a Christian life, separable in thought, but continuous in reality—Justification, Sanctification, Salvation.

§ 2 proceeds to the ground of Justification. We are justified **only for the merit of our Lord and Saviour Jesus Christ by faith, and not for our own works or deservings.** The meritorious cause, as the technical phrase goes, of our justification, that on account of (*propter*) which we are justified, is not faith, which is only the condition (*per*) of it, but the merits of Christ. The contrast here, as in the New Testament, is not between faith and works, but between our merits and Christ's (Rom. iv. 4, 5, 24, 25). The mediæval system encouraged men to think that they could earn forgiveness, and so resulted in a religious practice which had a very close resemblance to that legalism which S. Paul combated (Rom. iii. 20, 28; Gal. ii. 16). As against such notions, the Article re-affirms his doctrine that forgiveness is a free gift which we owe not to our own merits but to the redemptive work of our Lord (Rom. iii. 24). But on this point there is no disagreement among Christians. The Council of Trent equally affirms that 'the meritorious cause of justification is our Lord Jesus Christ, who merited justification for us by His passion'[1]; and divergences begin to arise not over such fundamental statements as that 'we have our redemption through His blood, the forgiveness of our trespasses according to the riches of God's grace' (Eph. i. 7; Tit. iii. 7), but upon the subsidiary point as to the office of faith in responding to it. 'By grace have ye been saved through faith; and that not of yourselves: it is the gift of God: not of works, that no man should glory' (Eph. ii. 8).

§ 3, to which all that precedes has been leading up, asserts that the office of faith is to be the condition of Justification on our part. **We are justified by faith only.**

(1) What then is meant by *faith*? In the New Testament it ranges over a wide field, and rises from mere belief or intellectual assent to a proposition, *e.g.* 'that God is one,' as when it is said that 'the devils also

---

[1] Sess. v. c. 7.

believe' this 'and shudder' (Jas. ii. 19), up to faith on (Acts xi. 17; Rom. iv. 5) or in (Acts x. 43; Gal. ii. 16; Phil. i. 29) a Person, Jesus Christ. This alone is justifying faith : for it is a faith like that of Abraham (Rom. iv. 21, 22) or of S. Peter (Matt. xvi. 16, *sqq.*), involving moral self-surrender to a Person, and reposing its confidence, not in a message about His atoning death, but in His own ever-present aid as the Risen Lord (Rom. iv. 24, 25; x. 9; 2 Cor. i. 9; iv. 13, 14; Col. ii. 12; 1 Pet. i. 21). The contrast to be observed is exactly that between the belief which Martha had, that there should be a resurrection, and the faith which our Lord required of her in Himself—'I am the resurrection. . . . Believest thou this?' (John xi. 24-27). Justifying faith is a thing not of the head but of the heart (Rom. x. 9).

(2) But why *faith only*? The expression does not occur in the New Testament, except for condemnation (Jas. ii. 24). We will return to that point presently. But S. Paul does affirm that faith is the sole condition of justification on our part. 'We reckon that a man is justified by faith apart from the works of the law' (Rom. iii. 28). It is true that the faith which justifies, springing as it does from personal devotion to a Person, is a 'faith working through love' (Gal. v. 6). But as in the first of these passages it is not meant to exclude any other instrument on God's part from the office of justifying, such as Baptism, which is 'unto remission of sins' (Acts ii. 38; Rom. vi. 6, 7), so in the second, all that is meant is to exclude works of charity from that office, not to exclude them altogether. Thus it is expressly 'to him that worketh not but believeth on Him that justifieth' that 'his faith is reckoned for righteousness' (Rom. iv. 5). *Faith only* is the condition of justification; and it is all-sufficient for the purpose because it carries with it, as a thing of the heart, the self-surrender of the whole man.

(3) It is this doctrine, then, **that we are justified by faith only**, which the Article describes as **a most wholesome doctrine and very full of comfort**. Words could not be better chosen. The condition of free forgiveness on our side is faith or whole-hearted self-surrender. Now

the *comfort* of this is that, in being offered on such terms, acceptance with God is placed within the reach of all. Head and hands can do little : we can neither understand much of God nor earn His favour : but there is no man who has not a heart to place at His disposal. But given such a change of heart, God receives a guarantee for the future, whose value cannot be equalled ; for 'personal adhesion' is 'the highest and most effective motive-power of which human character is capable.'[1] Here, then, in its promotion of moral effort (Rom. iii. 31), lies the *wholesomeness* of the doctrine; and it is only in its perverted forms, when faith is taken to mean something less than an entire self-surrender, that it ceases to be wholesome. Unwholesome perversions are such as were condemned by S. James and maintained by Luther.

(*a*) *The relation of SS. Paul and James* to each other is one of verbal contradiction, but substantial agreement. Both start from the case of Abraham (Gen. xv. 6 ; Rom. iv. 3 ; Jas. ii. 23), a standing thesis for discussions in the Jewish schools (*cf.* 1 Macc. ii. 52), and come to exactly opposite conclusions, S. Paul that 'To Abraham his faith was reckoned for righteousness' (Rom. iv. 9), S. James, that 'by works a man is justified, and not only by faith' (Jas. ii. 24). But (*a*) they give different senses to 'faith.' With S. James, it is only assent to a proposition (Jas. ii. 19), an affair of the head ; with S. Paul, an affair of the heart (Gal. v. 6 ; Rom. x. 10) ; and 'faith' in S. James corresponds to 'knowledge' (1 Cor. viii. 1) in S. Paul. (β) They give different meanings to 'works.' The works that S. Paul condemns are 'works of law' (Rom. iii. 20 ; R.V. marg.) ; those which S. James requires are works of charity (Jas. ii. 15-17). (γ) They attach different ideas to 'justification,' S. Paul using it of the initial act by which God, of His free grace, puts a soul into a right relation with Himself ; St. James, of its final vindication before Him (Jas. ii. 14 and 24). (δ) Each, moreover, had a different type of error to deal with. S. Paul writes, as a theologian, against theories of human merit ; S. James, like a prophet, indignantly asks of a

---

[1] Sanday and Headlam, on *Romans*, p. 34.

barren and unsympathetic orthodoxy, 'Can that faith save?' (Jas. ii. 14). It is probable that S. James, so far from being at variance with S. Paul, was employing carefully guarded language to correct a misuse by others of teaching peculiarly exposed to misrepresentation (*cf*. Rom. iii. 8; 2 Pet. iii. 16).

(*b*) *Luther*, who had to face a condition of practical error not unlike that which confronted S. Paul, understood him well; but, in his dread of admitting anything that savoured of human merit, he went too far. He rightly took justification to mean forgiveness or acquittal, and insisted that faith only is the condition upon which we receive it. But the reaction carried him beyond this point. He reduced faith to the level of mere belief. He made it that on account of (*propter*, διά with acc.) which, instead of that through (*per*, διά with gen.; *cf*. Gal. ii. 16) which, we are justified; or, in other words, treated it as the meritorious cause, rather than the condition, of our justification. He extended justification to cover more than the initial act by which God receives us into favour, and made it do duty for sanctification and salvation as well. Thus with Luther, 'We are justified through faith only' tended to mean 'We are saved by mere belief'; and this accounts for both types of excess which dogged the heels of his reformation, though with neither had he any personal sympathy. His disparagement of the good works naturally accompanying a faith which worketh by love led to antinomianism. His ascription to faith of the office, not of justifying only, but of saving as well, is Solifidianism. This is an error which makes faith only (*sola fides*) the be-all and end-all of religion, and is responsible for that neglect of the Church and the Sacraments as means of grace which has been characteristic of Protestantism since Luther's day.

ARTICLE XII

De Bonis Operibus.

‡ Bona opera, quae sunt fructus fidei et justificatos sequuntur, quanquam peccata nostra expiare et divini judicii severitatem ferre non possunt, Deo tamen grata sunt et accepta in Christo, atque ex vera et viva fide necessario profluunt, ut plane ex illis aeque fides viva cognosci possit atque arbor ex fructu judicari.‡

Of Good Works.

Albeit that good works, which are the fruits of faith and follow after justification, cannot put away our sins and endure the severity of God's judgment, yet are they pleasing and acceptable to God in Christ, and do spring out necessarily of a true and lively faith, insomuch that by them a lively faith may be as evidently known as a tree discerned by the fruit.

(i) **Source.**—Composed in 1563, the first clause, in **thick type**, being based on the Confession of Würtemberg.

(ii) **Object.**—This Article, like the next, is of the nature of an appendix to the statement of Art. 11, that 'we are justified by faith only.' Solifidianism denied the necessity, the Council of Trent, in its session of January 13, 1547,[1] asserted the merit, of Good Works. The first position was a corollary of, the second a revulsion from, Luther's extravagant depreciation of good works in the justified as sin. This led to antinomianism. The Article seeks to check it[2] by assigning to good works an acceptable and necessary, yet not a meritorious, place in God's sight.

(iii) **Explanation.**—Very little is needed. We have already seen that **good works** is almost a technical expression for works of Christians done in a Christian spirit and from Christian motives. Thus they necessarily **follow after justification**, and their office may be

---

[1] Sess. vi. can. 32.   [2] *Cf.* p. 137, above.

described (*a*) negatively and (*b*) positively. They (*a*) **cannot put away our sins.** The condition of justification, or remission of sins, on our part, is faith, not works; and its instrument, on God's part, baptism. Then only do we become Christians; and then *good works*, in the above sense of Christian works, become possible, but not till then. Yet even they cannot *put away* or expiate our sins. Only the blood of Christ can do that (1 John i. 7); nor, in view of the imperfection even of our best deeds (Ps. cxliii. 2; Rom. iii. 23) can they **endure the severity of God's judgment.** Thus in no sense can they be meritorious, or, as the Schoolmen said, deserve grace *de condigno*, *i.e.* be rewarded as deserving reward. Yet (*b*) they have their necessary place, and a positive value of their own. If only it be remembered that faith, as moral self-surrender to a Person, has an enthusiastic element in it as 'working through love' (Gal. v. 6), it will be obvious that **good works . . . are the fruits of faith . . . and do spring out necessarily of a true and lively faith,** and are its sole evidences (Matt. vii. 16-20; Tit. iii. 8; Jas. ii. 17 *sqq.*) to men. But they have a further value as **pleasing and acceptable to God.** 'Our great God and Saviour Jesus Christ . . . gave himself for us that He might . . . purify unto Himself a people for His own possession, zealous of good works' (Tit. ii. 13). God is thus represented as entering upon the plan of redemption with a view to the pleasure He would derive from our good works. But they are only acceptable **in Christ,** *i.e.* because of our union with His Son. We are 'created in Christ Jesus for good works' (Eph. ii. 10). We can only 'offer up spiritual sacrifices acceptable to God through Jesus Christ' (1 Pet. ii. 5).

ARTICLE XIII

De Operibus ante Justificationem.

Opera quae fiunt ante gratiam Christi et Spiritus ejus afflatum, cum ex fide Jesu Christi non prodeant, minime Deo grata sunt, neque gratiam (ut multi vocant) de congruo merentur: imo cum non sint facta ut Deus illa fieri voluit et praecepit, peccati rationem habere non dubitamus.

Of Works before Justification.

Works done before the grace of Christ and the inspiration of His Spirit, are not pleasant to God, forasmuch as they spring not of faith in Jesus Christ, neither do they make men meet to receive grace, or (as the School authors say) deserve grace of congruity: yea, rather for that they are not done as God hath willed and commanded them to be done, we doubt not but they have the nature of sin.

(i) **Source.**—Composed in 1552-3, and unchanged since.

(ii) **Object.**—To condemn the Scholastic theory of congruous merit. It is a second attempt to define the precise value of good works, and so to protect from invasion the true doctrine of Justification by Faith only, as contained in Art. 11.

(iii) **Explanation.**—(1) First note that the *text does not agree with the title*.[1] The title speaks of **Works before Justification.** The Article concerns **Works done before the grace of Christ**: and it is clear from Scripture that the *grace of Christ* sometimes precedes justification. Thus the grace of compunction (Acts ii. 37) was at work upon the hearts of those who heard S. Peter's sermon at Pentecost. But they were not yet justified; for they still had to 'repent and be baptized . . . unto the remission of their sins' (ii. 38). Again, S. Paul received grace at his conversion, for it was announced to Ananias, 'Behold, he prayeth' (ix. 11): but he was not justified till he

---

[1] For inexact titles, *cf*. Arts. 10, 31.

was baptized (ix. 18) 'three days' (ix. 9) afterwards. The initial grace of God may therefore precede justification, nor is it for us to say by how long an interval. Consequently the area of **works not pleasant to God** is more limited than at first sight of the title might appear. The earliest draft of the Edwardian Articles, that numbering forty-five and signed by the six royal chaplains (1552),[1] spoke in the text of 'works done before justification' as not pleasing to God: and a hundred years later the Westminster Divines suggested an emendation in this direction.[2] Cranmer, on the publication of the Forty-two Articles in 1553, brought the *text* of the Article into conformity with Scripture: but the *title* was left unaltered. For a similar discrepancy between title and text see Arts. 10 and 31. The titles, of course, must give way.

(2) Art. 12 has laid it down that 'good works . . . which follow after justification . . . are pleasing to God.' The question next arises, 'What of works that precede the grace of God?' The former are acceptable because they are the 'fruits of faith.' The latter **are not pleasant to God, forasmuch as they spring not of faith in Jesus Christ** (Rom. viii. 7, 8; John xv. 5). But **the School authors** thought otherwise. They were the systematic theologians of the Middle Ages, who made it their business at first to harmonise faith and reason, and afterwards to give a rational explanation for whatever the Church had thought fit to do. Merit was, in fact, attached to good works: and the Schoolmen justified the current practice by their doctrine of a twofold merit attaching to human actions. To such works as are done with the assistance of grace they ascribed merit *de condigno*: by which they meant that a reward was due as a matter of justice. This position is condemned in Art. 12. Such *works* as are done by man's own unaided strength *before the grace of God*, would, they held, be rewarded out of God's liberality: for, as fitting in with, or being in harmony with, the will of God, **they make men meet to receive grace**, or . . . **deserve grace (de congruo)** of

[1] Vol. i. p. 25.   [2] *Ib.*, p. 61.

congruity. God was not indeed bound to reward such actions, but it was congruous or fitting that He should. The instance usually adduced was that of Cornelius, whose 'prayers and alms came up as a memorial before God' (Acts x. 4), and were held to have drawn down God's grace upon him. But the instance is not to the point. It cannot be shewn that Cornelius' prayers and alms were done in his own unaided strength and before the grace of God. It is the assertion that they were, and were fittingly rewarded by God as a matter not of right but of equity, that the Article condemns. And this condemnation rests on two grounds: (*a*) that of Art. 10, that the initial grace in man's salvation comes from God; (*b*) that of the unacceptableness in God's sight of all that is not of faith (Rom. xiv. 23; Tit. i. 15; Heb. xi. 6). **For that they are not done as God hath willed and commanded them to be done, we doubt not but they have the nature of sin.** The last phrase, '*have the nature of sin*' (*cf.* Art. 9), would seem to hint the element of imperfection in all human effort as a further reason why the works in question can have no merit of congruity. At the same time, it stops short of calling them worthless or sinful. In signing this Article, therefore, we are not called upon to regard the heathen's efforts after good as sins: only to deny that they are unaided by God's grace, and *deserve grace of congruity*. If there is a light that lighteth every man (John i. 9) and grace at work even outside the covenant, whatever is good in any man is to be ascribed to it: and is only not acceptable so far as it is imperfectly Christian.

ARTICLE XIV

De Operibus Supererogationis.

Opera quae Supererogationis appellant non possunt sine arrogantia et impietate praedicari. Nam illis declarant homines non tantum se Deo reddere quae tenentur, sed plus in ejus gratiam facere quam deberent: cum aperte Christus dicat: Cum feceritis omnia quaecunque praecepta sunt vobis, dicite, Servi inutiles sumus.

Of Works of Supererogation.

Voluntary works besides, over and above, God's commandments which they call Works of Supererogation, cannot be taught without arrogancy and impiety. For by them men do declare that they do not only render unto God as much as they are bound to do, but that they do more for His sake than of bounden duty is required: Whereas Christ saith plainly, When ye have done all that are commanded to you, say, We be unprofitable servants.

(i) **Source.**—Composed in 1552-3, and unchanged since.

(ii) **Object.**—To define more accurately the place of Good Works by condemning the tenet of Works of Supererogation taught by some of the Schoolmen.

(iii) **Explanation.**—(1) The term *Supererogation* is the English of a Latin word which occurs in the Vulgate version of the parable of the Good Samaritan. 'Take care of him: and whatsoever thou spendest more (*quodcunque supererogaveris*), I, when I come back again, will repay thee' (Luke x. 35). **Works of Supererogation** was thus the technical expression for **voluntary works besides over and above God's commandments:** 'extras,' in fact, which the saints did but were not required to do, and which thus constituted for them an excess of merit.

(2) The value attached to Works of Supererogation

appears but late in the history of *Indulgences*. The word
'Indulgence,' which has now a sinister sound, was originally borrowed from the law-books of the Roman
Empire, and meant simply (*a*) a remission of punishment or taxation. The Church, in early days, had her
disciplinary system: and, as a rule, visited those who
had lapsed in time of persecution with penalties, such
as exclusion, more or less complete, from her ordinances,
lasting over a term of years. It rested, however, with
the bishop, as administrator of this penitential discipline,
to remit the penance, or part of it, where he saw evidence of true contrition. Such a lightening of ecclesiastical penalties was of the nature of an Indulgence. But
so far an Indulgence was no more than (*b*) the remission
of canonical penance imposed by the Church herself: and
she might fairly claim to exercise the right both of imposing and remitting on the ground that Our Lord left
her authority to 'bind' and 'loose' (Matt. xviii. 18).
So things stood till the seventh century. There was
then a civil institution called 'Wehrgeld,' by which, in
case a man had been injured or slain, compensation had
to be paid by the offender to him or to his relatives. The
Western Church now commuted the penalties formerly
exacted for sins into monetary fines, assessed at a fixed
tariff in her 'Penitentials.' This commutation of penance
for money could not but be demoralising. Men ceased
to look upon a definite penance as attached to a particular sin; and came to think that by certain gifts or
acts the penalties due to sin in general might be escaped.
This was at last explicitly stated in the eleventh century.
To go on the Crusade, was, by a grant of the Council
of Clermont, 1095, to 'count instead of all penance':
and similar remissions were presently attached to less
onerous acts of piety, such as giving alms, undertaking
a pilgrimage, or making the journey to Rome for a Papal
Jubilee. In the year 1300 Boniface VIII. established the
Jubilee, and promised 'the fullest forgiveness of all sins'
to such as took part in it. Thus an Indulgence was now
(*c*) a remission of the temporal penalties for sin in return
for acts from which the Church profited. The phrase of
Pope Boniface covers more: but it must not be forgotten

EXPLANATION

that the great theologians of the thirteenth century, in shaping the theory of Indulgences, confine them to remissions of the temporal penalty (*poena*) as distinct from the eternal guilt (*culpa*) of sin. Guilt is forgiven in absolution; but the purely temporal penalties remain. It was now held that, if not duly performed or authoritatively remitted in this life, they might be reduced, or even wiped off, by Indulgence in purgatory; for purgatory, as falling between death and the Judgment, belongs not to eternity but to time. For this purpose Indulgences might be obtained by the living and transferred to the account of departed friends: and it thus became one of the first of pious duties to accumulate a store of Indulgences for their benefit as well as for one's own.

(*d*) All that was now necessary was to set the current religious practice on an intelligible basis. This was first taken in hand by the Schoolmen of the thirteenth century, who invented the doctrine of the Treasury of Merits which received formal authorisation from Clement VI. in 1343. In Christ's sacrifice there was a large supererogatory element. He did far more than was necessary for the world's salvation. The same is true in their degree of the Blessed Virgin and the Saints. These supererogatory merits, or *voluntary works besides over and above God's commandments*, constituted a spiritual treasure, which the Church, as represented by the Pope, who has the keys of heaven (Matt. xvi. 19) and so of purgatory, is able to apply to the benefit of souls there.

(3) This is the theory that the Article summarily rejects: and had it not been a maxim with the Schoolmen to defend at all costs whatever the Church had thought fit to do, it is difficult to see how such a theory could have been seriously put forward, or held to require a grave repudiation. There is certainly a distinction traceable in the New Testament between 'precepts' and 'counsels' (1 Cor. vii. 25). There are duties for all alike: and there are states of life, to which some only are called, such as Vows of Marriage, or Vows, like those of a 'Religious,' to poverty (Matt. xix. 21) or chastity (1 Cor. vii. 26, 32 *sqq.*), which Our Lord recognises even with

special approbation[1] (Matt. xix. 12; *cf.* Rev. xiv. 4). But in such cases, once the call has come, the 'counsel' becomes a 'precept,' a duty to the particular soul concerned, though not to others. 'He that is able to receive it, *let him receive it*' (Matt. xix. 12). There can therefore be no excess of merit. We may well wonder what is the need for the merits of the saints in this connection, when Christ's merit is infinite; for they would only be finite, and could not be added to His, still less increase it. But the real offence of the theory is its **arrogancy and impiety.** The notion that men can **not only render to God as much as they are bound to do,** but that they may actually **do more for His sake than of bounden duty is required,** is directly contrary to His own words: **When ye have done all that are commanded to you, say, We be unprofitable servants** (Luke xvii. 10).

[1] Cf. *The Christian Year*, for Wednesday before Easter.

ARTICLE XV

De Christo qui solus est sine Peccato.

Of Christ alone without Sin.

(§1) Christus in nostrae naturae veritate per omnia similis factus est nobis, excepto peccato, a quo prorsus est immunis, tum in carne tum in spiritu. Venit ut agnus absque macula esset, qui mundi peccata per immolationem sui semel factam tolleret: et peccatum, ut inquit Johannes, in eo non erat. (§2) Sed nos reliqui, etiam baptizati et in Christo regenerati, in multis tamen offendimus omnes: et, si dixerimus quia peccatum non habemus, nos ipsos seducimus, et veritas in nobis non est.

(§1) Christ in the truth of our nature was made like unto us in all things, sin only except, from which He was clearly void, both in His flesh and in His spirit. He came to be the lamb without spot, Who by sacrifice of Himself once made, should take away the sins of the world: and sin, as S. John saith, was not in Him. (§2) But all we the rest, although baptized and born again in Christ, yet offend in many things: and if we say we have no sin, we deceive ourselves, and the truth is not in us.

(i) **Source.**—Composed in 1552-3, and since unchanged.

(ii) **Object.**—Uncertain: but, if we may judge by the position of the Article, next to Art. 14, and by its structure,[1] according to which Christ's unique sinlessness and satisfaction seem to be emphasised in § 1 in order to lead up to the assertion in § 2 of the sinfulness of all the rest of mankind, it may fairly be supposed that it was intended to supplement and strengthen the denial of supererogatory merits as simple impossibilities. This universality of the taint of sin was also denied by the Anabaptists; and by certain Schoolmen who taught the Immaculate Conception of the Blessed Virgin Mary, *i.e.* her freedom from Original Sin. The Article excludes

[1] *Cf.* Arts. 7, 10, 11, 16, 20, 21, 31, 32, 36.

the errors of both extremes. It need hardly be added that the doctrine of the Immaculate Conception of Our Lady was not erected into a dogma by the Roman Church till December 8, 1854.

(iii) **Explanation.**—§ 1. Sin is no part of human nature, but 'the fault and corruption' of it (Art. 9). Our Lord, therefore, when He took flesh (John i. 14), came 'in the likeness of sinful flesh' (Rom. viii. 3), in this sense that His flesh, though real, was not sinful flesh. He was thus not only actually sinless, as His enemies (John viii. 46) and His earliest followers (2 Cor. v. 21; Heb. vii. 26, 27; 1 Pet. ii. 22) alike confessed, but incapable of sin (Heb. iv. 15), as His own conscience testified (John xiv. 30). This gave its supreme worth to His satisfaction. He was **the Lamb without spot** (John i. 29; 1 Pet. i. 19) whose sacrifice, as **the sacrifice of Himself to take away sins**, was a full expiation (1 John iv. 10); as **once made** (Heb. ix. 26; *cf.* Art. 31) was unique; and as able to **take away the sins of the world** (1 John ii. 2) was all-availing. This was possible, for **sin, as S. John saith, was not in Him** (1 John iii. 5). But § 2 it is in us. **Although baptized and born again in Christ** we yet **offend in many things** (Jas. iii. 2) and commit *actual* sin. We suffer too from the effects of *original* sin: for **if we say that we have no sin, we deceive ourselves and the truth is not in us** (1 John i. 8). Only set Christ's sinlessness and our sinfulness thus side by side, and the silent conclusion, which the Article points to but does not name, is the impossibility of any merit attaching to works of ours. Merit is exclusively His.

ARTICLE XVI

De Peccato post Baptismum.

(§1) Non omne peccatum mortale post Baptismum voluntarie perpetratum, est peccatum in Spiritum Sanctum, et irremissibile. Proinde lapsis a Baptismo in peccata locus poenetentiae non est negandus. (§2) Post acceptum Spiritum Sanctum possumus a gratia data recedere atque peccare, denuoque per gratiam Dei resurgere ac resipiscere. Ideoque illi damnandi sunt qui se quamdiu hic vivant, amplius non posse peccare affirmant, aut vere resipiscentibus veniae locum denegant.

Of Sin after Baptism.

(§1) Not every deadly sin willingly committed after Baptism is sin against the Holy Ghost, and unpardonable. Wherefore the grant of repentance is not to be denied to such as fall into sin after Baptism. (§2) After we have received the Holy Ghost, we may depart from grace given and fall into sin, and by the grace of God we may arise again and amend our lives. And therefore they are to be condemned, which say they can no more sin as long as they live here, or deny the place of forgiveness to such as truly repent.

(i) **Source.**—Composed in 1552-3, and but slightly changed since.

(ii) **Object.**—Directed against Anabaptist errors to the effect that 'sinners after baptism cannot be restored by repentance,'[1] and that the 'regenerate cannot sin'[2] or fall from grace. The Council of Trent, the *Reformatio Legum*, and Calvin all bear out the testimony of the Article to the existence of such errors.

(iii) **Explanation.**—§ 1 states that *deadly sin is not unpardonable*. This is merely a negative proposition, intended to meet that of the Anabaptist with a direct denial. **Not every deadly sin willingly committed after Baptism is sin against the Holy Ghost, and unpardonable.** The Article is not concerned to define the nature of the unpardonable sin: and in 1563 Archbishop Parker deliberately struck out Art. 16 of the Edwardian series, *Of Blasphemy against the Holy Ghost*,[3] which attempted

[1] See 32 Henry VIII. c. 49 §11, vol. i. p. 18.
[2] See Hooper's letter, vol. i. p. 33.
[3] See Appendix.

the task. There are, however, two sets of passages in the New Testament which deal with deadly sin; and the question is, Do they support the assertion that it is not unpardonable? (1) The first series consists of those in which Our Lord speaks of Blasphemy against the Holy Ghost (Matt. xii. 31, 32; Mark iii. 28, 29; Luke xii. 10). Taking S. Mark's account, as the fullest, it appears (*a*) that Our Lord does not speak in general terms of sin against the Holy Ghost, but of one sin; (*b*) that this particular sin is 'blasphemy,' a sin of the tongue; (*c*) that it 'hath never forgiveness' because it is not so much an act as a condition, 'an eternal sin'; and (*d*) that its character is further limited by S. Mark's explanation, 'because they said, He hath an unclean spirit.' Thus the unpardonable sin is of a special kind. It is not even said that the Pharisees on that occasion had actually committed it, though it is implied that they were on the verge of doing so: and what they were doing was wilfully ascribing to diabolic agency that which manifestly could only be the work of the good God. Probably the unpardonable sin has been rightly defined as 'an *outward expression* of an inward hatred of that which is recognised and felt to be divine':[1] and it is unpardonable not because God ever willingly refuses His grace, but because the hatred which prompts such 'blasphemy' is so settled as to be eternally incapable of fulfilling the conditions of forgiveness. 'An eternal sin' necessarily involves an eternal punishment. But whether this definition be right or not, Our Lord's words give no countenance to the proposition that every deadly sin willingly committed after baptism is sin against the Holy Ghost and unpardonable. (2) But do the other passages, usually alleged for the purpose? In (*a*) Heb. vi. 4-6, the writer is speaking of Christians who had been both baptized and confirmed (4) and 'then fell away' by a definite act of apostasy. Of such persons he says that 'the while' (R. V. marg. *i.e.* 'so long as')'they crucify' (*pres.* 'go on crucifying') 'to themselves the Son of God afresh, and put (*pres.* 'go on putting') Him to an open

---

[1] Ellicott, *Lectures on the Life of our Lord*, p. 187 n. 1. (The italics are his.)

shame, it is impossible to renew them again unto repentance.' But there is nothing said as to the impossibility of doing so, if they should forego their opposition and return. Similarly in (*b*) Heb. x. 26-29 the 'fearful expectation of judgment' is denounced only to those who, after full knowledge of Christ (26), deliberately reject Him (29) and go on sinning wilfully (26): while in (*c*) Heb. xii. 14-17 it is not said that Esau sought diligently for a place of repentance and failed to find it, but that he failed to find it because what he sought was not the place of repentance but the blessing. In all three passages the failure to find pardon is described as due not to God's refusal to forgive but to the sinner's unwillingness to comply with His conditions of forgiveness. Finally (*d*) S. John, in the passage on which the distinction between mortal and venial sin is based (1 John v. 16, 17), does not define 'sin unto death,' *i.e.* the sin whose natural issue would be death, nor does he absolutely forbid intercession for it: and there is nothing to show that in his judgment it might not be forgiven, if repented of and forsaken, like any other sin. Thus the Scripture lends no support to the statement that all deadly sin after Baptism is unpardonable. It follows that **the grant of repentance is not to be denied to such as fall into sin after Baptism**: and the best proof of this is S. Paul's treatment of the incestuous man at Corinth. Of the deadly nature of his sin (1 Cor. v. 1), and of his delivery to Satan (5) there can be no doubt: but the punishment was inflicted 'that his spirit might be saved in the day of the Lord Jesus,' and, if 2 Cor. ii. 5-11 refers, as is commonly held, to the same case, he afterwards obtained not only *the grant of repentance* (*locus penitentiae*) when he was reinstated by the Church (7), but also **the place of forgiveness (locus veniae)** when he was forgiven by the Apostle 'in the person of Christ' (10).

§ 2 *repudiates the doctrine that the regenerate cannot sin, i.e.* that grace is indefectible. The Article unhesitatingly affirms that **after we have received the Holy Ghost we may depart from grace given and fall into sin, and by the grace of God we may arise again and amend our lives. And therefore they are to be condemned which say they can no more** sin as long as they live here. The last assertion found apparent support from the language of S. John, *e.g.* 'Whosoever abideth in Him sinneth not (1 John iii. 6) ... Whosoever is begotten of God doeth no sin' (9; *cf.* v. 18). But S. John had previously said, 'If we say that we have no sin, we deceive ourselves' (i. 8): and in iii. 6-9 the expression 'sinneth not' is explained by 'doeth no sin,' an expression which is so phrased in the original as to make it clear that what he asserts to be impossible to the regenerate is the habit and practice of sin rather than isolated acts of sin. He is only saying, in his own aphoristic way, what S. Paul puts in mixed exhortation and argument, that if we would but reckon ourselves to be dead unto sin, as indeed we are by our Baptism, sin need not reign in us that we should obey the lusts thereof (*cf.* Rom. vi. 2, 11-14). But it is there, and there is danger of sinning. If this were not so, all the hortatory parts of the Epistles would be gratuitous, particularly any such caution as that of S. Peter, to 'make your calling and election sure' (2 Pet. i. 10). So would Our Lord's own warnings that the good seed might become unfruitful (Matt. xiii. 22), the salt lose its savour (Matt. v. 13), the branch in the vine be cast forth (John xv. 6): passages addressed to His hearers as the future citizens and Apostles of His Kingdom, *i.e.* as baptized.

It only remains to add that the Calvinists, while rejecting the doctrine that the regenerate cannot sin, substituted for it the tenet of Final Perseverance, to the effect that they cannot finally, though they may temporarily, fall from grace. They would have admitted reluctantly that *we may depart from grace*: but they would have said not that *by the grace of God we may*, but that we must, *arise again and amend our lives*. This is quite inconsistent with S. Paul's fear that he might 'be rejected' (1 Cor. ix. 27) or fail to 'apprehend' (Phil. iii. 12): and it was a happy thing that only failure attended the repeated attempts of the Puritans, from 1572 onwards, to get the article amended so as to make room for their unscriptural tenet of the irresistibility of grace.[1]

---

[1] See vol. i. pp. 54 *sqq.*

ARTICLE XVII

De Praedestinatione et Electione.

(§ 1) Praedestinatio ad vitam est aeternum Dei propositum, quo, ante jacta mundi fundamenta, suo consilio, nobis quidem occulto, constanter decrevit eos, quos ‡ in Christo ‡ elegit ex hominum genere, a maledicto et exitio liberare, atque ut vasa in honorem efficta per Christum ad aeternam salutem adducere. (§ 2) Unde qui tam praeclaro Dei beneficio sunt donati, illi, Spiritu ejus opportuno tempore operante, secundum propositum ejus vocantur; vocationi per gratiam parent; justificatur gratis; adoptantur in filios Dei; unigeniti ejus Jesu Christi imagini efficiuntur conformes; in bonis operibus sancti ambulant; et demum ex Dei misericordia pertingunt ad sempiternam felicitatem.

(§ 3) Quemadmodum Praedestinationis et Electionis nostrae in Christo pia consideratio dulcis, suavis, et ineffabilis consolationis plena est vere piis et his qui sentiunt in se vim Spiritus Christi, facta carnis et membra quae adhuc sunt super terram mortificantem, animumque ad coelestia et superna rapientem,

Of Predestination and Election.

(§ 1) Predestination to life is the everlasting purpose of God, whereby, before the foundations of the world were laid, He hath constantly decreed by His counsel secret to us, to deliver from curse and damnation those whom He hath chosen in Christ out of mankind, and to bring them by Christ to everlasting salvation as vessels made to honour. (§ 2) Wherefore they which be endued with so excellent a benefit of God be called according to God's purpose by His Spirit working in due season; they through grace obey the calling; they be justified freely; they be made sons of God by adoption; they be made like the image of His only-begotten Son Jesus Christ; they walk religiously in good works; and at length by God's mercy they attain to everlasting felicity.

(§ 3) As the godly consideration of Predestination and our Election in Christ is full of sweet, pleasant, and unspeakable comfort to godly persons and such as feel in themselves the working of the Spirit

tum quia fidem nostram de aeterna salute consequenda per Christum plurimum stabilit atque confirmat, tum quia amorem nostrum in Deum vehementer accendit: ita hominibus, curiosis carnalibus et Spiritu Christi destitutis, ob oculos perpetuo versari Praedestinationis Dei sententiam perniciosissimum est praecipitium, unde illos diabolus protrudit vel in desperationem vel in aeque pernitiosam impurissimae vitae securitatem.

(§ 4) Deinde promissiones divinas sic amplecti oportet, ut nobis in sacris literis generaliter propositae sunt; et Dei voluntas in nostris actionibus ea sequenda est quam in verbo Dei habemus deserte revelatam.

of Christ, mortifying the works of the flesh and their earthly members and drawing up their mind to high and heavenly things, as well because it doth greatly establish and confirm their faith of eternal salvation to be enjoyed through Christ, as because it doth fervently kindle their love towards God: so for curious and carnal persons, lacking the Spirit of Christ, to have continually before their eyes the sentence of God's Predestination is a most dangerous downfall, whereby the devil doth thrust them either into desperation or into wretchlessness of most unclean living no less perilous than desperation.

(§ 4) Furthermore, we must receive God's promises in such wise as they be generally set forth to us in Holy Scripture; and in our doings that will of God is to be followed which we have expressly declared unto us in the word of God.

(i) **Source.**—Composed in 1552-3: and since retained as it then stood, except for the addition of 'in Christo' in § 1, and the omission in § 4 of 'although the decrees of Predestination are unknown to us,' after 'Furthermore.'

(ii) **Object.**—To allay the angry disputes upon Predestination, already rife in England in 1552, as we learn from the *Reformatio Legum*; and to guard against the extravagances both of belief and practice consequent upon the tenet of Reprobation.

(iii) **Explanation.**—§ 1 merely explains *what is meant by Predestination and Election*, and that in the language of Scripture without note or comment. It is chiefly based on Eph. i. 3-11, with allusions to Rom. viii. 28-30; ix. 21.

We note (1) the restraint of its language, and this in two directions. (*a*) The Article only observes that

Predestination to life is the everlasting purpose of God. It avoids saying that the election of some implies the rejection of all the rest, and so declines to be committed to the doctrine of Reprobation, according to which all who are not predestinated to eternal life were held to be predestinated to eternal death. (β) It says nothing about the motive or cause of such predestination, and refuses to enter into the question whether it proceeds from the arbitrary decree of God's absolute will, irrespective of anything in those predestinated, or whether it is somehow consequent upon God's foreknowledge of their ways, good or bad. The Article is content merely to state the fact that **He hath constantly decreed by His counsel . . . to deliver . . . those whom He hath chosen**, and to emphasise the truth that this counsel is **secret to us**, a mystery we are not to pry into.

On the other hand (2) the positive statements of the Article, so far as they go, faithfully reflect the Scriptural doctrine of Predestination and Election in its double aspect. (a) In the main drift of Holy Scripture the 'elect people of God' are chosen to privilege. They consist of those who have been brought within the covenant; in the Old Testament, of circumcision, in the New Testament, of baptism (cf. Ex. xix. 5; 1 Pet. i. 1, 2; ii. 9). There the elect or chosen are the **chosen in Christ**, or the baptized (Col. iii. 1, 9, 10, 12). Thus S. Paul addresses his readers as the 'called' (Rom. i. 6), and S. Peter as the 'elect' (1 Pet. i. 1). Both imply that some of their converts were in danger of falling away (1 Cor. x. 6 *sqq.*; 1 Pet. v. 8): and S. Peter definitely charges his people to 'make their calling and election sure' (2 Pet. i. 10). Clearly then, in the Apostolic Epistles, the elect are elect to grace only, and not to final glory (*cf.* John vi. 70). But (β) in the Gospels, Our Lord expressly distinguishes between the called and the elect. 'Many are called but few chosen' (Matt. xxii. 14): while in the language of Rom. ix. 21, 22, there is a corresponding contrast drawn between 'vessels of wrath fitted unto destruction,' and 'vessels of mercy which God afore prepared unto glory.' The latter it is definitely said that God predestinated unto life, though it is not said that *He* fitted the former unto destruction. A potter never makes vessels merely for destruction. But the distinction between the called and the elect remains in fact; and thus the teaching of Scripture, taken as a whole, reflects, in its main drift, what is known as the doctrine of Ecclesiastical Election, viz., that some men are elect to privilege; but it also recognises the further truth that there are, too, some elect to glory; though it is not part of this truth either that those elect to glory are known to us, or that those who are not of the number are foreordained to reprobation.

It will now be clear that the language of § 1 is so drawn as to cover the Scriptural doctrine of predestination to life in its entirety; but with special care to avoid unwarranted and extravagant statements already current, such as those which afterwards became familiar to Englishmen through the works of Calvin (1509-1564). He held that 'by Predestination we mean the eternal decree of God, by which He has determined with Himself what He would have to become of each individual man. For all are not created in like condition, but for some eternal life, and for others eternal damnation, is foreordained. Therefore, according as each one was created for one of these two ends, we say that he is predestinated either to life or to death.'[1] He repudiated the denial of Reprobation as illogical, 'since election itself would not stand unless it were opposed to reprobation.'[2] He taught that Predestination and Reprobation proceeded from a purely arbitrary decree of God. 'Those, therefore, whom God passes over, He reprobates, and that from no other cause than that He wills to exclude them from the inheritance which He predestinates for His sons.'[2] His followers summed up his system in the nine Lambeth Articles and the Five Points of orthodox Calvinism.[3] But by the moderation of § 1 of Art. 17, by its precise repudiation of the most dangerous of Calvin's tenets, that of particular redemption in § 4, as well as by the teaching of Arts. 9 and 16, the Calvinistic scheme was

---

[1] *Institutes*, III. xxi. 5.   [2] *Ib.*, xxiii. 1.   [3] See vol. i. pp. 55, 57.

effectually prevented, by anticipation, from obtaining a footing in our formularies. This has been an unmixed blessing, for it is an immoral creed.

§ 2 proceeds to describe *the course of the predestinate.* In close dependence on Scripture, it enumerates seven stages in their progress from their original election to their final glory: (1) Vocation; (2) Obedience to vocation through grace; (3) Free justification; (4) Sonship by adoption; (5) Conformity to the likeness of Our Lord; (6) A religious life; (7) Everlasting felicity. The enumeration is based on Rom. viii. 28-30; and seems to be inserted with a view to providing against antinomian perversions of the doctrine of predestination to life. Such election on the part of God, though it does not proceed, as was afterwards contended by Arminius (1560-1609), from any foreseen merit of ours (*cf.* Rom. ix. 10-13), and is therefore not to be thought of as a consequence of God's foreknowledge, does require in the elect a real correspondence to His grace (Rom. xi. 21-24).

§ 3 states *the practical effect of the doctrine of Predestination,* with an eye to the fascination which the discussion of these high mysteries exercised over the sixteenth century mind. Happily we are not given to speculation of this sort in the nineteenth; but there are people still whom it attracts. It is well to be cautioned, as we are here, that while the thought of our predestination to life is full of consolation to a good man, for the merely inquisitive and carnally minded it is a topic to be avoided, as certain to lead in their case either to despair, if they come to believe that they are not predestinate to life, or to recklessness, if they believe that they are.

§ 4 provides *two rules for the interpretation of Scripture,* as safeguards against abuse of the doctrine. (*a*) The first is aimed at the tenet of particular redemption, which held that God's predestination had reference not to mankind at large, but to this and that particular individual (*cf.* Calvin's definition in § 2). On the contrary, says the Article, **We must receive God's promises in such wise as they be generally set forth to us in Holy Scripture.** *Generally* means 'universally,' as in the

Catechism, when it is said that there are two sacraments 'generally necessary to salvation,' *i.e.* necessary for all mankind (humano generi), 'where they may be had.' Accordingly the rule laid down is that God's promises, such as that of Predestination and Election, are to be taken as applicable to all men, not to a favourite few, nor to individuals. (*b*) The second rule is aimed at the doctrine of Reprobation. **In our doings that will of God is to be followed, which we have expressly declared to us in the word of God.** That will is certainly that all men should be saved (1 Tim. ii. 4; *cf.* John iii. 16); and if that is God's purpose, we cannot say that he has reprobated any. Some of the Anabaptists, however, 'maintain,' as Hooper wrote in 1549, 'a fatal necessity; and that beyond and besides that will of His, which He has revealed to us in the Scriptures, God hath another will by which He altogether acts under some kind of necessity.'[1] This is mere fatalism: and the Article rejects it not tacitly only, as when it insists that our election *in Christ* (*cf.* §§ 1, 3) is the only election with which we are concerned, but explicitly by this rule, which lays down that we are only concerned with *that will of God . . . which we have expressly declared to us in the Word of God.* Taken together, the two rules further imply that we have only to do with the positive assurances of God, and are not at liberty to assert their contradictories by way of conclusions drawn from His Predestination of some to His Reprobation of others; still less to apply such conclusions where we like.

[1] Vol. i. p. 33.

ARTICLE XVIII

De speranda aeterna salute tantum in nomine Christi.	Of obtaining eternal salvation only by the name of Christ.
Sunt et illi anathematizandi qui dicere audent unumquemque in lege aut secta quam profitetur esse servandum, modo juxta illam et lumen naturae accurate vixerit: cum sacrae literae tantum Jesu Christi nomen praedicent in quo salvos fieri homines oporteat.	They also are to be had accursed that presume to say that every man shall be saved by the law or sect which he professeth, so that he be diligent to frame his life according to that law and the light of nature. For Holy Scripture doth set out to us only the name of Jesus Christ, whereby men must be saved.

(i) **Source.**—Composed in 1552-3, and since unchanged.

(ii) **Object.**—To condemn a latitudinarian theory of a school of Anabaptists which held that, if men were only sincere in following out their own systems, even their rejection of Jesus Christ would prove no obstacle to their salvation. The tenet in question is noticed and condemned in the *Reformatio Legum*.

(iii) **Explanation.**—(1) At first sight the Article might seem to deny that salvation is open to the heathen, and such as have never heard the name of Christ. But this is not its purpose. (*a*) *The title*[1] should be strictly translated 'of hoping for eternal salvation,' etc. Such a phrase shows that the Article only refers to those who live within the sound of the Gospel, and is meant to assert, in effect, that they have no right to expect salvation but on God's terms, *i.e.* 'in the name of Christ.' This is clear from (*b*) its *contents*. **They also are to be had accursed, etc.** The connecting particle *also* appears to run back to the last clause of Art. 16, where it is said that *they are to be condemned which . . . deny the place of forgiveness to such as truly repent.* Both clauses point, in short, to the

---

[1] For inexact titles, *cf.* Arts. 10, 13, 31.

specific teaching of a particular set of persons. The question whether the heathen can be saved is not raised. If the Article asserts the truth of Acts iv. 12 (*cf.* 1 Tim. ii. 5, 6; 1 John v. 11, 12), this is not to deny the possible salvation of the heathen. 'God is the Saviour of all men,' and not only, though 'specially, of them that believe' (1 Tim. iv. 10). A heathen who is saved, will be saved not **by the law or sect which he professeth**, though he will be saved *in* it: for, if saved, it will be by virtue of service done (unconsciously, it may be, but really done) to Jesus Christ (Matt. xxv. 31-46), and by fidelity to 'the light which lighteth every man,' which is not **the light of nature**, but Christ Himself (John i. 9).

(2) But the Article leaves this question on one side. It is really aimed at the lax opinion which maintains that one religion is as good as another, and which has for its logical basis the denial of all objective truth whatever. The Anabaptists, claiming for themselves as they did a continuous or immediate inspiration, held that they were above the necessity of acknowledging as authoritative any body of revealed truth. They went so far as to draw the logical conclusion that they might reject Christ with impunity. 'There are such libertines and wretches,' writes Hooper, 'who are daring enough in their conventicles not only to deny that Christ is the Messiah and Saviour of the world, but also to call that blessed seed a mischievous fellow, and deceiver of the world.'[1] This was their sin, to hold that, after having received it, they could let the revealed faith go with impunity. It is condemned as explicitly in Holy Scripture as in the Article (Mark xvi. 16; John iii. 18, 19; xii. 48; 1 Pet. iv. 17).

There are few errors of the Anabaptists that find favour to-day, but none is more common than the deliberate adoption by a Christian of the latitudinarian position that a man's creed does not matter if his life is right. It is the only error definitely anathematised in the Articles, as in the Athanasian Creed: and it is as distinctly condemned by Our Lord Himself.

[1] *Cf.* vol. i. p. 33.

Group C. Articles dealing with **Corporate Religion**, or **the Church, the Ministry, and the Sacraments** (Arts. 19-31).

(i) After defining **the Church** and denying infallibility to any one part of it (19), the formulary treats of (*a*) the authority of the Church and its limitations (20); (*b*) General Councils as the voice of the Church (21); (*c*) certain doctrines sanctioned by Councils claiming to be General (22).

(ii) Next, of **the Ministers** of the Church; as to (*a*) their call and mission (23), and (*b*) the language proper to their ministrations (24).

(iii) Then, of **the Sacraments**; (*a*) in general, as to their nature and number (25), and the principle of their efficacy (26); (*b*) in special, of Baptism (27), and the Eucharist, with reference to the Eucharistic Presence (28, 29), Communion in both kinds (30), and the Eucharistic Sacrifice (31).

ARTICLE XIX

De Ecclesia.

(§ 1) Ecclesia Christi visibilis est cœtus fidelium, in quo verbum Dei purum praedicatur et sacramenta, quoad ea quae necessario exiguntur, juxta Christi institutum recte administrantur. (§ 2) Sicut erravit Ecclesia Hierosolymitana, Alexandrina, et Antiochena: ita et erravit Ecclesia Romana, non solum quoad agenda et caeremoniarum ritus, verum in his etiam quae credenda sunt.

Of the Church.

(§ 1) The visible Church of Christ is a congregation of faithful men, in the which the pure word of God is preached and the sacraments be duly ministered according to Christ's ordinance in all those things that of necessity are requisite to the same. (§ 2) As the Church of Jerusalem, Alexandria, and Antioch have erred: so also the Church of Rome hath erred, not only in their living and manner of ceremonies, but also in matters of faith.

(i) **Source.** — Composed by the English Reformers, 1552-3.

(ii) **Object.**—Probably polemical, and intended (*a*) to give such a definition of the visible Church as should exclude the claim of the Roman Church to be the only true Church, and, at the same time, shut out the various sects of Anabaptists: and (*b*) to deny the claim of the Roman Church to infallibility.

§ 1 offers *a definition of* **the visible Church.**

(1) The word *Church* is the customary English equivalent of the Greek Ἐκκλησία, which was naturalised in the Latin Ecclesia, but not in our own tongue. As used in the New Testament, Ecclesia once appears (*a*) in its classical sense of an assembly such as that to which, in a free Greek city, the transaction of public affairs was entrusted (Acts xix. 32, 39, 41). The Greek assemblies were called by a herald, and, consisting as they did of such only as enjoyed the rights of citizenship, were called out or elected from a larger population. Both these ideas are expressed in the word Ἐκκλησία, and have their counterpart in the Christian's calling (2 Tim. i. 9) and election (Rom. xi. 7; *cf.* 2 Pet. i. 10). There was thus a measure of fitness in the adoption of the heathen term Ecclesia to be the title of the Christian community. But, before its adoption, its associations had ceased to be exclusively, or even mainly, Greek; for it passed to the Christian Church not direct but through the Septuagint. (*b*) Ecclesia, with the Alexandrian translators of the Old Testament, was the standing, though not the invariable, equivalent of *Kahal*, 'the congregation' of Israel: which the Revised Version translates now by 'company' (Gen. xxviii. 3; xxxv. 11; xlviii. 4), now by 'assembly' (Deut. xviii. 16; Josh. viii. 35; Judg. xx. 2; xxi. 5, 8), and now by 'congregation' (Ezra ii. 64; x. 1; Neh. viii. 2; Joel ii. 16): and twice in the New Testament the word occurs in this sense (Acts vii. 38; Heb. ii. 12), where it is translated in the former passage by 'church' and in the latter by 'congregation.' Everywhere it conveys the notion (*a*) of numbers compacted into an organised body, *i.e.* of a congregation as distinct from a mere aggregation, and

EXPLANATION

(β) of the congregation of Israel, or assembly of the whole people gathered together for religious purposes. It contrasts, in the original, with *Adah*, which, for the most part, is represented in the LXX. by 'synagogue'; and, though translated in the Revised Version now by 'congregation' (Ex. xii. 3; Lev. iv. 13; x. 17; Num. i. 16; Josh. ix. 27), and now by 'company' (Num. xvi. 5; Ps. cvi. 17), signifies no more than an informal massing of individuals, and can even be used of a swarm of bees (Judg. xiv. 8) or 'a multitude of bulls' (Ps. lxviii. 30). Ecclesia was thus naturally appropriated by Our Lord as the name of His new society (Matt. xvi. 18): and that as conveying two ideas, that the Church was to be (a) an organised body, and (β) the new 'assembly of the people of God' (Judg. xx. 2). Had Ecclesia been taken over direct from its Greek usage, it would have suggested only that the Church was called out of a larger body, and not that it was intended to take the place of the Jewish theocracy as the new 'people for God's own possession' (1 Pet. ii. 9; *cf.* Acts xx. 28; Eph. i. 14). (c) Thus in the New Testament Ecclesia became the regular designation for the new society. Sometimes it designates the Church as a whole throughout the world (Matt. xvi. 18; 1 Cor. xii. 28; and especially in Eph. *e.g.* i. 22, etc.; *cf.* Acts xx. 28): sometimes the Church in a particular place (Acts viii. 1; 1 and 2 Thess. i. 1; 1 Cor. i. 2; 2 Cor. i. 1; Rom. xvi. 1; Rev. ii. 1): and, not infrequently, a particular congregation accustomed to meet in somebody's house (1 Cor. xvi. 19; Rom. xvi. 5; Col. iv. 15; Philem. 2): and this variety of usage is faithfully reflected in the Articles which speak of 'the Church' (Art. 20), of 'the visible Church' (Art. 19) as a whole, and again of 'every particular or national church' (Art. 34) such as 'the Church of Jerusalem, Alexandria, and Antioch,' or 'the Church of Rome' (Art. 19). It would seem from the Gospels that the conception of the Church as a whole (Matt. xvi. 18) historically preceded that of the local church (Matt. xviii. 17). With S. Paul, 'the idea of the local church, as a unit in itself, is more prominent in the earlier Epistles: that of individual Christians forming part of the great body of believers (the Church Catholic) is more prominent in the later.'[1] But we cannot conclude from this that the use of Ecclesia for the local church necessarily came first in order of time: nor that the conception of the Church as a whole is not logically prior to that of the different churches, or of its individual members who are spoken of as 'added to' the Church (Acts ii. 47). In order of thought the plan of a building precedes its parts, though in order of time the parts precede the whole. Our Lord, as the architect of His Church, constituted it in effect when, in order to describe it, He adopted the term Ecclesia with all its Old Testament antecedents. S. Paul, 'as a wise masterbuilder' (1 Cor. iii. 10), would naturally be pre-occupied with the parts until the entire building rose before him in its ideal proportions, as at length it does in the Epistle to the Ephesians.

(2) The Church, so planned by Our Lord, was of necessity **the visible Church**: for it inherited the name, and was to step into the place, of the old theocracy.

(a) The foreign reformers, who had but an inadequate sense of the obligation of Church unity, endeavoured to justify their separation from the historic Church by setting up a doctrine of *the Invisible Church,* which consisted of true believers known only to God. As if with an eye merely to the Greek associations of Ecclesia, they spoke of a Church of the elect: and, decrying all organisation as mere externalism, they affected to regard membership in any or no ecclesiastical unity as indifferent by the side of membership in the Invisible Church. S. Augustine had, indeed, opened up an ulterior distinction between the *corpus Christi verum* and the *corpus Christi mixtum.*[2] He made an 'interior' Church of those only who were predestined to adhere permanently or 'perseveringly' to their Lord.[3] But, for all this, he never lost sight of the visible Church as a Divine institution, nor set up the 'interior' Church as a rival to the actual, of which it was but a subdivision. This antagonism was

---
[1] Sanday and Headlam, on the *Romans,* p. 15.
[2] *De Doctrina Christiana,* iii. 32.
[3] Bright, *Lessons, etc.,* p. 281.

EXPLANATION

first set up by Wyclif (d. 1387), who defined the Church as 'the congregation of all the predestinate,' and contrasted it with the corrupt Church of his day. Wyclif's definition was taken up by Hus (d. 1415), and through him the doctrine became common property with the continental reformers, though Luther was the first to embody it in the actual phrase of 'the Invisible Church' in his lectures on *the Galatians* (1516-19). Melanchthon, however, who will not hear of an invisible Church apart from the visible, had sufficient influence to keep the tenet out of the Lutheran formularies, whose definitions of the Church run on lines similar to those of Art. 19. But the Swiss were less cautious. They firmly believed that the Church is one: but by seeking its unity in the invisible Church rather than in the visible, they necessarily set up the one as a rival to the other. Their formularies now draw a distinction between the visible and the invisible Church, and speak of the true Church as invisible. In England, Swiss influences on this point made themselves felt as early as the reign of Henry VIII.: for both the Bishops' Book of 1537 and the Thirteen Articles of 1538 assert that the Church has two senses in Scripture, and means either 'the whole congregation of them that be christened and profess Christ's Gospel' or 'the number of them only which belong . . . to everlasting life.' It is only visible in the first sense: it is only one in the second. These distinctions are traceable to Zwingli, and are reproduced in the language of his English disciple Hooper. Hence their entire rejection, in the later and authorised English formularies, is no less significant than providential. Such currency as this doctrine of the Invisible Church still retains it owes to the exigencies of apology for the sects (including the new sect of unsectarianism) and not to sound learning. The notion that, for instance, 'S. Paul regarded membership of the universal Ecclesia as invisible and exclusively spiritual . . . seems . . . incompatible with any reasonable interpretation of S. Paul's words.'[1]

(*b*) *The evidence that Our Lord intended to found a*

---

[1] Hort, *The Christian Ecclesia*, p. 169.

visible Church appears both in (a) the plan of action which He adopted, and in (β) the language which He used to describe His work.

(a) *His plan* was not to scatter His teaching broadcast for men to make what they could of it, nor to set it down in a book; but to organise a society to which it should be entrusted. Thus, after He had offered Himself as Messiah to the rulers of the old theocracy at Jerusalem (John ii. 18 and iii. 1-15) and been rejected (John iv. 1), He retired to Galilee (Mark i. 14), and left Judea to itself (John iv. 3). In the Galilean ministry, He at once proceeded to gather round Him a band of disciples (Matt. iv. 18-22; Luke vi. 13), out of whom He chose twelve (Mark iii. 13; *cf.* John xv. 16) to be apostles (Luke vi. 13). Thus provided with the nucleus of His new society, His next step was to legislate for it (Matt. v.-vii.). He then trained the apostles for their future work by sending them out on temporary missions (Mark iii. 14, 15; *cf.* Luke viii. 1; Matt. x.-xi. 1), by revealing His real claims (Matt. xvi. 16) and intentions (Matt. xvi. 18) to them alone (Matt. xvi. 20), by correcting their notions of the means by which His Kingdom would be attained (Matt. xvi. 21; xvii. 22; xx. 18), and of the sort of Kingdom which it would be (Matt. xviii. 1; xx. 21; *cf.* John xviii. 36). Finally, He instituted in the two sacraments of Baptism (Matt. xxviii. 19) and the Eucharist (Matt. xxvi. 26; 1 Cor. xi. 23) rites of admission into (John iii. 5), and maintenance in (John vi. 53), the new society, which were of an essentially visible and corporate (1 Cor. x. 17) character, and entrusted the administration of them to His apostles, who also received, under the warrant of successive commissions, power to legislate for (Matt. xvi. 19; xviii. 18), absolve (John xx. 22, 23), and feed (Luke xii. 42) the Church, together with a last injunction to gather 'all the nations' into its obedience (Matt. xxviii. 19). In this work, the Apostles were to regard themselves as enjoying a mission identical with that which the Lord Himself had received from the Father (John xvii. 18; xx. 21 *a*), as acting under the escort (John xx. 21 *b*; *cf.* Matt. xxviii. 20) of His perpetual presence, and the guidance of the Spirit (John

xvi. 13); and that with a view to all their converts being 'perfected into one,' with a unity organic enough to bear a true likeness to the Unity of the Trinity, and visible enough to convince the world (John xvii. 20-23). The Gospels, then, leave no doubt that Our Lord's purpose was to found a society at once organised and visible. On turning to the Acts and the Epistles, we find that His work was immediately carried forward on these lines. There was at first but 'a multitude of persons' (Acts i. 15), though with the Apostles at their head (i. 13, 14). After the Pentecostal outpouring of the Spirit they became not merely a larger (Acts ii. 41), but an organised, body (ii. 42). There was 'one body and one Spirit' (Eph. iv. 4). Functional developments of organisation followed (Eph. iv. 11 *sqq.*) under Apostolic guidance. Thus the Apostles appointed (Acts vi. 3; xiv. 23) deacons (vi. 1-6) and elders (xi. 30; xiv. 23) as need arose; exercised discipline (v. 1-11; 1 Cor. v. 3-5); led the way in prayer and preaching (v. 42; vi. 4); presided over the administration of the sacraments (x. 48; xix. 5; 1 Cor. i. 17; Acts xx. 7); and took the chief part in legislating for the Church (xv. 22). Men were invited to have fellowship with the Church in order to have fellowship with God (1 John i. 3); if they became converts, they were admitted through the visible rite Baptism (Acts ii. 38), and regarded as having been 'added to' a body previously existing (41); so long as they remained in it 'they continued stedfastly in the Apostles' teaching and fellowship,' in the Eucharist and the public prayers (ii. 42). It is quite in accordance with this development that the Epistles frequently describe the Church under such outward figures as a body (1 Cor. xii. 12 *sqq.*), a building (iii. 9), a temple (iii. 16), a household (Gal. vi. 10), a city (Eph. ii. 19), and a kingdom (Col. i. 13). These Epistles, moreover, are addressed to definite societies (1 Thess. i. 1; Rev. ii. 1), which include bad (1 Cor. v. 1) as well as good among their members, and have both a local habitation (1 Cor. i. 2) and officers of their own (Phil. i. 1). Nothing, in short, can be clearer than that Our Lord's plan was to found a visible Church, and that Christianity everywhere presented itself under this aspect in the Apostolic age.

(β) The society thus launched into the world was spoken of by its Founder as *the Kingdom of God*. The meaning of this phrase was well understood by the Jews, as is clear from the fact that Our Lord was never at pains to explain it. He had only to announce it (Matt. iv. 17), and make it from the first (John iii. 5) the substance of His teaching (Matt. xiii. 11, 19) and that of His disciples (Matt. x. 7; Luke x. 9; *cf.* Acts xx. 25; xxviii. 31) for it to be welcomed with enthusiasm (Luke xiv. 15). The exact phrase, indeed, does not occur in the Old Testament, nor in the apocalyptic literature; but the thing itself is frequently alluded to, specially in the Book of Daniel, a book which had much influence at the time of Our Lord's ministry. There it was promised that God would 'set up a Kingdom which shall never be destroyed' (Dan. ii. 44; vii. 14; *cf.* Matt. xvi. 18), under the rule of 'one like unto a son of man' (vii. 13), and in the hands of Israel, 'the people of the saints of the Most High' (27). Jewish Messianic expectation was building on these prophecies when Our Lord appeared: and He not only adopted the tone of one declaring the accomplishment of that which His hearers hoped for (Matt. iv. 17), but employed imagery already associated with the glories of the Kingdom (Luke xiii. 28, 29; *cf.* Is. lix. 19; Mal. i. 11) to describe it. The Jews, however, expected that the Kingdom would take shape in the renewal of an empire like that of David (Mark xi. 10). So secular were their notions of it that Our Lord had to transform, before He could accept, them. Thus He refused to be a king after their own heart (John vi. 15), and in the end it was their disappointment at this refusal which led to His death. 'Pilate executed Him on the ground that His Kingdom was of this world: the Jews procured His execution precisely because it was not'[1] (*cf.* John xviii. 33-37; xix. 12-16). So we find two sides to Our Lord's teaching about the Kingdom. As opposed to current expectation, He laid stress on its spiritual and moral character. The Jews thought it would be a kingdom of the material order (Matt. xx. 21). He taught that

---

[1] *Ecce Homo*, p. 27 (ed. 20).

it would be for 'the poor in spirit' (Matt. v. 3), and described it as the highest moral good (Matt. vi. 33). They thought that it was still to come (Luke xix. 11; xxiii. 42). He said that the final stage was yet in the future (Matt. vi. 10; Luke xxii. 18); but that it was actually among[1] them (Luke xvii. 21), suffering violence (Matt. xi. 12); for He Himself had brought it (Luke xi. 20). They believed that it was a perquisite of their nation, to which they had an hereditary right. He assured them that it was His Kingdom (Matt. xiii. 41); that it would be taken from them (Matt. xxi. 43); and that the conditions of entry into it were not Jewish birth, but a New Birth (John iii. 5) and conversion (Matt. xviii. 3). In the Sermon on the Mount He described the character of its citizens (Matt. v.-vii.), and He devoted the parables of the Kingdom to insist now on its mixed and outward aspect (Matt. xiii. 1-32, 47-50), now on its hidden life (33, 45, 46). At last He was justified in identifying the Kingdom, so purified in idea, with His Church (Matt. xvi. 18, 19). It was to be a visible society 'in,' but 'not of, this world'; not a Kingdom of heaven in the sense that its seat was solely there, but in the sense that it was from heaven and 'not from hence' (John xviii. 36), and its character heavenly.

Attempts are current to obscure the outward aspect of the Kingdom of heaven, and to question its identification with the Church. For this purpose the genuineness of Matt. xvi. 18, 19 is questioned, though without reason: and stress is laid on the fact that, in the Epistles, the Kingdom of God appears only on its inward side[2] (Rom. xiv. 17) or as a thing to be attained in the future (1 Cor. xv. 50). It is then added that the Church is merely the community of believers looked at as an institution; while the Kingdom of heaven, which Our Lord made the kernel of the Gospel, is Christianity in its essence and spirit. Undoubtedly, the Kingdom of God stands for the whole sphere of the Divine Sovereignty, and is used sometimes for God's rule over the world (Ps. xxii.

---

[1] 'In the midst of you' (marg.). His questioners were Pharisees, and it was not 'within' *them*.
[2] But *cf.* Col. i. 12.

28) or in men's hearts and wills (Ps. cxlv. 11), sometimes of His ultimate triumph (Matt. xxv. 34). It is therefore a larger conception than that of the Church: but the Church is the present manifestation of the Kingdom, and is so far identical with it. This identification, moreover, is not confined to one passage in the Gospel (Matt. xvi. 18, 19): for when S. Peter asked a question about forgiveness arising out of the precept upon Church discipline (Matt. xviii. 15-17), he was immediately answered with a parable about the Kingdom of heaven (xviii. 23-35). On the other hand, the ideal and spiritual aspect of the Church appears in the Epistles (1 Cor. iii. 16, 17), and is exactly that which is elaborated in the Epistle to the Ephesians side by side with its corporate organisation. Certainly the Christian community is usually spoken of in the Gospels as the Kingdom of God and in the Epistles as the Church: but there is no reason to suppose that the Apostles lapsed from Our Lord's spiritual idea of the Kingdom and discarded it for an inferior and materialised one when they spoke of the Church instead. Both Church and Kingdom have a double aspect, each having its organised life and its inward principles. But there is a solid reason for the substitution of 'Church' for 'Kingdom' as the usual name for the Christian community in Apostolic times. Ecclesia, like Logos, was a word which had a meaning for the Greek as well as for the Jew. To the Gentile as to Pilate (John xviii. 33-8) the name Kingdom of God would convey little or nothing. The Apostles, having the mind of Christ, were not at pains to quote Him. They boldly conveyed His teaching by using the word which their hearers would best understand.

The Gospels then, in what they tell us alike of Our Lord's plan and of the title which He used to describe His Church, tell us that He meant it to be *the visible Church*.

(3) **The visible Church** is further described as **a congregation of faithful men.** *Congregation*, as we have seen, is here used not in its modern sense of a number of Christians assembled for worship in a particular place, but in its Scriptural sense of the whole people of God: and again, of the whole as an organised body, not a mere

EXPLANATION 171

aggregation. The Church is further limited as a body of *faithful men*, but nothing is implied as to the character of their faith. To make the possession of a lively faith the test of Church membership would be to make havoc of the visibility of the Church, and to read into the later part of its definition as here given what is contradictory of the first. 'Faithful men,' or 'the faithful,' are such as have received and profess the faith, whether good or bad. In Art. 26 it is stated that 'in the visible Church the evil be ever mingled with the good.' If, for all its mixed character, 'the visible Church' is yet defined as 'a congregation of faithful men,' it is obvious that 'faithful' can mean no more than such as have received the faith in Baptism (Mark xvi. 16). The parables of the Wheat and the Tares (Matt. xiii. 24-30), the Draw Net (47, 48), and the Marriage Feast (xxii. 2-14) are enough to show that of such was the Church in Our Lord's intention. It was to be a school for sinners, and not a museum of saints.

(4) The definition concludes with *the notes of the Church*.

(*a*) The first is that in it **the pure Word of God is preached.** That the Church was to be a dogmatic institution is clear from Our Lord's last commands to the Apostles. They were to 'make disciples of all the nations,' not only 'baptizing them,' but 'teaching them to observe all things' which He had commanded (Matt. xxviii. 19). So their earliest converts 'continued stedfastly in the Apostles' teaching' as well as in their 'fellowship' (Acts ii. 42): while they themselves went out to 'preach the Gospel' (1 Cor. i. 17), and enjoined it as a last duty upon their successors to 'preach the Word' (2 Tim. iv. 2), and 'hold the pattern of sound words' (2 Tim. i. 13). Their writings everywhere imply that a definite body of teaching was committed to the Church (2 Thess. ii. 13-15; 1 Tim. vi. 20, 21; 2 Tim. i. 12-14), and the Church committed to the teaching (Rom. vi. 17): and this, as we have seen, is what is meant by the Word of God or the Gospel Message.[1] For us, it

---

[1] See vol. i. p. 112.

is preserved in the Creed: and where the Church delivers the Creed, there *the pure Word of God is preached*, and the first note of the Church satisfied.

(b) A second note is that in it **the sacraments be duly ministered, according to Christ's ordinance, in all those things that of necessity are requisite to the same.** The Church is the home not only of truth but of grace. Our Lord accordingly instituted the two 'Sacraments of the Gospel,'[1] both of which were to be used until His coming again (Matt. xxviii. 19, 20; 1 Cor. xi. 26; *cf.* Luke xii. 42, 43). Stedfastness, therefore, in sacraments and sacramental worship (Acts ii. 42; xx. 7; Heb. x. 19-25) was regarded as equally necessary with stedfastness in doctrine. For the due administration of the sacraments the requisites are a right *Matter* and a right *Form*; the 'matter' of Baptism being water, and of the Eucharist bread and wine, the 'form' being in Baptism the use of the Threefold Name, and in the Eucharist the recitation of the words of consecration. In their requirement, however, of a duly ordained *Minister* the two sacraments are not on a par. Lay baptism is allowed, in case of need, because there are indications in Scripture that the act of baptizing was sometimes delegated to others by the Apostles, even when to all appearance no other ordained person was present beside themselves (Acts x. 48; *cf.* Acts xix. 5, 6, and 1 Cor. i. 14-17). But for a valid Eucharist, a duly ordained minister is also one of *those things of necessity requisite to the same.*

(c) A third note is only implicitly stated in the Article. The sacraments cannot be **duly ministered** without 'the right use of ecclesiastical discipline.'[2] The Church received from Our Lord 'the authority of the keys to excommunicate notorious sinners, and to absolve them which are truly penitent'[2] (Matt. xvi. 19; xviii. 18; John xx. 23); and the English Ordinal recognises this third note of the Church when it requires every priest 'so to minister the Doctrine and Sacraments and the Discipline of Christ, as the Lord hath commanded.'

[1] *Cf.* Art. 25.
[2] Homily for Whitsunday, part 2. Cf. *The Homilies*, p. 462 (ed. Oxford, 1859).

§ 2, while it is not concerned to charge the Church of Rome with apostasy or heresy, denies her claim to infallibility by observing that, as a mere matter of history, **as the Church of Jerusalem, Alexandria, and Antioch have erred, so also the Church of Rome hath erred.** Those Eastern Churches all compromised their orthodoxy for a time during the Arian controversy. The Church of Rome similarly erred when in 358 Liberius signed an Arianising creed; when in 417 Zosimus declared Pelagius a man 'of entirely sound faith'; or again, in 634 when Honorius supported Monothelitism. The errors of the Church of Rome have thus embraced not only errors of **living**, as in the corrupt moral tone of Western Christendom at the end of the Middle Ages, for which the Court of Rome was mainly responsible; nor only **manner of ceremonies** such as the denial of the Chalice to the laity or the superstitious use of relics and images; they have extended to **matters of faith**. As a matter of fact the Roman Church has erred, like other churches. It follows that she is no more infallible than they.

ARTICLE XX

De Ecclesiae Auctoritáte.

Of the Authority of the Church.

Habet Ecclesia ritus statuendi jus et in fidei controversiis auctoritatem; quamvis Ecclesiae non licet quicquam instituere quod verbo Dei scripto adversetur, neque unum Scripturae locum sic exponere potest, ut alteri contradicat. Quare licet Ecclesia sit divinorum librorum testis et conservatrix; attamen, ut adversus eos nihil decernere, ita praeter illos nihil credendum de necessitate salutis debet obtrudere.

The Church hath power to decree rites or ceremonies and authority in controversies of faith; and yet it is not lawful for the Church to ordain anything contrary to God's word written, neither may it so expound one place of Scripture, that it be repugnant to another. Wherefore, although the Church be a witness and a keeper of Holy Writ: yet, as it ought not to decree anything against the same, so besides the same ought it not to enforce anything to be believed for necessity of salvation.

(i) **Source.**—Composed by the English Reformers, 1552-3, with the exception of the first clause, in **thick type**, which was added in 1563 from the Confession of Würtemberg. There has been some doubt as to the authority of this clause (1). It is *not found* in (*a*) the Latin MS. of the Articles which received the signatures of the bishops on January 29, 1563; nor in (*b*) an English 'minute' of the Articles dated January 31, 1563, and now preserved among the Elizabethan State Papers; nor in (*c*) the English edition printed by Jugge and Cawood in 1563, which was the edition referred to by 13 Eliz. c. 12. But the value of this evidence rests on the

EXPLANATION

assumption that these copies present us with the Articles as finally authorised. On the other hand, (2) the clause *is found* in (*a*) an early but undated Latin draft of the Articles preserved among the Elizabethan State Papers, where it was inserted, in the same hand, after the draft itself was made; and in (*b*) the earliest Latin edition, which was published by Wolf the Queen's printer, and contains her imprimatur. It is possible that the clause was added by the Lower House of Convocation after the Bishops had signed their final draft: but it is more probable that it was added at the bidding of the Queen. In either case the clause was deficient in full synodical authority. This was made good in 1571: and when Archbishop Laud was charged, at his trial, with having added the clause himself, he was able to produce a transcript of the records of Convocation, attested by a notary public, containing the words in question.

(ii) **Object.**—To give a clear and balanced statement of the authority of the Church in view of attempts made by some to minimise, and by others to exaggerate, it. The Anabaptists denied it altogether, and were sufficiently met by the claim of the Church to 'expound' Scripture which underlay the Article as it stood in 1553. The additional clause prefixed in 1563 was wanted in view of the Puritan claim, then rising into prominence, that the Church had no power to enforce rites or ceremonies other than those for which explicit sanction might be found in Scripture. This was the familiar position of the Swiss reformers, who held that the Bible and the Bible only is the rule both of faith and practice: and the Article repudiates it, as Luther did. On the other hand, it equally repudiates the position to which the Roman Church had committed herself in 1546,[1] that in doctrine the Church is not limited by what is contained in Scripture or may be proved thereby.

(iii) **Explanation.**—Under the general subject of *the authority of the Church and its limitations*, the Article deals with three points:—(1) The *legislative* power of the Church. The ambiguity of the word 'Church' makes it

---

[1] *Conc. Trid.* Sess. iv.

a little uncertain whether the Article refers to the authority of the universal Church or of particular Churches. The statement that **the Church hath power to decree rites or ceremonies** would be true of the Church as a whole ; for the Council of Nicaea, in 325, fixed the time for keeping Easter. But in 1563, when the statement was first prefixed to the Article, the opposition was to the exercise of such power by the national Church. Probably, therefore, 'Church' is used in the more restricted sense: and the clause thus merely anticipates the fuller statement of the last clause of Art. 34, also added in 1563, to the effect that 'every particular or national church hath authority to ordain, change, and abolish ceremonies or rites of the Church ordained only by man's authority, so that all things be done to edifying.' As a matter of fact, such changes have usually been made on the authority of local Churches. The earliest liturgies are those belonging to particular Churches : and it is only the greater influence of some particular Church that has led to the growth of the later uniformity in rites and ceremonies. Thus the importance of the Church of Constantinople has led to the adoption of her liturgies of S. Basil and S. Chrysostom throughout the orthodox East ; while the unique position of the Roman See in the West has resulted in the abandonment of the Mozarabic and Gallican rites in favour of the liturgy of the local Roman Church. In the sixteenth century the English Church reverted to the principle that, as a local *Church*, she *hath power to decree rites or ceremonies* for herself. A *rite* is the 'order'[1] or 'form' of service, as expressed in words, for any particular purpose, *e.g.* 'The Order for Morning Prayer,' or 'The Form of solemnization of Matrimony.' Such rites the Church of England has not hesitated to modify whether by way of omission, re-arrangement, or addition. Thus, at the last revision of the Prayer Book in 1662, she omitted explicit prayer for the departed ; retained that sequence in the parts of the Eucharistic rite which was first adopted in 1552 ; and prefixed to the

---

[1] In Canon 23 of 1604 '*ritus*' is translated 'order.'

EXPLANATION

Order of Confirmation an additional rite for the renewal of the baptismal vows. In dealing with *ceremonies*, which are the gestures or acts[1] accompanying the rite, she has exercised the same discretion; retaining in use kneeling at the Communion, the sign of the Cross at Baptism, and the ring at Marriage, though all were ceremonies once sharply contested; and abandoning others whether in the interests of simplification or of edification (*cf.* 'Of Ceremonies' in the Prayer Book).

But the Church claims this power only under *limitations*:—(a) *In principle*, it is not lawful for the Church to ordain anything that is contrary to God's word written: and again, it ought not to decree anything against the same. Thus, on the ground that 'both the parts of the Lord's sacrament, by Christ's ordinance and commandment, ought to be ministered to all Christian men alike,' Art. 30 condemns the denial of the Chalice to the laity, *i.e.* not as a doctrinal, but as a disciplinary, error. But short of this, where Scripture is silent about rites and ceremonies, it need not be consulted. To hold, as the Puritans held, that every rite and ceremony must have express warrant in Holy Writ, is to misconceive its purpose. Scripture is 'profitable for teaching, for reproof, for correction, for instruction which is in righteousness' (2 Tim. iii. 16; *cf.* Rom. xv. 4). It is the supreme authority in matters doctrinal and moral, but not in matters disciplinary. On the contrary, questions of practice were left, as the Scriptures themselves testify, to be settled by the authority of the Church. Thus the Jewish Church added the observance of the Feasts of Purim and of the Dedication (John x. 22) to the round of feasts divinely ordained (Deut. xvi. 1-17); and Our Lord not only sanctioned its claim by His presence at the Feast of the Dedication, but recognised in the Jewish hierarchy an authority equal to that of Moses for such purposes (Matt. xxiii. 2, 3) and in its minor ceremonial precepts an obligation, secondary indeed, but still real (Matt. xxiii. 23). When the Christian Church was set up, similar powers were

[1] Canon 18 speaks of kneeling, standing, and bowing as 'outward ceremonies and gestures.'

exercised by its leaders. In the absence of express precept, it is difficult to attribute the substitution of Sunday for the Sabbath to any authority short of Apostolic; which must also be held responsible for the connection of the Eucharist with the earliest hours of 'the first day of the week' (Acts xx. 7). At any rate, this is the authority which regulated the conduct of worship. Thus, S. Paul orders that men should pray with head uncovered (1 Cor. xi. 4) and hands uplifted (1 Tim. ii. 8); that women should be veiled (1 Cor. xi. 5), and be in silence (1 Cor. xiv. 34; 1 Tim. ii. 12); that the prophets should exercise their gift in turn (1 Cor. xiv. 29 *sqq.*). Details, apparently of direction for celebrating the Eucharist, he reserves till he come (1 Cor. xi. 34). Meanwhile he lays down general principles for the conduct of worship. It is to have an eye first to edification (1 Cor. xiv. 26) and then to decency and order (1 Cor. xiv. 40), and where doubts arise, they are to be settled by appeal to the 'custom' delivered by Apostles (1 Cor. xi. 2) or prevalent among 'the churches of God' (xi. 16). It is abundantly clear then that powers of regulating rites and ceremonies are assigned, in Scripture, to the Church: and later history shows that they have been freely exercised by local churches.

(β) *In practice* the English Church is further limited, in legislating upon rites and ceremonies for herself, by the existing conditions of Establishment. When in 1532 she permitted the Crown to rob her synods of the right of meeting, debating, and legislating for her needs at their own pleasure,[1] she lost all freedom of self-government; and when she allowed herself, as in the successive Acts of Uniformity, to accept from Parliament coercive powers for the enforcement of the Prayer Book, she bartered away her liberty of reviewing it without the consent of the civil power, then but not now necessarily Christian. Hence deadlocks have arisen. But in theory it is still to the Church and not to the civil authority, whether Crown or

---

[1] By the 'Submission of the Clergy,' afterwards incorporated in 25 Henry viii. c. 19 (1534).

Parliament, that such power to decree rites or ceremonies belongs. As in former days, 'When any cause of the law divine happened to come in question, or of spiritual learning, then it was declared, interpreted, and showed by that part of the . . . body politic, called the spiritualty, now being usually called the English Church, which . . . is . . . sufficient and meet of itself . . . to administer all such offices and duties as to their rooms spiritual doth appertain':[1] so now, 'If any difference arise about the external policy, concerning the Injunctions, Canons, and other Constitutions whatsoever thereto belonging, the Clergy in their Convocation is to order and settle them, having first obtained leave under Our Broad Seal so to do: and We approving their said Ordinances and Constitutions; providing that none be made contrary to the laws and customs of the land.'[2]

(2) The *judicial* power of the Church. **The Church . . . hath authority in controversies of faith.** (a) The *nature* of this authority is judicial. It is an authority to **expound.** In a civilised state, the legislature makes the laws, but it is the office of the judge to interpret them: and while the legislature may make new laws, the powers of the judicial bench are confined to the interpreting of laws already in existence. It is so with the Church. She possesses a less absolute authority in questions of doctrine than of discipline. For, while she 'hath power to decree rites or ceremonies,' she only 'hath authority in controversies of faith' to the extent of expounding what revelation means. For example, the Council of Nicaea had no hesitation in making a new regulation for the time of keeping Easter: but, in dealing with Arianism, it went no further than to declare the sense of Scripture as to Our Lord's Divinity. There was indeed a development; but it was an explanatory, not an accretive, development: not an addition to the substance of the faith such as might proceed from a lawgiver, but an exposition of its contents such as is proper to a judge. (b) The *Scriptural warrant* for the assumption by the

[1] 24 Henry VIII. c. 12.
[2] His Majesty's Declaration, prefixed to the Articles.

Church of such an 'authority in controversies of faith' is found in Our Lord's grant to the Apostles of the power to 'bind' and 'loose,' *i.e.* prohibit or permit by declaring a thing lawful or unlawful after the manner of a judge (Matt. xvi. 19; xviii. 18), to feed with discrimination (Luke xii. 42), and to teach (Matt. xxviii. 19).; again, in Apostolic practice, as when at the Council of Jerusalem a doctrinal question involving the Catholicity of the Church was decided by 'the Apostles and the elders with the whole Church' (Acts xv. 22); and also in the language of S. Paul. He bids the elders of Ephesus 'to feed the Church of God' and guard it against false teachers (Acts xx. 28-30). He urges Timothy to 'guard the deposit' (1 Tim. vi. 20), and the elders under Titus to 'hold to the faithful word which is according to the teaching' (Tit. i. 9). Here he assumes that Christian teachers are responsible for judging between truth and falsehood;[1] and his language is only intelligible on the supposition that he regarded them as the official interpreters of the mind of the Church, which he describes as 'the pillar and ground of the truth' (1 Tim. iii. 15). But (c) like all judicial authority this right of the Church to discriminate and decide has its *limitations*. Thus it belongs to the Church as a whole. Only to the Apostles as a body is the presence of Christ (Matt. xxviii. 20) and the guidance of the Holy Spirit (John xiv. 26; xvi. 13) promised: just as indefectibility is assured only to the whole Church (Matt. xvi. 18). It is true that local churches have taken upon themselves to define doctrine: but usually under some necessity, as of checking local error or of making provisional arrangements where circumstances rendered a final settlement by the whole Church unattainable. Thus Montanism was condemned by Asiatic Synods in the second century; Pelagianism, on its appearance in Africa, by the Synod of Carthage in 412; Anabaptism by the English Convocation of 1536. Where such local synods received more than local weight, it was in proportion to the extent of their acceptance in later times. Thus the Synod of Orange, which

---

[1] *Cf.* 2 Tim. ii. 15.

EXPLANATION 181

condemned Semi-Pelagianism in 529, though only a little Gallican Council, earned the respect and gratitude of the entire West; while the Council of Constantinople, which in 381 put Apollinarianism and Macedonianism under its ban, eventually came to be recognised as the second Œcumenical Council. Their decisions were for a long time of local or temporary authority. Similarly the theologians of the English Reformation repeatedly affirmed that their doctrinal formularies were in no sense final but temporary expedients, awaiting the confirmation of a free Council representative of the whole Church. But even were 'authority in controversies of faith' exercised by the whole Church, it would still be under the further limitation that no decision would be binding if it either contravened the terms, or added to the substance, of Holy Scripture. **The Church may not so expound one place of Scripture that it be repugnant to another ... so besides the same ought it not to enforce anything to be believed for necessity of salvation.** But this has already been dealt with under Art. 6.[1]

(3) What then is *the relation of the Church to the Scriptures*? **The Church is described as a witness and a keeper of Holy Writ.** (*a*) As a *witness*, her chief function is to testify what books are to be regarded as Scripture, *i.e.* what is Scripture, as also to expound what Scripture means. (*b*) As a *keeper*, she is, like the Jewish Church, 'entrusted with the oracles of God' (Rom. iii. 2). She is not the mistress but the steward of Scripture. Her duty is not to reveal truth, but to guard the truth as revealed (Jude 3). As against the Roman position, she is not the oracle of truth; nor are we to look for any such institution as would relieve us of the mental and moral discipline involved in the obligation to search for truth in the spiritual as in the scientific region. On the other hand, as against the Protestant claim that every man is to discover the truth in Scripture for himself, the Article teaches that not the individual but the Church is the keeper of Holy Writ. The Scriptures themselves bear witness to their proper function. Both Gospels and

---

[1] Vol. i. pp. 95 *sqq.*

Epistles were addressed to men already instructed in the faith (Luke i. 4; 2 Thess. ii. 15; iii. 6; 1 Cor. xv. 1-4; Heb. v. 12), and were never intended either to take the place of a teacher, or to serve as a mine out of which each man was to quarry the truth for himself. The Church is the teacher, the Scriptures are the test, of truth. The Ethiopian eunuch was obliged to allow that he was but half equipped for arriving at the truth by his possession of the Scriptures: but when the representative of the 'teaching Church' expounded them in the person of Philip, he speedily attained it and was baptized (Acts viii. 27-38). Everywhere the Apostles follow the same method. They teach first: and prove, or bid men prove for themselves, by appeal to the Scriptures afterwards (Acts ii. 14-36; xiii. 16-42; xvii. 2, 3, and 11).

ARTICLE XXI

De auctoritate Conciliorum Generalium.

(§ 1) Generalia Concilia sine jussu et voluntate principum congregari non possunt. (§ 2) Et ubi convenerint, quia ex hominibus constant, qui non omnes Spiritu et verbo Dei reguntur, et errare possunt, et interdum erraruut, etiam in his quae ad normam pietatis pertinent. (§ 3) Ideoque quae ab illis constituuntur, ut ad salutem necessaria, neque robur habent neque auctoritatem nisi ostendi possint e sacris literis esse desumpta.

Of the authority of General Councils.

(§ 1) General Councils may not be gathered together without the commandment and will of princes. (§ 2) And when they be gathered together, forasmuch as they be an assembly of men, whereof all be not governed with the Spirit and word of God, they may err and sometime have erred, even in things pertaining unto God. (§ 3) Wherefore things ordained by them as necessary to salvation have neither strength nor authority, unless it may be declared that they be taken out of Holy Scripture.

(i) *Source.*—Composed by the English Reformers, 1552-3.

(ii) *Object.*—Art. 21, standing as it does between one that treats 'Of the Authority of the Church,' and another that repudiates certain doctrines, as 'Of Purgatory,' etc., put forward on that authority, serves as the natural sequel to the one and the necessary introduction to the other. The authority of the Church, as the position of the Article implies, is normally expressed through General Councils; but, as its text goes on to affirm, the doctrines sanctioned by Councils claiming to be General cannot be accepted unless brought to the test of Holy Scripture. There is thus no intention to disparage the authority of such Councils as were really General: a point which is further established by the structure and the historical affinities of the Article. As with other Articles,[1] its main statement is reserved for its final clause, which simply affirms that, in matters doctrinal, a council has no function beyond that of declaring the sense of Holy Scripture: and again, the *Reformatio Legum*, which proceeded from the same hands as the Articles under Edward VI., professes that we reverently accept the four great Œcumenical Councils, and defer to the decisions of many later synods. There was, however, a special object in defining the degree of this deference at the time. A council, claiming to be Œcumenical, was sitting at Trent: and the English Divines, by pointing out that it was merely an assembly summoned by the Pope and confined to bishops of the Papal obedience, *i.e.* neither free nor representative, rid themselves by anticipation of any responsibility to it.

(iii) **Explanation.**—The Article makes three statements as to § 1 *the right of convening*, § 2 *the fallibility of*, and § 3 *the authority of, General Councils*.

§ 1 affirms that *the right of convening* **General Councils belongs to the civil power. They may not be gathered together without the commandment and will of princes.** This was certainly the authority by which the six councils, generally accepted as Œcumenical, were assembled. The Council of Nicaea in 325 was summoned by the Emperor Constantine: and even the plan of such a gathering was probably his own. The Council of Constantinople in 381 was convened by Theodosius I. to deal with the errors of Macedonius. The Council of Ephesus, which met in 431 to condemn the Nestorian heresy, was called together by his grandson Theodosius II. The Council of Chalcedon, assembled in 451 to put down Eutychianism, at the request of Pope Leo the Great addressed to the Emperor Marcian, who formally convened it. In 553 the second Council of Constantinople was summoned by Justinian, in the course of the Monophysite controversy: and in 680 the third Council of Constantinople met at the bidding of the Emperor Constantine Pogonatus, and

Cf. the structure of Arts. 4, 7, 10, 11, 15, 16, 20, 31, 32, 36.

EXPLANATION

condemned Monothelitism. Thus every Council, which can claim recognition as Œcumenical, was 'gathered together' at 'the commandment and will of princes.' Upon the decadence of the Roman power in the West, the Pope became the legatee of the imperial right of summoning councils: but, when he also came to be regarded as the successor of S. Peter and spiritual head of the whole Church, his right acquired additional sanction on that ground. At length, however, the decline of the Papacy led men to call in question its sovereign claims: and when, with the growth of the great nations of Western Europe into sovereign states, imperial authority was exercised by each monarch for himself, the right to have a voice in the summoning of Councils was at once claimed for the civil power as part of it. Probably no more than this was in the mind of the framers of Art. 21: for, in the previous reign, the Convocation of Canterbury had expressed itself to this effect: 'We think that neither the bishop of Rome nor any one prince . . . may, by his own authority, . . . summon any general council, without the express consent . ·. of the residue of Christian princes, and especially such as have within their own realms and seigniories *imperium merum*, that is to say, of such as have the . . supreme government . . over all their subjects.'[1] It is a question of precedent rather than of inherent right. In the sixteenth century the civil power, when it wished to secure itself against papal pretensions, reverted to ideals drawn from the practice of later Roman, or earlier mediæval, emperors, chief among which was the imperial right to summon Councils. Imperial authority being now, as it were, in commission, it was argued that this prerogative was in commission too. In the present age, were a General Council possible, the states of the civilised world would be more likely to act on the principle that the interests of religion were no concern of civil government. But as they have the power, and by precedent might claim the right, to intervene, it is still true, though somewhat of an academic truth, that *General Councils*

[1] Pocock's *Burnet*, vol. iv. p. 300.

may not be gathered together without the commandment and will of princes.

§ 2 asserts *the fallibility* of General Councils; but it 'must be understood,' as Bishop Burnet justly observed, 'of councils that pass for such.' **They may err, and sometime have erred, even in things pertaining to God.** Two propositions are made here, that councils, when assembled, are (1) liable to err, and (2) have actually erred.

(1) It might have been thought that God, having entrusted His Church with a revelation of supreme moment, would have taken care that a body summoned to represent the whole Church would be protected from possibility of error. But this is not so: and the mechanical theory of conciliar infallibility is of later growth. In the fourth century 'the very continuance of the Arian controversy, subsequent to the Council of Nicaea, is enough to shew that no such ideas of the finality of a General Council as are now current were then held in the Church.'[1] The language of the orthodox leaders at that time points to the same conclusion. S. Athanasius, with all his veneration for 'the great and holy synod,' maintains that it is not to be preferred before the earlier, but local, Synod of Antioch in 269, nor is that to be preferred before the Council of Nicaea; since both alike did nothing new, but fell back upon the words of those who went before them.[2] So too Pope Julius, while contending that 'a General Council ought not to be set aside by a few individuals,' declares that it is within the power of one Council to revise the decisions of another, and refers to the Council of Nicaea as having laid down this principle.[3] Accredited theologians then expressly declined to attribute to General Councils any inherent authority. In other words, they recognised that *they may err.*

(2) That they *sometime have erred* is mere matter of history. Not only were Councils, such as that of Ari-

---

[1] Professor Collins, on *The Authority of General Councils* (Church Historical Society Lectures, Series ii. p. 167), to whom the writer is indebted for the general treatment of this Article.
[2] *Cf.* Ath., *de Synodis*, §§ 43, 46, 47.
[3] *Cf.* Julius' letter in Ath., *Apol. c. Ar.*, §§ 22, 25.

EXPLANATION

minum in 359, which met with all the appearance of truly representative numbers, actually betrayed into making havoc of the faith, but others, lawfully called and widely attended, were repudiated by contemporaries and revised by subsequent synods. For instance, the Council which met at Ephesus in 449 to acquit Eutyches was immediately denounced by S. Leo as 'no court of justice, but a gang of robbers' (Latrocinium), and its decisions were reversed at the Council of Chalcedon, 451. The Article is thus amply justified in its statement that neither the formal convocation of a Council, nor its numbers, can ensure to it rectitude of proceedings or immunity from error. It should be noted that the statement, thus effectually grounded, was aimed, in all probability, at certain mediæval synods, which, while commonly taken for General Councils, were representative only of Latin Christendom, and were responsible for the promulgation of mere errors, such as the dogma of Transubstantiation, which was first imposed by the Lateran Council of 1215, and was afterwards re-affirmed at Trent.

§ 3 states, in conclusion, *the authority* of General Councils. **Things ordained by them as necessary to salvation have neither strength nor authority, unless it may be declared that they be taken out of Holy Scripture.** This is only to re-affirm the root principle of the English Reformation, the sufficiency of Scripture in matters of faith; and the function of General Councils was never more than to declare its sense. But this is essentially the Catholic position. To S. Athanasius the merit of the Council of Nicaea is that it exactly declared the sense of Scripture. 'Divine Scripture is sufficient above all things; but if a council be needed on the point, there are the proceedings of the Fathers: for the Nicene bishops did not neglect this matter, but stated the doctrine so exactly, that persons reading their words honestly, cannot but be reminded by them of the religion towards Christ announced in the Divine Scriptures.'[1] Nor is this a function of inferior moment. At the present time Christendom is hardly conscious that there have ever been

---

[1] Ath., *de Synodis*, § 6.

differences as to those parts of the Faith on which General Councils were directly called upon to declare the sense of Scripture. The doctrines of the Trinity and the Incarnation, once the most disputed and still the most mysterious, are exactly the doctrines most universally accepted. It is with points that have arisen since the days when, in the undivided Church, General Councils were possible, that controversy is now mainly concerned. It rages round the constitution of the Church, the nature of the Presence and the Sacrifice in the Eucharist, and the source and character, sacerdotal or otherwise, of the Ministerial Commission. Limited as it is by Holy Scripture, nothing testifies so eloquently to the authority of General Councils as the continuance of division without them. The Article is concerned to emphasise their limitations rather than their authority. Hence it dwells on their less favourable aspects, the passions that found scope in them, and their liability to error. But they have another side. Indefectibility was not promised to Church assemblies, nor to the Church of any one age or country, but it was promised to the Church as a whole (Matt. xvi. 18; xxviii. 20; John xiv. 26; xvi. 13). Thus, while there never was any guarantee for the inerrancy of a Council at the moment, once its decisions were received throughout the whole Church it took rank as a General Council, and its doctrine was rightly regarded as infallible. Of such, the English Church recognises 'six Councils which were allowed and received of all men.'[1]

[1] Homily against Peril of Idolatry, p. 197 (ed. Oxford, 1859).

ARTICLE XXII

De Purgatorio.

Doctrina Romanensium (§ 1) de Purgatorio, (§ 2) de Indulgentiis, (§ 3) de veneratione et adoratione tum Imaginum tum Reliquiarum, nec non (§ 4) de Invocatione Sanctorum, res est futilis, inaniter conficta, et nullis Scripturarum testimoniis innititur; imo verbo Dei contradicit.

Of Purgatory.

The Romish doctrine concerning (§ 1) Purgatory, (§ 2) Pardons, (§ 3) worshipping and adoration as well of Images as of Relics, and also (§ 4) Invocation of Saints, is a fond thing vainly invented, and grounded upon no warranty of Scripture; but rather repugnant to the word of God.

(i) **Source.**—Composed by the English Reformers, 1552-3, and unchanged since, except for the substitution in 1563 of 'the Romish doctrine' for 'the doctrine of the School authors.'

(ii) **Object.**—The effect of this change was to direct the condemnation against a type of practice and teaching current within recent memory rather than against the system of the Schoolmen whose day was past. The party with which this teaching was current was known as the 'Romanensian' or 'Romish' party, a name given to the extreme Mediævalists, and not descriptive of the Roman Church as a whole. Consequently it must not be assumed that the tenets here condemned are identical with those of the Church of Rome. The Article could not have been aimed, either in its original or in its amended form, at her authoritative teaching on the points in question; for that teaching was not laid down till the last session of the Council of Trent, December 4, 1563. But the Council, while rejecting the extravagances of current practice, retained the underlying doctrines, at least in their main outlines: and so far the Article, while not intended to condemn the teaching of the Church of Rome, does reject it at certain points. The degree of condemnation, however, has to be examined by taking each subject on its merits.[1]

(iii) **Explanation.**—The Article deals with four topics.

§ 1. The **Romish** doctrine concerning **Purgatory** was of gradual growth.

(1) *In the New Testament* the intermediate state between death and the Judgment is represented as one of sleep, both for those who departed this life before the Gospel era (John xi. 11-13) and for 'the dead in Christ' (1 Thess. iv. 13-16), or Faithful Departed. But this figure, while it suggests rest (John xi. 13; Rev. xiv. 13), must not be pressed to mean that the dead are in a state of somnolent insensibility. Even the Old Testament conceptions of a future life rise above this level:[2] and the language of Our Lord forbids the notion. In the parable of the Rich Man and Lazarus, it is clear that, after death and before the final judgment, there is (*a*) an anticipatory separation of good and bad (Luke xvi. 22, 23, 26); next (*b*), consequent upon this, a state, for the good of 'comfort,' and for the bad of 'anguish' (25); and again (*c*), a vivid consciousness for each soul not only of its own condition but of that of others, whether departed, where it reaches to what is taking place on either side of the 'gulf' in Hades (23, 26), or still living, where, however, it is represented only as memory of the past (25, 27, 28; *cf*. Rev. vi. 9-11). It may be questioned how much we are at liberty to infer from the details of a parable: but this much, at any rate, seems to be covered by Our Lord's reply to the Sadducees 'as touching the dead, that they are raised' (Mark xii. 26). The dead, He says, are really living: 'for all live unto God' (Luke xx. 38): and our life is no life without conscious activity. The Epistles illustrate the directions of this activity. The souls of the faithful enter at death upon a condition of immediate communion with God, the prospect of which tempted S. Paul (Phil. i. 23), and gladdened the thief upon the Cross (Luke xxiii. 43).

---

[1] *Cf.* vol. i. p. 31.   [2] *Ibid.*, p. 107.

They also (for life means progress) continue their advance toward perfection 'until the day of Jesus Christ' (Phil. i. 6 ; *cf.* 1 Cor. i. 8). Thus there is a real element of truth in the doctrine of purgatory, so far as it provides for a discipline, or purgation, of character in the intermediate state, and recognises (what natural religion would require) that the souls of the faithful, departing as they do in every stage of spiritual and moral growth, need a season, some more, some less, not of fresh probation indeed, which is over once for all at death (2 Cor. v. 10), but of further education for the presence of God.

(2) It is on this principle that, *with the early Christians*, prayer for the dead was an habitual practice. Natural piety and the New Testament doctrine of the intermediate state alike encourage it. As living unto God, the souls of the Faithful Departed are capable of progress, and capable therefore of being aided by our prayers. The literary remains of the first century are so scanty that actual evidence of the custom only begins with the second. But then it occurs on epitaphs such as those of the Catacombs, 'Irenaea, mayest thou live in God, A.Ω.,' and in the Liturgies, where it invariably formed part of the Great Intercession. Such prayers, however, consistently imply belief in the peace and bliss of the Faithful Departed, and lend no countenance to the notion that the destiny of any soul can be changed by prayer of ours. At the end of the Middle Ages a great perversion had taken place. Popular religion looked upon the condition of the departed Christian soul as one of pain, which could be relieved by the prayers, alms, and Masses of surviving friends. The English Reformers, convinced of the difficulty of dissociating prayer for the departed from such perversions, omitted explicit retention of it in the public services. But they expressly refrained from condemning what, apart from later accretions, they knew to be a primitive and Catholic practice. The Article, as it stands in the draft of the Forty-five Articles signed by the six Royal Chaplains in October 1552, contains an express condemnation of prayer for the dead. This was deliberately omitted by the authors of the Forty-two Articles: and prayer for

the dead was not the doctrine rejected by the English Church.

(3) But the later mediæval or *Romish doctrine concerning Purgatory* was rejected. It originates, in Western theology, with S. Augustine. Not without some hesitation, he transferred Origen's belief in the purgatorial nature of the fires of the Last Day to the period in between death and the Judgment. Gregory the Great (Pope, 590-604) erected this speculation into a certainty. 'For certain lighter sins,' he taught, 'we are to believe in a purgatorial fire before the Judgment': and he ascribed to prayers and 'the sacred oblation of the salutary Host' the power to mitigate its severities. Legend,[1] from the seventh century, lent support to the doctrine. By the ninth, it had given rise in practice to solitary Masses and superfluous altars; early in the eleventh to the institution of the Feast of All Souls; and, from the thirteenth onward, to the Chantry system. Meanwhile the Schoolmen, at the end of the twelfth century, had set the reigning system on a rational basis by elaborating the distinction between 'pain' and 'guilt':[2] the latter being an accompaniment of sin forgiven in absolution, but the former an accumulation of consequences to be worked off either in this world or in a penal purgatory. The doctrine was at last authoritatively formulated by the so-called General Council of Florence in 1439, which laid it down that 'if such as be truly penitent die in the grace of God before they have made satisfaction for their sins by worthy fruits of penance, their souls are purged after death with purgatorial punishments: and, for the relief of such pains, they may be aided by the suffrages of the faithful still living, such as the sacrifices of Masses, prayers and alms, and other works of piety.'[3] As might be expected under such a system, the dominant aspect of religion in the later Middle Ages was, with the people, either one of carelessness or else of calculation and fear. If religious, a man's chief object was to reduce the pains

---

[1] *Cf.* Bede, *Eccl. Hist.*, iii. 19, v. 12: and Milman, *Latin Christianity*, ix. 93.   [2] See above, on Art. 14, p. 145.
[3] *Cf.* Denzinger, *Enchiridion*, p. 159.

in prospect by purchasing a store of Masses and Pardons. If irreligious, he could safely leave it to his friends to help him, by the same means, after his death; and enjoy life while he had it. With the clergy religion became equally a business. They only sold what the laity wanted to buy. These evils the Council of Trent fully admitted when in its decree touching Purgatory it deprecated the discussion of 'the more difficult and subtle questions' in 'popular discourses before the uneducated multitude'; and bade bishops prohibit those 'which tend to a certain kind of curiosity or superstition, or which savour of filthy lucre.' Nevertheless it did not condemn the root error that the state of the faithful departed is one of suffering. The Council affirmed that 'there is a Purgatory, and that the souls there detained are relieved by the suffrages of the faithful, but chiefly by the acceptable sacrifice of the altar.'[1] But the *Catechismus Romanus* goes further and describes 'the fire of Purgatory' as one 'in which the souls of the just are purified by torment for a stated time (*cruciatae expiantur*).'[2] It is unnecessary to examine further into the *Scripturalness* of such a doctrine. The passage most often alleged is 1 Cor. iii. 13-15: but it is not to the point. 'The fire' which 'shall prove each man's work of what sort it is' is spoken of as a destructive, not as a cleansing, agency: again, as having effect on every man and not only on the faithful departed; and, once more, as connected in operation not with the prolonged interval between death and the Judgment, but with the conflagration which is to accompany the moment of Our Lord's appearing at the Last Day (13; *cf.* 2 Thess. i. 7, 8; 2 Pet. iii. 10-13). At the same time, it should be remembered that it is not all doctrine of purgatory, but only this 'Romish doctrine' of a penal purgatory, that the Article rejects.

§ 2. **Pardons** have already come under review as Indulgences in the Article on Works of Supererogation;[3] but they have a natural place in the Article on Purgatory, because Pardons dispensed out of the Treasury of Merits

---

[1] Sess. xxv.
[2] Pars I. cap vi. qu. 3.
[3] Art. 14, see above, p. 144.

constituted the chief means, along with the sacrifices of Masses,[1] for shortening its pains. At the end of the Middle Ages the theory of Indulgences was so uncertain that in 1522 the Cardinals dissuaded Adrian VI. from attempting to define it; but there was no hesitation about their use. Eagerly bought by the faithful, they had a high value simply as a piece of papal finance. But the thing itself, apart from its sale, was an offence to religion. Tetzel's Indulgence, *e.g.*, assigns to the purchaser four grants or 'graces': (*a*) 'the plenary remission of all sins, . . . by which remission of sins the penalties which a man must pay in Purgatory . . . are most fully remitted'; (*b*) liberty to choose his own confessor; (*c*) a share in the spiritual wealth of the Church. For all these, some formal expression of penitence is necessary. The fourth 'grace' is (*d*) 'for souls actually in Purgatory, namely a plenary remission of all sins':[2] and for this, payment alone is necessary. Religion could not but suffer under such a system. The distinction between forgiveness of sins and the remission of the penalties due to sin is obscured in the very language in which the Indulgence is drafted. Much less was it likely to be regarded by the popular preachers of the Indulgence who advocated their wares as a good investment;[3] or by the man in the street, who believed, as the German Princes told Adrian VI. in their Hundred Grievances, that 'licence to sin with impunity is granted for money.' Moreover, even were the Indulgence not for sale, the personal element in religion disappeared where its characteristic acts were prompted by fear of punishment. The Council of Trent abolished the worst features of 'the Romish doctrine concerning Pardons,' and rendered the Pardoner, as painted by Chaucer, a person of the past.[4] But the Roman Church, in still 'enjoining the use of Indulgences' and defending them with greater subtilty, at once admits their former abuse and retains their chief offence. Whatever their defence,

---

[1] See below, on Art. 31, for the repudiation of Masses with this object.
[2] Gieseler, *Eccl. Hist.*, v. p. 255, n. 10.
[3] *Ib.*   [4] Sess. xxi. c. 19 (*de Reformatione*).

they are still represented as more than a remission of ecclesiastical penance imposed by the Church: and while this much, which may be called the older doctrine, of Indulgences is certainly covered by Our Lord's grant to her of the power to 'bind' and 'loose,' there is nothing in Scripture to extend her power over the soul into the other world.

§ 3. **The worshipping and adoration as well of Images as of Relics** may be taken together.

(1) **Images** had no place in the worship of the early Christians. As Jewish converts, many had no sympathy with the plastic arts. As Christians, living in close contact with heathenism, they could hardly conceive of art except as associated with the cultus of what was vile. The earliest Christian art therefore confined itself to symbolism: and even for the use of emblems on Church furniture we have no testimony before that of Tertullian (c. 200), who mentions 'The Good Shepherd whom thou paintest on the Chalice.'[1] An advance from symbolism to portraiture appears about the end of the third century: for the Council of Elvira, 305, forbade the painting of pictures on the walls of churches in order to guard against the representation of the objects of worship. But in the fourth century, despite occasional protests, the admission of painting became general. Statuary, which far more than painting was identified with idolatry, has left but few traces of its adoption by Christians during the first five centuries. In the East, the aversion to a 'graven image' (Ex. xx. 4) continues to this day: for the Eastern Church interprets the Second Commandment in its strict sense, and uses only painted representations of Our Lord and the Saints called Icons ($\varepsilon \mathring{\iota} \kappa \omega \nu$ = an Image). But it was with the use of such paintings and mosaics that superstitious practices arose. In the West, Gregory the Great (d. 604) had to insist that 'pictures were placed in churches *only* to instruct the minds of the ignorant'; in the East, by the beginning of the eighth century, the worship of Icons, many of them supposed to be miraculous, had become such a scandal that

---

[1] *De Pudicitia*, c. 10.

they were destroyed by the Imperial Edict of Leo the Isaurian (716-741). His action led to the Iconoclastic Controversy of the eighth and ninth centuries: a long struggle, which finally issued in the admission not only of images but of the veneration of images by the Council of Nicaea in 787, a Council accepted both by Greeks and Latins as the seventh General Council. It decreed that images should be set up and 'treated as holy memorials, worshipped, kissed, only without that peculiar adoration (λατρεία) which is reserved for the Invisible, Incomprehensible God.'[1] The doctors of the Western Church in the Middle Ages went much further: for S. Thomas Aquinas (1224-74) allowed to images of Christ and to the Cross the same worship as to Christ Himself, *i.e.* latria.[2] This was a fatal confusion. It was worse confounded as impressed on our own countrymen in the Constitutions of Archbishop Arundel, 1408, which ordered that 'all henceforth preach up the veneration of the Cross, and of the image of the Crucifix, and other images of saints':[3] where the distinction implied by S. Thomas between the veneration due to the image of Christ and to those of the Saints is lost sight of altogether. Of the superstitions consequent upon image-worship history is eloquent. It stimulated the thirst for the miraculous by impostures such as the Rood of Boxley, and it substituted a grotesque polytheism for the pure worship of Christ: effects for which we have unimpeachable testimony in the writings of Erasmus and Sir Thomas More, the former no friend to Protestantism, and the latter a martyr for the mediæval faith. The Council of Trent, in elaborately safeguarding the 'lawful use of images,' confirms their testimony to the abuses that had existed.

---

[1] Milman, *Latin Christianity*, ii. p. 392. The word προσκυνεῖν, like 'worship' in old English, did not necessarily imply divine worship, and this Council compares the veneration paid to sacred pictures with that paid to the Gospels, and with the salutation given by David to Jonathan (1 Sam. xx. 41). *Cf.* Hefele, *Councils*, vi. p. 375.
[2] *Summa Theologica*, III., xxv., Arts. 3 and 4.
[3] Johnson, *Canons*, ii. p. 469.

EXPLANATION

It would be waste of time to search the Scriptures for a defence of image-worship: but it should be observed that the Second Commandment forbids the adoration of images, not their employment in religious art and as adjuncts of worship. The Jews were alive to this distinction. They set up the Cherubim over the Mercy Seat (Ex. xxv. 18) and the twelve oxen upholding the molten sea (1 Kings vii. 25) without scruple, but destroyed the Brazen Serpent when it became an object of adoration (2 Kings xviii. 4). So far, too, as the image of God in Christ is concerned, the commandment has been modified by the Incarnation. So it was on a theological question that the retention of images rightly turned in the Iconoclastic controversy, the question as to the permanent reality of Our Lord's Human Nature. If, as Catholics hold, He is very man now, then He still wears a human frame; and may be represented in art without prejudice to the spirituality of the Godhead: for now God ever exists in human form. It is, however, for the Church of each age and country to say how far this truth can be safely applied in practice without fear of superstition. In the sixteenth century the English Church took a line amply justified by her late experience, and yet not so rigid as to exclude from God's service that most powerful of all incentives to worship—the appeal to the eye.

(2) **Relics** were as dear to the first Christians as images were distasteful. Their reverent care for the dead bodies of the brethren is explained by that consecration of the material to be the instrument of the spiritual which follows from the Incarnation, as well as by their belief that the body is a 'temple of the Holy Ghost' (1 Cor. vi. 19) and so an heir of the Resurrection (Rom. viii. 11). This instinct of reverence was greatly intensified in the age of the persecutions. How could they but honour the remains of those who had played the true 'athlete'[1] in their 'agony' of witness to Christ? But it was

---

[1] $ἀθλήτης$=a combatant, and $ἀγωνία$=the contest, in which he strove for the victor's crown: a figure freely applied by the Christians to the martyr's triumph.

satisfied by giving the martyrs fitting burial, and meeting for worship at their tombs. Thus the Church of Smyrna, in its account of the martyrdom of S. Polycarp, 155, indignantly repudiates the insinuation that Christians can worship any but Christ. 'Him we worship, as the Son of God, but the martyrs we deservedly love, as the disciples and imitators of the Lord. . . . So we took up his bones, of more worth than precious stones and more valuable than gold, and laid them where it was fitting. There being gathered together, as we have opportunity, the Lord shall grant unto us to celebrate the birthday of His martyrdom, both for a memorial of those that have finished their contest before us and for the exercise and preparation of them that are about to enter upon it.'[1] No sentiment could be purer. But in the fourth century there was a change. An impetus was given to the appetite for relics by the Empress Helena's discovery of the Cross: and even a superstitious value began to be set on relics of martyrs and other saints, which rapidly increased, partly through the influx of half-heathen converts into the Church when the Emperors declared for Christ, but also through the attestation of their healing virtues by great doctors of the Church. Throughout the Middle Ages relic-worship prevailed. It received a further impetus from the Crusades, when the imagination of Europe was fired by the thought of the Holy Places. From that time, and specially about the fourteenth century, Western Christendom was flooded with remnants of the true Cross, limbs of the saints, and like treasures: some spurious, all 'gainful.'[2] Of the genuineness of the relics of local saints there need be no doubt. Those of S. Thomas were adored in Canterbury, and enriched the place where he lived and died. Less, but no little, profit accrued to the fortunate possessors of a phial of the Holy Blood at Hales in Shropshire, or of Our Lady's Milk at Walsingham in Norfolk. For a picture of old Church life, with its pilgrimages and relic-worship,

---

[1] Eus., *H. E.*, iv. 15.
[2] Homily of the Peril of Idolatry—*Homilies*, p. 236 (ed. Oxford, 1859).

which, by joining religion with travel and amusement, at least made it part of common life, the student may read Erasmus' account of his visit to Canterbury with Colet early in the sixteenth century.[1] It sounded the first note of a reaction as fervent as the devotion which it displaced. Of this reaction the Homily against Peril of Idolatry preserves the tone in full vigour. The Article merely forbids 'the worshipping and adoration of relics,' which the Council of Trent retained with words of caution against 'superstition.'[2] But Scripture does not direct the preservation of relics for purposes of veneration. The bodies of the saints were honourably buried (Acts viii. 2). Their raiment wrought cures (xix. 12); but it was not preserved for that purpose after their death: and even the grave-cloths of Our Lord were left in the tomb (Luke xxiv. 12; John xx. 5-10).

§ 4. **Invocation of Saints**, however exaggerated in 'the Romish doctrine,' (1) rests ultimately on two great truths of *Scripture*. The faithful departed are represented (*a*) by Our Lord as 'living unto God' (Luke xx. 38), so that each is in a state of consciousness and can pray; and (*b*) by S. Paul as equally 'in Christ' with ourselves (1 Thess. iv. 14, 16), so that all, being members of the same body (Heb. xii. 22, 23), have a common interest in prayer for each other. (2) These truths were felt by the *primitive Church* to justify the practice of what is sometimes distinguished as Comprecation of Saints,[3] *i.e.* the practice of asking God for the benefit of the prayers of the departed. Of its lawfulness, as of its utility, there was no question: for it differs from Invocation in this respect, that, while in Invocation the words 'Pray for us' are directly addressed to the Saints, in Comprecation the request for their prayers is addressed to God. On this point the Catechetical Lectures of S. Cyril (315-386) illustrate the teaching traditional in the Church of Jerusalem by the middle of the fourth century. 'Then

[1] Dixon, *History of the Church of England*, i. pp. 64 *sqq.*
[2] Sess. xxv.
[3] *Cf. The Church Quarterly Review*, Jan. 1899, in an article on Invocation of Saints, to which the present writer begs to acknowledge his debt.

we make mention also (*sc.* in the Eucharist) of those who have fallen asleep before us, first, of patriarchs, prophets, apostles, martyrs, that God would at their prayers and intercessions receive our supplication : then also [we pray] for the holy fathers and bishops who have fallen asleep before us, and, indeed, for all who have already fallen asleep from among us, believing that the greatest help will be gained for the souls for whom the intercession of the holy . . . oblation is offered.'[1] Here, as in the Liturgy on which S. Cyril comments, we observe a distinction already recognised between the great Saints and the general body of the faithful departed, between those whose prayer is asked for and those for whom the Holy Sacrifice is pleaded : 'not,' as says the text, after commemoration of the Blessed Virgin and the Apostles, 'that we are worthy to make mention of their blessedness, but that they also standing before Thy terrible and awful throne, may in turn make mention of our sad estate, and that we may find grace and mercy in Thy sight, O Lord, to help us in time of need.'[2] But the distinction was not universally established in the official worship of the Church of the fourth century. The Liturgy of the Nestorians prays God to 'accept this offering for all the Holy Catholic Church and for all the just and righteous fathers who have been well pleasing in Thy sight, and for all the prophets and the apostles, and for all the martyrs and confessors.'[3] The Roman Canon of the Mass, which, in the parts concerned, can be safely assumed to have remained unchanged since 400, is a monument to this day of the stage of hesitation or development at which the doctrine of the Saints departed then stood : it refrains from praying *for* those who are now accounted the Saints, but it also refrains from praying *to* them. (3) Meanwhile, *patristic* rhetoric and piety carried the distinction of greater and lesser saints to a higher degree of certainty than was found in the official worship of the Church. To ask the Saints for the benefit

---

[1] *Cat. Myst.*, v. 9.
[2] Brightman, *Liturgies Eastern and Western*, i. p. 57.
[3] *Ib.*, p. 285.

of their prayers to God was a habit which in the East could plead the authority of S. Basil (329-379) and in the West of S. Augustine (354-430). It was the task of (4) *the Middle Ages* to justify it on theological grounds. Custom, inherited from the Fathers, restricted Invocation to canonised Saints: but, even so, the twofold difficulty arose, (*a*) How do our petitions reach the Saints? and (*b*) How, once heard, is their help afforded? In answer, it was held (*a*) that the Saints became cognisant of our requests from their vision of 'the glory of Almighty God'; and this explanation, emanating from Pope Gregory the Great (*d*. 604), became traditional with the schoolmen from Peter Lombard (*d*. 1164) to S. Thomas (*d*. 1274), and was adopted by typical post-Tridentine theologians such as Bellarmine (1542-1621). It was further affirmed (*b*) that the help to be expected of the Saints was no more than the help of their prayers. The Catechism of the Council of Trent, in teaching that to God and the Saints 'we employ two different forms of prayer: for to God we properly say, "Have mercy on us, hear us"; to a Saint, "Pray for us,"'[1] merely perpetuates the doctrine of S. Thomas. Such was the defence of the practice in mediæval theology.

Whether the Article forbids Invocation of Saints as thus limited is open to doubt. There is evidence that in the earlier English formularies of 1537 and 1543 'Invocation' was used to denote prayers for gifts of grace such as God only can give;[2] and it is Invocation of this kind, *i.e.* such forms of it as infringe the prerogatives of God, that is the real object of attack in the second part of the Homily concerning Prayer. The English formularies have indeed been deliberately denuded of all Invocation of Saints in public worship: but it is one thing to condemn a doctrine and another to dismiss practices based on it which might encourage abuse. It would appear then that the English Church has exercised a double caution. She has refrained from condemning all doctrine of Invocation of Saints. She

---

[1] Pars IV. c. vi. qu. 3.
[2] Lloyd, *Formularies of Faith*, pp. 141, 304-5.

has also put away all open practice of it. She had ample justification for both courses. On the one hand, the Reformers had before their eyes the popular saint-worship of the later Middle Ages, in which the elaborate safeguards of the Schoolmen were overlooked, and the Saints supposed to be addressed directly, and to render help which went far beyond the help of their prayers. 'We set every saint in his office,' is the testimony of Sir Thomas More to the extravagances of his own side, 'and assign him such a craft as pleaseth us: S. Loy a horse-leech, S. Ippolytus a smith, S. Apollonia a tooth-drawer, S. Syth women set to find their keys, S. Roke we appoint to see to the great sickness, and S. Sebastian with him. Some saints serve for the eye only, others for a sore breast.' This was mere paganism, the last development of the principle so emphatically repudiated at Nicaea, 325, when the Council, by its rejection of the Arian Christ as a mere demigod, condemned once for all the offering of any sort of worship to intermediate beings, no less unequivocally than such homage, whether to them (Col. ii. 18; Rev. xix. 10; xxii. 9) or to men (Acts x. 25; xiv. 13 *sqq.*), is condemned in Holy Scripture. On the other hand, short of such worship, a limited use of Invocation may be held to be left open. Even by the Council of Trent it is taught under safeguards, and only as 'good and useful,'[1] not as necessary to salvation. But before teaching it a wise and thoughtful Christian will need to be convinced that, in practice, all risk of misunderstanding is past; and that, in doctrine, there is some solid ground for believing that our petitions can reach the Saints. The warning which the whole history of the Church has bequeathed to us on the one point is no less eloquent than the inscrutable silence which Scripture maintains on the other.

[1] Sess. xxv.

ARTICLE XXIII

De vocatione Ministrorum.

Of Ministering in the Congregation.

(§ 1) Non licet cuiquam sumere sibi munus *publice praedicandi aut administrandi sacramenta in ecclesia, nisi* prius fuerit ad haec obeunda *legitime vocatus et missus.* (§ 2) Atque illos legitime vocatos et missos existimare debemus, qui per homines, quibus potestas vocandi ministros atque mittendi in vineam Domini publice concessa est in ecclesia, co-optati fuerint et asciti in hoc opus.

(§ 1) It is not lawful for any man to take upon him the office of public preaching or ministering the sacraments in the congregation, before he be lawfully called and sent to execute the same. (§ 2) And those we ought to judge lawfully called and sent, which be chosen and called to this work by men who have public authority given unto them in the congregation to call and send ministers into the Lord's vineyard.

(i) Source.—Art. 23 is derived from the Confession of Augsburg, through the medium of the Thirteen Articles. The parts of § 1 printed in *italics* are all but verbally identical in the three formularies: and the substance of § 2 is similar to the language employed in the second. But with one significant omission. In 1538, when the commission of Anglican and Lutheran divines was endeavouring to find a basis of agreement, it was necessary, since the Lutherans had abandoned Episcopacy, to take refuge in generalities upon the question, With whom lay the right to ordain? The Thirteen Articles left it with those 'to whom it belonged . . . by the Word of God and the laws and customs of each country.' In 1553, when the Article was remodelled for the use of the English Church alone, the phrase, which suggested that the constitution of the Church might vary in different lands, was dropped. There has been no change in the Article since that time.

(ii) **Object.**—Simply to condemn 'a characteristic error of the Anabaptists, who maintained that any one believing himself to be called to the work of the ministry, was bound to exercise his functions as a preacher in defiance of all church authority.'[1] The error was but one instance of their defiant attitude to all external authority, civil or ecclesiastical, which they justified by their doctrine of 'continuous inspiration.' According to it, each individual Christian, as illuminated by 'the Spirit' which 'breatheth where it listeth' (John iii. 8 marg.), enjoys an authority that renders him independent of all outward order in Church or State. The Article is merely concerned to negative this position, so far as it applies to the Ministry; and does so by insisting on the necessity of an external call and mission. It is not concerned with (a) the need of an internal call, which was admitted by the Anabaptists no less than by the English Ordinal, and was, in fact, the one qualification they required; nor with (b) the further definition of those *who have public authority given unto them in the congregation, to call and send ministers.* The Articles of 1553 gave themselves no airs of systematic rotundity. They were supplements to earlier reformed formularies such as the Ordinals of 1550 and 1552, which are quite explicit in maintaining that this authority pertains to Bishops, as had never been questioned up to that date, and as has been the invariable rule of the English Church since.

(iii) **Explanation.**—§ 1 affirms *the need of an external call and mission.* **It is not lawful for any man to take upon him the office of public preaching or ministering the sacraments in the congregation, before he be lawfully called and sent to execute the same.** *Called* and *sent* refer to two different things. (1) The *call* is the summons to enter the Ministry; and is necessary, in addition to the internal call,[2] because the Minister being the organ of the

---

[1] Hardwick, p. 102 (ed. 1884).
[2] *Cf.* the first question addressed to Deacons in the Ordinal.

corporate action of the congregation or Church[1] in worship and discipline, must be appointed in a formal and public way. Of this principle Scripture is full. 'No man taketh the honour unto himself but when he is called of God, even as was Aaron. So Christ also glorified not Himself to be made a high priest' (Heb. v. 4, 5); but waited for the open call to come at His Baptism (Matt. iii. 16, 17); and both displayed Himself (John v. 36; viii. 42; xi. 42, etc.), and impressed upon His disciples (John xv. 16; xvii. 18; xx. 21), a strong sense of the need of such an open call. It is quite true that, under the Old Testament, God raised up prophets from time to time (Deut. xviii. 18; Amos vii. 14, 15) beside the Aaronic priesthood: and that, under the New Testament, S. Paul received his Apostolate not from men, neither through man, but through Jesus Christ (Gal. i. 1). But the extraordinary ministry of prophets and apostles was authenticated by signs externally recognisable (Deut. xviii. 21, 22; 2 Cor. xii. 12). When prophecy and miracles became rarer, then the laying on of hands, which had been used from the first whether apart from or in company with (1 Tim. iv. 14; *cf.* i. 18) miraculous attestations of a call, became the normal means of bestowing it upon all orders of the Ministry (Acts vi. 6; xiv. 23; 2 Tim. i. 6). In either case the principle of an externally attested call is asserted : and it has ever since been maintained in the Church by the use of prayer and laying on of hands as the essentials of Ordination. (2) But every Minister must be *sent* as well. Such *mission* is as necessary as the call, and is the commission *to execute the same* within a given sphere. If only the call were given, several rightly ordained persons might be found exercising their office in the same place. Mission is simply the result of authoritative arrangement (*cf.* 2 Cor. x. 13 *sqq.*; Rom. xv. 19, 20; Gal. ii. 7), based upon the general principle that 'God is not a God of confusion, but of peace' (1 Cor. xiv. 33), and that His work is to be 'done decently and in order' (40).

---

[1] For the identification, as in Art. 19, see pp. 162 and 170 above: and note *Ecclesia* in the Latin here.

§ 2 describes *those who are empowered to give the call*. **Those we ought to judge lawfully called and sent, which be chosen and called to this work by men who have public authority given unto them in the congregation to call and send ministers into the Lord's vineyard.** This language is vague; but, apart from the supplementary force of the Ordinal and Art. 36, there is one phrase in the Latin which gives light where the English is dark. When it is said that the clergy are to *be chosen and called* to their work, the Latin (co-optati et asciti) implies that their choice and call must proceed from above, *i.e.* by way of their co-option and adoption into an order through the agency of some already endowed with it. So in Scripture. The 'brethren' elected the 'seven' deacons; but it lay with the Apostles to 'appoint' them (Acts vi. 3, 6). Timothy again was approved 'with (μετὰ) the laying on of the hands of the presbytery' (1 Tim. iv. 14); but he received the gift 'through (διὰ) prophecy,' and 'through (διὰ) the laying on of the Apostle's hands' (*ib.* and 2 Tim. i. 6).

ARTICLE XXIV

De precibus publicis dicendis in lingua vulgari.

Of speaking in the Congregation in such a tongue as the people understandeth.

‡ Lingua populo non intellecta publicas in Ecclesia preces peragere aut sacramenta administrare, verbo Dei et primitivae Ecclesiae consuetudine plane repugnat.‡

It is a thing plainly repugnant to the word of God and the custom of the primitive Church, to have public prayer in the Church, or to minister the sacraments in a tongue not understanded of the people.

(i) **Source.**—Composed by the English Reformers, 1552-3, but rewritten in 1563.

(ii) **Object.**—As thus rewritten, the Article was probably aimed at a recent decision of the Council of Trent, which, in September 1562, anathematised those who say that 'the Mass ought only to be celebrated in the vulgar tongue.'[1] The Article of 1553 had not said as much : but only that 'it is most seemly and most agreeable to the word of God that in the congregation nothing be openly read or spoken in a tongue unknown to the people.' As if to take up the challenge, it was now recast in a stronger form. It is worth while, however, to note that where the Articles thus directly challenge the official teaching of the Roman Church, the points in dispute are points of discipline not of doctrine, such as service in the vernacular (Art. 24), communion in both kinds (Art. 30), and the marriage of the clergy (Art. 32). Where the traditional doctrines are condemned by the Articles, they are those of the Mediævalist ; which are not necessarily, nor commonly, identical with the reformed theology of the Church of Rome.

[1] Sess. xxii. can. 9.

(iii) **Explanation** is hardly necessary. It is simply affirmed that the use of **a tongue not understanded of the people** is contrary to (1) **the word of God**, and (2) **the custom of the primitive Church.** (1) *In Scripture,* 'Let all things be done unto edifying' (1 Cor. xiv. 26) is, for S. Paul, the rule of Christian worship. Prophecy is accordingly to be preferred to the gift of tongues (xiv. 3); and the celebration of the Eucharist is to be governed by this principle (xiv. 16, 17). This is quite decisive: and was so regarded by (2) *the primitive Church.* The early liturgies were all in the vulgar tongue: 'Kyrie eleison,' in the Roman Mass, itself being but a relic of the time when the Roman Church was Greek and her service in Greek. There is no special sanctity about Latin. The best plea for its retention, as for that of any other dead language, lies in the danger of promoting false conceptions of Christian truth by having to express it in popular speech. But, whether in preaching or worship, the choice must remain between expressing it thus or not at all!

ARTICLE XXV

De Sacramentis.

(§ 1) *Sacramenta a Christo instituta non tantum sunt notae professionis Christianorum, sed certa quaedam potius testimonia et efficacia signa gratiae atque bonae in nos voluntatis Dei, per quae invisibiliter ipse in nobis operatur, nostramque fidem in se, non solum excitat, verum etiam confirmat.*

(§ 2) ‡ Duo a Christo Domino nostro in Evangelio instituta sunt Sacramenta, scilicet, Baptismus et Coena Domini. ‡

(§ 3) ‡ Quinque illa vulgo nominata Sacramenta, scilicet, Confirmatio, Poenitentia, Ordo, Matrimonium, et Extrema Unctio, pro Sacramentis Evangelicis habenda non sunt, ut quae partim a prava Apostolorum imitatione profluxerunt, partim vitae status sunt in Scripturis quidem probati, sed Sacramentorum eandem cum Baptismo et Coena Domini rationem non habentes, ut quae signum aliquod visibile seu ceremoniam a Deo institutam non habeant.‡

(§ 4) Sacramenta non in hoc instituta sunt a Christo ut spectarentur aut circumferrentur

Of the Sacraments.

(§ 1) Sacraments ordained of Christ be not only badges or tokens of Christian men's profession, but rather they be certain sure witnesses and effectual signs of grace and God's good will towards us, by the which He doth work invisibly in us, and doth not only quicken, but also strengthen and confirm, our faith in Him.

(§ 2) There are two Sacraments ordained of Christ our Lord in the Gospel, that is to say, Baptism and the Supper of the Lord.

(§ 3) Those five, commonly called Sacraments, that is to say, Confirmation, Penance, Orders, Matrimony, and Extreme Unction, are not to be counted for Sacraments of the Gospel, being such as have grown partly of the corrupt following of the Apostles, partly are states of life allowed in the Scriptures; but yet have not the like nature of Sacraments with Baptism and the Lord's Supper, for that they have not any visible sign or ceremony ordained of God.

(§ 4) The Sacraments were not ordained of Christ to be

sed ut rite illis uteremur. Et in his duntaxat qui digne percipiunt, salutarem habent effectum: qui vero indigne percipiunt, damnationem, ut inquit Paulus, sibi ipsis acquirunt.

gazed upon or to be carried about, but that we should duly use them. And in such only as worthily receive the same, have they a wholesome effect or operation: but they that receive them unworthily, purchase to themselves damnation, as S. Paul saith.

(i) **Source.**—Ultimately from the Confession of Augsburg through the Thirteen Articles, but with important changes at each revision. Thus § 1 in *italics*, which stood last in 1553, was put first in 1563, and took the place of a clause from S. Augustine then dropped. In substance it is identical with Art. 9 of 1538, which, in its turn, repeats the language of 1530: but with the significant addition, that the Sacraments are **effectual signs of grace . . . by the which God doth work invisibly in us.** §§ 2, 3 between ‡ ‡ were composed in 1563. § 4 dates from 1553, but with an important omission. As it then stood, it contained a condemnation of the phrase *ex opere operato*, which, as used by the later Schoolmen, covered the comfortable notion that the Sacraments operate mechanically like charms, 'without requiring any inward impulse of good in the recipient.'[1] This was 'no godly but a very superstitious sense.' But *ex opere operato* had also been used to affirm that the Sacraments confer grace on condition of the outward action being performed, to which God has attached grace by His promise, and not simply *ex opere operantis, vel suscipientis*, as if their grace depends solely on the devotion of minister or recipient. In 1547 the Council of Trent by adopting *ex opere operato* to exclude the notion that 'faith alone in the Divine promise suffices for obtaining the grace' of the Sacraments,[2] at once cleared it of ambiguity and rendered it of permanent value. It could now be used simply to safeguard the undoubted truth that the Sacraments are 'effectual' not because of our faith but 'because of Christ's institution

---

[1] 'Non requiritur bonus motus interior in suscipiente' (Gabriel Biel, *d.* 1485).   [2] Sess. vii. can. 8 (de Sacramentis).

EXPLANATION

and promise': [1] and in 1563 the condemnation of it was accordingly withdrawn.

(ii) **Object.**—§ 1 repudiates the Anabaptist depreciation of Sacraments. §§ 2 and 3 improve upon the mediæval theology of the Sacraments by limiting the number of 'Sacraments of the Gospel,' and by insisting on the necessity of right conditions in the recipient.

(iii) **Explanation.**—The Article deals with three subjects: (1) **Sacraments ordained of Christ**, as to § 1 their *nature*, and § 2 their *number*; (2) **Those five rites commonly called Sacraments**, § 3; and (3) the *right use of Sacraments*, § 4.

§ 1 is not concerned with Sacraments in general, but only with **Sacraments ordained of Christ**. Its definition of the *nature* of Sacraments is closely parallel to that of the Catechism, which also confines itself to Sacraments (*a*) 'ordained by Christ Himself.' Next, (*b*) both formularies regard them as signs. As 'outward and visible signs' they be . . . **badges or tokens of Christian men's profession**. This was the only sense in which they were acknowledged either by the Anabaptists, who 'will' them 'to be nothing else than outward signs of our profession and fellowship as the badges of captains be in war'; or by Zwingli, who, though not always consistent with himself in regarding them as mere signs, would never really allow that they were more. Hence the name of Sacramentaries [2] first given by Luther to him and his followers. 'Badges' or signs the Article allows that they are, but insists that they are **not only** signs: (*c*) **rather they be certain sure witnesses** . . . **of grace and God's good-will toward us**, as 'pledges to assure us thereof.' It was to this obsignatory function of the Sacraments, as he called it, that Calvin and his school confined their purpose. They looked upon them as seals or testimonies of the Divine grace, perhaps then and there but perhaps also independently bestowed. They denied that they could properly be said to work grace in, or confer grace on, the

---

[1] See vol. i. pp. 36, 44-47: and Art. 26, below.
[2] *Ib.*, p. 17, Sacramentum=signum: *cf.* S. Aug. 'sacramenta, id est, sacra signa.'—*Opera*, viii. 599 B. (ed. Ben.).

recipient. Hence, while admitting the truth in the Calvinistic definition of the Sacraments, the Article proceeds to supplement it by asserting that they are signs effecting what they signify, or (*d*) **effectual signs of grace . . . by the which** God **doth work invisibly in us.** Here the Article rises to the essential position of the Catholic theology of the Sacraments. With that part of the Catechism, which was added in 1604 to complete the sacramental teaching of the English Reformation on its Catholic side, it asserts that they are more than 'pledges to assure us' of 'the inward and spiritual grace given unto us.' They are 'means whereby we receive the same.' When it is added that by them God (*e*) **doth not only quicken but also strengthen and confirm our faith in Him**, the intention seems to be to apply to Baptism and the Eucharist respectively the general principle that the Sacraments are really means of grace. In Baptism we are 'quickened' by a gift of new life (John iii. 5), which is 'strengthened' within us by the Eucharist (John vi. 54).

§ 2, dealing with their *number*, says **there are two Sacraments ordained of Christ in the Gospel, that is to say, Baptism and the Supper of the Lord.** To this statement, (1) on its *positive* side, no exception can be taken. Baptism and the Eucharist are the only rites which Our Lord is recorded in the Gospels to have instituted, by commanding their use (Matt. xxviii. 19 ; 1 Cor. xi. 24, 25); and that as Sacraments, by Himself connecting the outward sign with the inward grace (John iii. 5 ; Matt. xxvi. 26, 28 ; Mark xiv. 22, 24). They occupy a unique position therefore as the two 'Sacraments of the Gospel,' and as alone 'generally (*i.e.* universally) necessary to salvation,' where they may be had[1] (John iii. 5 ; vi. 53). But the statement has its (2) *negative* aspect, brought out with more emphasis in the Catechism. '*Q.* How many Sacraments hath Christ ordained in His Church? *A.* Two only,' etc. Yet in thus limiting the 'Sacraments ordained of Christ' to two, the Catechism and Articles place no such limit

---

[1] For this important qualification see the order of *The Ministration of Baptism to such as are of riper years.*

on Sacraments in general. 'Sacrament' has always had a wider, as well as a stricter, meaning. In Western theology, as the equivalent of the Greek μυστήριον,[1] it was indifferently applied, from the second century onwards, to a sacred truth or a sacred rite; 'to any mystery,' in fact, 'where more was meant than met the eye or the ear.'[2] Thus S. Augustine defines it as 'a sign of a holy thing,' and gives it a wide range of application, not only to the Lord's Prayer, the Creed, the Imposition of Hands, but even to Jewish ordinances. But as contrasted with the multiplicity of the latter, he insists, in terms which formed the first clause of this Article in 1553, that the Sacraments of the new dispensation are 'most few in number . . . as is Baptism and the Lord's Supper.' Their number was first fixed at seven by Peter Lombard, d. 1164: and this became the received teaching of the Schoolmen, and was finally adopted by the Council of Trent in 1547. 'If any one shall say that the Sacraments of the new law were not all instituted by Jesus Christ our Lord, or that they are more or less than seven, . . . let him be anathema.'[3] Thus the Reformers had a double use of the word 'Sacrament' before them, the wide sense common with the Fathers and the restricted sense traditional with the Scholastics. The Henrician formularies waver as to the number of the Sacraments, owing to differences of opinion upon the definition of the word. But by 1553 the influence of S. Augustine had asserted itself: and, as a result of the definition of § 1, while Baptism and the Eucharist retained their pre-eminence as the only Sacraments of the Gospel, the other five rites took rank as Sacraments, but not 'such Sacraments as Baptism and the Communion are.'[4] The difference is simply that in their case the grace is not known to have been annexed to the sign by Christ Himself. In this connection it should be noted that the Roman Church, though maintaining that (*a*) the

[1] *Cf.* 1 Cor. ii. 7, and xiii. 2, where O. L. has 'sacramentum': and Eph. v. 32, 1 Tim. iii. 16, where Vulgate has 'sacramentum.'
[2] Trench, *On the Study of Words*, p. 104 (ed. 2).
[3] Sess. vii. can. 1 (de Sacr.).
[4] *The Homilies*, p. 355 (Oxford, 1859).

Sacraments are neither more nor less than seven, and that (*b*) all were instituted by Our Lord, is not committed to the position that in every case the visible sign was of His institution, and expressly repudiates the tenet that all the seven are of equal dignity.[1] The question between England and Rome is mainly one of definition: but also of differences of temperament characteristic of the two Churches in their attitude towards fact. The English Church is unwilling to allow that all were instituted of Christ, when the New Testament records as much only of two.

§ 3 intends no disparagement of **those five commonly called Sacraments** by so designating them any more than 'The Nativity of Our Lord' is slighted by being 'commonly called Christmas-Day.'[2] It simply affirms that they are **not to be counted for Sacraments of the Gospel**, on two grounds: (1) *positive*—**being such as have grown partly of the corrupt following of the Apostles, partly are states of life allowed in the Scriptures.** The sentence is carelessly expressed. But its first clause would seem to refer possibly to Penance, as corrupted by mediæval accretions from the 'godly discipline' of 'the Primitive Church'[3]; but certainly to Extreme Unction, which, from being administered to the sick according to Apostolic precept (Jas. v. 14, 15) after the earlier unctions of Baptism and Confirmation came to be known as the last unction (*extrema unctio*), and afterwards, by 'a corrupt following of the Apostles,' was sometimes mistakenly reserved for administration at the point of death as an unction *in extremis*.[4] The second clause probably alludes to Orders and Matrimony, for both are 'states of life approved in the Scriptures.' But neither clause can refer to Confirmation, which is not a 'state of life' at all, and is retained by the English Church 'after the example of the Holy

---

[1] Conc. Trid., Sess. vii. can. 3.
[2] Rubric before Collect for Christmas Day.
[3] Commination Service.
[4] It should be noted that the mediæval English rite was faithful to the primitive idea in enjoining prayers for the sick man's recovery, and in expressly allowing the unction to be repeated.

Apostles.'[1] (2) The *negative* difference between the two *Sacraments of the Gospel* and *the five commonly called Sacraments* is that the latter **have not the like nature of Sacraments with Baptism and the Lord's Supper, for that they have not any visible sign or ceremony ordained of God.** Thus **Confirmation**, though a Sacrament with laying on of hands for its sign, and the gift of the Holy Ghost for its grace (Acts viii. 14-17; xix. 1-6), can only be traced to Apostolic origin, so that we cannot directly assert that its 'outward and visible sign' was 'ordained by Christ Himself.' **Penance** (John xx. 23) and **Orders** (21, 22) were ordained of Christ, and **Matrimony** 'adorned and beautified by His presence and first miracle that He wrought in Cana of Galilee'[2] (John ii. 1-11): but in Penance and Matrimony there is no 'sign' of Divine appointment, while in Orders the laying on of hands is, so far as we can positively assert, only of Apostolic institution (Acts vi. 6). The name **Extreme Unction** disappeared in the Prayer Book of 1549, and all Unction in that of 1552; possibly as having been misused, possibly from the idea that Jas. v. 14, 15, which treats it indeed as a sacrament or. holy rite, only implied that it was to be continued so long as miraculous gifts of healing (1 Cor. xii. 9) remained in the Church.

§ 4 deals with *the use of* the **Sacraments**. (1) **They were not ordained of Christ to be gazed upon, or to be carried about.** Despite the plural, the reference is only to the Eucharist; for Baptism could not be *carried about*, nor is there any evidence that it was superstitiously *gazed upon*. The Eucharist, intended by Our Lord for Communion, was not utterly neglected by the mass of Church people as it is now; but, with the same impulse to avoid the responsibility of communicating, it was used merely as a sacrifice to attend and 'gaze upon,' or as an object of worship to 'gaze upon' and 'carry about' in Procession, especially since the greater prominence given to the feast of Corpus Christi in 1264. Such uses are not forbidden but deprecated in comparison with the primary end for which Our Lord instituted the Eucharist. There was real danger of

---

[1] The Order of Confirmation.
[2] The Form of Solemnisation of Matrimony.

the Sacraments being resorted to as charms. Hence it was well to state further (2) that **we should duly use them and that in such only as worthily receive the same have they a wholesome effect or operation.** They do not operate mechanically but only on condition of faith on the part of the recipient; for lack of which they **that receive them unworthily purchase to themselves damnation**[1] (1 Cor. xi. 29, R.V., judgement), **as S. Paul saith.**

[1] = condemnation.

ARTICLE XXVI

De vi institutionum divinarum, quod eam non tollat malitia Ministrorum.

(§ 1) *Quamvis in Ecclesia* visibili *bonis mali* semper *sunt admixti, atque interdum ministerio verbi et sacramentorum* administrationi *praesint; tamen cum non suo sed Christi nomine* agant, ejusque *mandato et auctoritate ministrent, illorum ministerio uti licet* cum *in verbo Dei audiendo* tum *in sacramentis percipiendis. Neque per illorum malitiam effectus* institutorum Christi tollitur *aut gratia donorum* Dei *minuitur* quoad eos qui fide et *rite* sibi oblata percipiunt, quae *propter* institutionem *Christi et promissionem* efficacia sunt, licet *per malos* administrentur.

(§ 2) Ad Ecclesiae tamen disciplinam pertinet, ut in malos ministros inquiratur, accusenturque ab his qui eorum flagitia noverint; atque tandem, justo convicti judicio, deponantur.

Of the unworthiness of the Ministers, which hinders not the effect of the Sacraments.

(§ 1) Although in the visible Church the evil be ever mingled with the good, and sometime the evil have chief authority in the ministration of the word and sacraments; yet, forasmuch as they do not the same in their own name, but in Christ's, and do minister by His commission and authority, we may use their ministry both in hearing the word of God and in the receiving of the sacraments. Neither is the effect of Christ's ordinance taken away by their wickedness, nor the grace of God's gifts diminished from such as by faith and rightly do receive the sacraments ministered unto them, which be effectual because of Christ's institution and promise, although they be ministered by evil men.

(§ 2) Nevertheless it appertaineth to the discipline of the Church that inquiry be made of evil ministers, and that they be accused by those that have knowledge of their offences; and finally, being found guilty by just judgment, be deposed.

(i) **Source.**—Derived from Art. 5 of the Thirteen Articles, words common to the two formularies being printed in *italics* as both reproduce in part the words, and generally the substance, of the Confession of Augsburg. Unchanged since 1553.

(ii) **Object.**—To repudiate the opinion held by Anabaptists that the validity of the Sacraments is destroyed by the personal unworthiness of the Minister.

(iii) **Explanation.**—§ 1. The *principle* here set forth is of vital importance, affecting, as it does, the religious interests of all Christ's people, so long as, by His institution, the Church is not composed of the perfect but is a school for the discipline of the erring. The parables of the Wheat and the Tares (Matt. xiii. 24-30), and of the Drawnet (47-50), as also the allegory of the unfruitful branches in the Vine (John xv. 2), are inapplicable but to a **visible Church** in which **the evil be ever mingled with the good**: and Our Lord expects at His coming to find 'chaff' as well as 'wheat' on His 'threshing-floor' (Matt. iii. 12), and 'both bad and good' among His 'guests' (xxii. 10). Thus His Church is not a pure but a mixed body (2 Tim. ii. 20), nor is its Ministry perfect. There was a Judas even among the Apostles (Luke vi. 16). This being so, the faithful soul requires to be assured that it suffers no spiritual or moral loss when ministered to by evil men. Such security is found in *the principle that they are but ministers* (1 Cor. iii. 5, 6) *or stewards* (iv. 1), *not authors, of God's grace,* and **the Sacraments** not theirs but Christ's, **effectual** therefore, not according to man's merit or demerit, but **because of Christ's institution and promise**. God is responsible for the bestowal of His own grace, and He accompanies[1] (John xx. 21) the official acts of His Ministers with His own presence (Matt. xxviii. 20) whether in the ministry of the Word (Luke x. 16; John xiii. 20; 2 Cor. v. 20) or of the Sacraments (Luke xii. 42). As His acts therefore they cannot be vitiated or impaired by human unworthiness. It was on this principle that Our Lord bade men listen to the Scribes and Pharisees (Matt.

---

[1] In John xx. 21 the first 'send' ($\dot{a}\pi o\sigma\tau\epsilon\lambda\lambda\omega$) means 'despatch' as a plenipotentiary: the second 'send' ($\pi\epsilon\mu\pi\omega$) implies that the sender escorts the person sent. Our Lord's disciples 'receive no new commission, but carry out His.'—Westcott, *ad loc.*

EXPLANATION 219

xxiii. 2, 3) as sitting in Moses' seat, and allowed the ministry of Judas to be as efficacious as that of the eleven (Mark vi. 7-13): that SS. Peter and John disowned the imputation of having cured the cripple by their 'own power' (Acts iii. 12): and that S. Paul could say of the Christian Ministry, 'We have this treasure in earthen vessels that the exceeding greatness of the power may be of God, and not from ourselves' (2 Cor. iv. 7). The principle was finally established by S. Augustine, c. 400, in controversy with the Donatists, who, anxious, like all Puritans before or since, for a pure Church and Ministry, held that sins, or even faults, in the Minister invalidate the Sacraments which he administers. On this assumption all ministerial and sacramental acts are uncertain; for who is to know but God whether this or that Minister is 'evil' or not? When S. Augustine shewed once for all that such a position was false 'for the simple but deeply significant reason that' the Minister 'was but the organ of the ever-present and never-failing Bestower of grace, the true, though invisible, Dispenser of ordinances, "whose Divine power is always present with His Sacrament," "who Himself consecrates His Sacrament," "who is Himself the Baptizer," and, we may add, Himself the Celebrant, Confirmer, Absolver, Ordainer,'[1] he did a lasting service to religion. He vindicated that momentous principle of the Divine action which not only throws the receiver of God's Word and Sacraments with absolute confidence upon God Himself for security that in them he has access to their intended grace, but sets up a permanent criterion to distinguish between the false sacerdotalism and the true, between that which puts the Ministers and Sacraments of the Church into the place of Christ, and that which teaches that they are indeed His agents and instruments but nothing more. To this truth, as to its perversion, the great theologians of the Middle Ages[2] were as fully alive as the Article itself; but, lest the assertion that the

---

[1] Bright, *Lessons from the Lives of Three Great Fathers*, pp. 154, 155.
[2] *Ib.*, Appendix xviii. *Cf.* S. Thos. Aq., *Summa*, III., lxiv. 5 ad 1: and *Imitatio Christi*, iv. 5.

Sacraments are real instruments of grace should be taken to mean that they operate mechanically, the Article enters a caveat to the effect that, while **the grace of God's gifts** is not conditional upon the merit or demerit of the Minister, its assimilation is conditional upon the faith of the recipient. It is to be had only by **such as by faith and rightly do receive the Sacraments.**[1]

§ 2 only adds that, however important the principle above laid down may be to the welfare of souls, it is no less essential that the Church should guard herself against suspicion of indifference to the character of her Ministers by the maintenance of a sound **discipline** (1 Tim. v. 19, 20).

[1] *Cf.* Art. 28, § 3.

ARTICLE XXVII

De Baptismo.

(§ 1) Baptismus non est tantum professionis signum ac discriminis nota qua Christiani a non Christianis discernantur, sed etiam est signum regenerationis, per quod, tanquam per instrumentum, recte baptismum suscipientes Ecclesiae inseruntur; promissiones de remissione peccatorum atque adoptione nostra in filios Dei per Spiritum Sanctum visibiliter obsignantur; fides confirmatur, et vi divinae invocationis gratia augetur.
(§ 2) ‡ Baptismus parvulorum omnino in Ecclesia retinendus est, ut qui cum Christi institutione optime congruat.‡

Of Baptism.

(§ 1) Baptism is not only a sign of profession and mark of difference whereby Christian men are discerned from other that be not christened, but is also a sign of regeneration or new birth, whereby, as by an instrument, they that receive baptism rightly are grafted into the Church; the promises of the forgiveness of sin, and of our adoption to be the sons of God, by the Holy Ghost are visibly signed and sealed; faith is confirmed, and grace increased by virtue of prayer unto God.
(§ 2) The baptism of young children is in any wise to be retained in the Church as most agreeable with the institution of Christ.

(i) **Source.**—Composed by the English Reformers, 1552-3, and since unchanged, except for the recasting of § 2 in more emphatic language, 1563.

(ii) **Object.**—To condemn Anabaptists and others who denied that Baptism was a means of grace, and repudiated Infant Baptism altogether.

(iii) **Explanation.**—§ 1 offers *a description of* (1) *Baptism* and (2) *its effects*.

(1) **Baptism is defined (*a*) negatively. It is not only a sign of profession and mark of difference whereby Christian men are distinguished from others that be not christened.**

This was the position of Anabaptists and Zwinglians. Sacraments to them were bare signs; and Baptism, accordingly, no more than a mark to distinguish between Christian and non-Christian as Circumcision served to distinguish between Jew and Gentile. Even this is to admit, what many now forget, that no man is a Christian who is not baptized,[1] and certainly 'Baptism doth represent unto us our profession';[2] but, apart from the nature of the grace bestowed and the mode of its bestowal, the promises held out in connection with Baptism by Our Lord (Mark xvi. 16) and His Apostles (Acts ii. 38) are empty words unless it be accompanied by actual blessings. Hence the Article proceeds to the (b) *positive* element in the definition: **Baptism ... is also a sign of regeneration or new birth.** As in Art. 25, *sign* must be interpreted as 'effectual sign,' and thus the whole expression will mean that in Baptism the blessing *of Regeneration* is not only signified but conveyed to the recipient through the sign. But what is *Regeneration*? As popularly used, when, *e.g.*, we speak of the regeneration of society and mean its amelioration, the word implies a *moral* change: and such a change may be part of the 'regeneration' alluded to in the first of the two passages in which the word occurs in the New Testament. (*a*) There Our Lord speaks of 'the regeneration, when the Son of man shall sit on the throne of His glory' (Matt. xix. 28), as S. Peter afterwards of 'seasons of refreshing' and of 'the times of restoration of all things' (Acts iii. 19-21)—all phrases descriptive of the Messianic blessedness. But this 'regeneration,' though it bring with it a moral change, is a future consummation affecting society as a whole, and so is unconnected with Baptism. But (*b*) 'regeneration' also appears as descriptive of a *spiritual* change, affecting individuals now: 'God ... saved us, through the washing of regeneration and renewing of the Holy Ghost, which he poured out upon us richly through Jesus

---

[1] Or 'christened.' Notice that 'Christiani' is translated first by 'Christian' and then by 'christened.'
[2] Public Baptism of Infants.

Christ' (Tit. iii. 5). Here, by the use of the aorist, by the mention of the Threefold Name and of the 'laver of regeneration' as the means of its bestowal, this change in our spiritual condition is plainly connected with Baptism; just as in Our Lord's teaching to be 'born again' is 'to be born of water and the Spirit' (John iii. 3-5). This is what is meant by Regeneration or New Birth as the special grace of Baptism: but it must be carefully distinguished both from Conversion and Renewal. As our ordinary birth is not dependent on ourselves, so our Regeneration or New Birth is God's act; whereas Conversion, or the surrender of the will to God, is, though prompted by His grace (John vi. 44), in a real and inalienable sense, ours. Again, as at birth we receive our ordinary life, so at Baptism we receive the gift of spiritual life. Regeneration thus effects a spiritual change in our condition, and that in a moment; but Conversion is a moral change, which may indeed appear in a moment as in the conversion of S. Paul (Acts ix.), but may equally be the work of a lifetime during which Christ is being formed in us (Gal. iv. 19), as we may suppose was the case with S. John. Both Regeneration and Conversion are indispensable to the true Christian (*cf.* Matt. xviii. 3, and John iii. 3-5); for as the Conversion (Acts ii. 37; xxii. 10; x. 31) of S. Peter's audience at Pentecost, of S. Paul, and of Cornelius did not preclude but led up to their baptism (Acts ii. 38; ix. 18; x. 48), so the initial grace of Regeneration bestowed on Simon Magus at his baptism (Acts viii. 13) availed him nothing, because his 'heart was not right before God' (21). But either may precede the other. S. Paul was converted before he was regenerated. The Prodigal, as we by baptism, was already a son before he 'came to himself' (Luke xv. 17) and resolved to return to his father. In the Apostolic age, as now in any heathen country, Conversion normally precedes Regeneration (Matt. xxviii. 19; Mark xvi. 16; Luke xxiv. 47): in our day and in a Christian land, Regeneration normally comes first. But both are essential, and both again require to be supplemented in the ordinary Christian life by that daily[1]

---

[1] *Cf.* the Order of Confirmation.

development of character which is called Renewal (*cf.* Collect for Christmas; and 2 Cor. iv. 16; Col. iii. 10; Rom. xii. 2). Baptism then is not an absolute security for a converted will or for a Christian character: but it places us within reach of new spiritual forces by effecting our *regeneration or new birth* into a new life, the life by which the Christian lives,[1] that is the risen life of Christ (Rom. vi. 3, 4; Gal. iii. 26, 27; Col. ii. 12, 13).

(2) Having thus described the cardinal gift of Baptism as 'a new birth unto righteousness,' the Article proceeds to enumerate the *effects* accompanying so great an event in the life-history of the soul as its transference (Col. i. 13) out of the merely natural into the Spiritual order. It is **a sign . . . whereby, as by an instrument,**[2] (*a*) *admission* into the Christian society is obtained, or **they that receive baptism rightly are grafted into the Church** (Rom. xi. 17), and (*b*) God's **promises** to the soul of *pardon* for the past (Eph. ii. 3) and *favour* for the future, or **of the forgiveness of sin and of our adoption to be the sons of God**, are guaranteed. In three words we may say that Baptism is the Sacrament of Initiation, of Justification (as its instrumental cause on God's part, faith being its condition on ours),[3] and of Adoption. Moreover, the promises of each of these blessings **by the Holy Ghost are visibly signed and sealed**, and by no one less: for in each of its aspects Baptism is His act (1 Cor. xii. 13; Acts ii. 38; Rom. viii. 15). When it is added that by Baptism **faith is confirmed and grace increased by virtue of prayer unto God**, the reference would seem to be to the faith of the bystanders, if, as seems likely, the Article contemplates Infant Baptism as the normal mode of its ministration. It makes the effect of Baptism contingent only upon its being received 'rightly,' and omits all such conditions as that it be 'worthily and with faith'[4] received. When, then, we note the strong resemblance between the clause now under consideration and the language put into the

---

[1] The life which he lives would require a different Greek word.
[2] A phrase equivalent to 'effectual sign' in Art. 25.
[3] See above, p. 135.
[4] *Cf.* Art. 28, where these additional requirements are demanded from recipients of the Eucharist.

mouths of those present at a Baptism, 'We give thee humble thanks for that thou hast vouchsafed to call us to the knowledge of thy grace and faith in thee: increase this knowledge and confirm this faith in us evermore'; the presumption is that the Article intends to give a complete description of the effects of Baptism by concluding with mention of its benefit to the bystanders as well as to the child baptized. Then follows naturally § 2 on *Infant Baptism*. **The Baptism of young children is in anywise to be retained in the Church, as most agreeable with the institution of Christ.** Here it is enough to say that, while it cannot be proved from Scripture that infants were baptized in the early days of the Church, and while of necessity baptism of adult converts would be the rule in the missionary stage of the Gospel, there is nothing to forbid it. On the contrary, it is certain from Our Lord's example that infants are capable of receiving Spiritual blessing. They cannot 'place a bar' to grace: and 'of such is the Kingdom of God' (Mark x. 13-16). In Apostolic language they are spoken of as 'holy' (1 Cor. vii. 14), *i.e.* admitted to the covenant, a privilege which, as not denied to Jewish infants through circumcision, cannot have been refused to the children of Christians in baptism. So the principle, if not the practice, of Infant Baptism is established in Holy Scripture. The prejudice which would now refuse it, rests upon no ground of Scripture: but either upon the denial of 'birth-sin' altogether, or more commonly upon the confusion of Regeneration with Conversion.

ARTICLE XXVIII

De Cœna Domini.

(§ 1) Cœna Domini non est tantum signum mutuae benevolentiae Christianorum inter sese, verum potius est sacramentum nostrae per mortem Christi redemptionis. Atque ideo rite digne et cum fide sumentibus, panis quem frangimus est communicatio corporis Christi: similiter poculum benedictionis est communicatio sanguinis Christi.

(§ 2) Panis et vini transubstantiatio in Eucharistia ex sacris literis probari non potest, sed apertis Scripturae verbis adversatur, sacramenti naturam evertit, et multarum superstitionum dedit occasionem.

(§ 3) Corpus Christi datur, accipitur, et manducatur in Cœna, tantum cœlesti et spirituali ratione. Medium autem quo corpus Christi accipitur et manducatur in Cœna, fides est.

(§ 4) Sacramentum Eucharistiae ex institutione Christi non servabatur, circumferebatur, elevabatur, nec adorabatur.

Of the Lord's Supper.

(§ 1) The Supper of the Lord is not only a sign of the love that Christians ought to have among themselves, one to another, but rather it is a sacrament of our redemption by Christ's death: insomuch that to such as rightly, worthily, and with faith receive the same, the bread which we break is a partaking of the body of Christ, and likewise the cup of blessing is a partaking of the blood of Christ.

(§ 2) Transubstantiation (or the change of the substance of bread and wine) in the Supper of the Lord, cannot be proved by Holy Writ, but is repugnant to the plain words of Scripture, ‡ overthroweth the nature of a Sacrament, ‡ and hath given occasion to many superstitions.

(§ 3) ‡ The body of Christ is given, taken, and eaten in the Supper, only after an heavenly and spiritual manner. And the mean whereby the body of Christ is received and eaten in the Supper is faith. ‡

(§ 4) The Sacrament of the Lord's Supper was not by Christ's ordinance reserved, carried about, lifted up, or worshipped.

EXPLANATION 227

(i) Source.—Composed by the English Reformers, 1552-3, Art. 28 underwent changes of the first magnitude ten years later. The formularies of Henry VIII. steadily maintained the real presence: and in 1550 Gardiner expressed himself content with the First Prayer Book of Edward VI. on the ground that 'touching the truth of the very presence of Christ's most precious body and blood in the Sacrament, there was as much spoken in that book as might be desired.' But before the book was published, Cranmer, its author, was already wavering: and in the three formularies of 1552-3, the Second Prayer Book, the Forty-two Articles, and the *Reformatio Legum*, by which he intended to complete respectively the devotional, the doctrinal, and the disciplinary settlement of the English Church, the presence of Our Lord in the Sacrament, as distinct from His presence only in the faithful recipient, was set aside. For this purpose, the third paragraph[1] of Art. 29 of 1553 contained an explicit denial of 'the real and bodily presence (as they term it) of Christ's flesh and blood in the Sacrament of the Lord's Supper.' But in 1563, not only was this denial expunged[2] by the Synod, and that in face of an attempt by the Primate to secure its retention, but in its place was inserted the statement of § 3, whose author has left it on record that by it he never intended to exclude 'the presence of Christ's body from the Sacrament, but only the grossness and sensibleness in the receiving thereof.'[3] The change was far from acceptable to the Puritans.[4] They saw that, technicalities apart, the question at issue was a simple one, Is the presence consequent upon Consecration or upon Communion? Is it in the Sacrament, or only in the worthy receiver? Is it real or contingent? The addition of § 3 committed the Church of England irrevocably to the former alternative: and this position received fresh emphasis in 1604 when, in the questions and answers on the Sacraments then added to the Catechism, a pregnant distinction was drawn between the component parts of Baptism and the Eucharist. In Baptism, the Catechism

---

[1] See Appendix. [2] See vol. i. pp. 44, 47.
[3] *Ib.*, p. 47.   [4] *Ib.*, p. 49.

recognises two parts only, 'the outward visible sign,' and 'the inward and spiritual grace.' In the Eucharist it marks three; and by asking, first, 'What is the outward part or sign?' next, 'What is the inward part or thing signified?' and, finally, 'What are the benefits whereof we are partakers thereby?' it reaffirms the old recognition of the *signum*, the *res*, and the *virtus*, in the Sacrament of the Eucharist. Cranmer and the reformers of his day did good service in exposing mediæval errors: but where their opinions are less Catholic than those of their successors, they are of merely historical interest. In 1563 and 1604 the English Church left their Protestant negations far behind, and for the official exponents of her Eucharistic teaching, as for her representative divines, we must go, not to the Edwardian leaders who inaugurated her reformation in doctrine, but to the later and more primitive theology of those who completed it in the following age.

(ii) **Object.**—After condemning § 1 Zwinglian, and § 2 mediæval errors, to state the truth of § 3 Christ's presence in the Sacrament, and § 4 to reduce certain practices connected with the Eucharist to their proper level.

(iii) **Explanation.**—§ 1, in giving *a description of the Eucharist*, keeps close to the language of Scripture; and, by way of rejecting the Zwinglian tenets less as false than as inadequate, follows the method of Arts. 25 and 27 by proceeding first negatively and then positively. Thus (1) the Article admits with the Sacramentaries that **the Supper of the Lord is ... a sign of the love that Christians ought to have among themselves one to another.** Its institution was immediately preceded by the feetwashing (John xiii. 1-11) and 'the new commandment'[1] ... that ye love one another' (34): while S. Paul argues from the common participation in the one loaf that 'we, who are many, are one body: for we all partake of the one loaf' (1 Cor. x. 17, marg.). Yet the Eucharist is **not only** thus a mere sign: but (2) **rather it is a sacrament of our**

---

[1] *Mandatum.* Hence 'Maundy-Thursday.'

redemption by Christ's death. In Our Lord's intention, indeed, the Eucharist was to be a memorial of Himself (Luke xxii. 19; 1 Cor. xi. 24, 25). It recalls His Person, and not merely His work or His death. But what He is in Himself is most perfectly shewn by His 'obedience unto death' (Phil. ii. 8): and so S. Paul, with an eye to the Lord's own teaching as to the significance of His death (Luke ix. 31; Matt. xx. 28), interprets the command, 'This do in remembrance of me,' with special reference to the preciousness of His death in the Father's sight (1 Cor. xi. 26). This is the Godward aspect of the Eucharist, considered as a Sacrifice: and, as we are taught in the Catechism, this was the primary object of its institution. '*Q*. Why was the Sacrament of the Lord's Supper ordained? *A*. For the continual remembrance of the sacrifice of the death of Christ,' etc. But it has also a function manward. It is a sacrament ... insomuch that to such as rightly, worthily, and with faith receive the same, the bread which we break is a partaking of the body of Christ, and likewise the cup of blessing is a partaking of the blood of Christ. These last are simply S. Paul's words (1 Cor. x. 16). They are prefaced by a statement insisting on the need of faith in the recipient (*worthily and with faith*) as well as on the observance of due order in the ministration of the Sacrament by the priest (*rightly*); but they lay stress on the fact that the presence is attached to the sign by virtue of the act of Consecration and is not consequent upon the act of Communion. It is not 'the bread which we *eat*,' but 'the bread which we *break*' and 'the cup of blessing[1] which we *bless*'[2] that is 'a communion of the body, and of the blood, of Christ'; though, of course, the Apostle is careful to affirm that the benefit which the communicant derives is entirely proportionate to his attitude of faith (1 Cor. xi. 27). The Catechism puts this beyond doubt. It is in answer to the question,

---

[1] A Hebraism for 'Eucharistic Cup.' *Cf.* Luke xvi. 8, 'the steward of unrighteousness'='the unrighteous steward,' and 'Sacrifice of praise and thanksgiving'=not 'a sacrifice which consists in praise and thanksgiving,' but 'Eucharistic Sacrifice.' *Cf.* Lev. vii. 12; Ps. cxvi. 17.

[2] 'Bless'='consecrate.'

not, 'What is the inward grace?' but, 'What is the inward part?' that it replies, 'The Body and Blood of Christ, which are verily and indeed taken and received by the faithful in the Lord's Supper.'

§ 2 deals with *the mediæval error of transubstantiation*. The word itself first appears in the twelfth century. But the doctrine is older: nor was it gratuitously invented. On the contrary, it was adopted in defence of the more reverential and ancient view of the Eucharist which, without formulating any theory to explain the real presence of Our Lord in the Sacrament, accepted it as a fact, but equally held to the permanence and reality of the outward elements of bread and wine even after the consecration. In the ninth century there were some, as now, who took the words 'This is my body' to mean no more than 'This is a figure of my body'; and their opponents, in order to secure the acceptance of Our Lord's words in their simple and natural sense, were betrayed into replying that by 'This is my body' He meant 'This is no longer bread.' The essence of their position was to provide for the real presence of His body by the simple expedient of asserting that the bread having ceased to exist its place was taken by another substance. But the teaching of either side was unsatisfactory. The one party explained the Words of Institution by explaining away 'the inward part or thing signified'; the other, by explaining away 'the outward sign.' The controversy slept till the eleventh century, when it was re-awakened by the attack of Berengarius on notions of a carnal presence which had now become current. They had such a strong hold that he was forced to recant, and to accept (1059) the revolting doctrine that 'the bread and wine . . . after consecration are not only a sacrament, but the very body and blood of Our Lord Jesus Christ; and are sensibly, not sacramentally only, but actually handled and broken by the hands of priests, and ground by the teeth of the faithful.' This was to say in effect that the material substances of bread and wine give place to the material substances of Christ's body and blood. It was a crude attempt to secure some real meaning to Our Lord's Words of Institution by the doctrine of a *physical* transubstantiation or change in the material elements. But the Schoolmen now came forward with a subtler defence in their philosophy of Reality. Using 'substance' not of the material thing as it affects our senses but as the equivalent of 'essence,' the Realists held that the 'substance' of a thing is not only that which makes it to be what it is or gives it reality, but also that which exists independently of its outward manifestations. This seemed to exactly meet the case of the Eucharist, where words were said and acts done, and no apparent change took place though a real change was effected. Hence the doctrine of a *metaphysical* transubstantiation was adopted. According to it, the 'substance' of the bread and wine is changed into the 'substance' of Christ's body and blood and so ceases to exist, though in their outward aspects bread and wine remain. This became the accepted theory for explaining the mystery of Our Lord's presence in the Sacrament. It was laid down by the Lateran Council, 1215, and re-affirmed by the Council of Trent, 1551, in its assertion that 'by the consecration . . . a conversion takes place of the whole substance of the bread into the substance of the body of Christ our Lord, and of the whole substance of the wine into the substance of His blood, which conversion is . . . called transubstantiation.'[1]

But though this decree immediately preceded the formulation of the English Article, it may be doubted whether the Article repudiates the doctrine as there set forth.

(1) The technical sense attached to 'substance' by the Schoolmen and the Roman Church, was not easily apprehended nor everywhere accepted. In England, where the influence of the Realists was less than that of the Nominalists, substance was commonly used, as we use it, of material substance. Hence, in the fifteenth and sixteenth centuries, it was the doctrine of a physical transubstantiation that prevailed. In 1413 the assent of the Lollard leader, Sir John Oldcastle, was required to the following article: 'That after the sacramental words be said by a priest in his Mass, the material bread that was

[1] Sess. xiii. c. 4.

before is turned into Christ's very body, and the material wine that was before is turned into Christ's very blood, and so there leaveth in the altar no material bread nor material wine, the which were there before the saying of the sacramental words' : and in 1556, after the publication of the Tridentine doctrine, Sir John Cheke was made to re-affirm at his recantation the very confession required of Berengarius. Moreover, it was not the doctrine of a metaphysical transubstantiation which Cranmer and his fellows cared to attack, but the doctrine of a mutation in the material elements which, by denying the existence, after consecration, of the bread and wine 'in their very natural substances,'[1] deprived the outward sign of all reality, and so abolished one of the two necessary parts of a sacrament.

But (2) this is put beyond all doubt by the case as presented in the Article itself against **transubstantiation or the change of the substance of bread and wine.** It is rejected on four grounds. (*a*) It **cannot be proved by Holy Writ.** This much is clear from the Words of Institution. They state the *fact* of the Real Presence. They neither offer nor invite, still less prove, any *theory* in explanation. (*b*) It **is repugnant to the plain words of Scripture,** which freely speaks of the elements as bread and wine after consecration (1 Cor. xi. 26, 28; Matt. xxvi. 29). (*c*) It **overthroweth the nature of a sacrament**: for a sacrament consists of two parts, and if bread and wine cease to exist upon consecration, there is no sacrament. (*d*) It **hath given occasion to many superstitions.** Thus it was the notion that the material elements only retain the similitude of bread and wine, but are really nothing else than the body and blood of Christ, that found expression in the multiplication of legends concerning bleeding Hosts.

Now these are valid reasons for rejecting the notion of a physical transubstantiation ; but they do not touch the official Roman theory of a metaphysical transubstantiation. Certainly this Roman theory 'cannot be proved by Holy Writ'; but neither can it be so

---

[1] *Cf.* the Black Rubric in the Prayer Book of 1552.

EXPLANATION

disproved, for it is not 'repugnant to the plain words of Scripture.' All the material phenomena of bread remain, and the Roman Church has no difficulty in speaking of the consecrated Host as 'bread' in the Mass nor in teaching that 'it has the appearance, and still retains the quality, natural to bread, of supporting and nourishing the body.'[1] Neither does this doctrine 'overthrow the nature of a sacrament'; for if what remains after consecration is thus bread, the outward as well as the inward part of the sacrament continues throughout. Nor again can it be said to have 'given occasion to many superstitions': for under its sanction worship is directed not to the elements but to Our Lord. Objections, however, do lie against the modern Roman theory. They are briefly two: (a) that the philosophy which holds that 'substance' has an existence of its own independently of its manifestations, was never undisputed and is now out of date; and (β) that no Church has a right to impose as essential to salvation a theory which is no part of the original faith of Christendom, even in defence of a fact like the Real Presence, which is a part of the original faith.

§ 3. The Article, having thus dismissed explanatory theories, now proceeds to state *the fact of the Real Presence*. **The body of Christ is given, taken, and eaten in the Supper.** Here we note that the subject of the sentence is not 'The sacrament' but *The body of Christ* or the 'inward part' of the sacrament: and that this is said to be not only *taken and eaten* by the recipient, but also to be *given* as well. That which passes from giver to receiver has an existence independent of both. In other words, Our Lord's body exists in the sacrament before it is imparted to the communicant. But lest this statement should seem to wear the taint of materialism, it is supplemented by two safeguards. (1) The whole action takes place **only after a heavenly and spiritual manner.** The meaning of this qualification is bound up with the Scriptural sense of 'spiritual,' which is never contrasted with 'bodily' but with 'carnal' (Rom. vii. 14), 'natural' (1 Cor. ii. 14), and 'worldly' (Heb. ix. 1, 23): and which

[1] *Catechismus Romanus*, II. iv. 38.

is never used of what is figurative, imaginary, and unreal, like much that owes its origin to the human spirit, but always of that, which, like the spiritual man (1 Cor. ii. 15), the resurrection-body (1 Cor. xv. 44), or the unity of the Church (Eph. iv. 3), is created and sustained by the Holy Spirit, and therefore is most real. In other words, the gift in the sacrament is effected by the Holy Spirit; and the presence, as being thus a spiritual presence, is at once a real presence and not a 'gross or sensible' one (*cf.* S. John vi. 52-63). (2) A second safeguard, directed against mechanical notions of the action of the sacrament, follows in the assertion that **the mean whereby the body of Christ is received and eaten in the Supper is faith.** *Given* is not repeated, but only *received and eaten.* The point is unmistakable. Faith neither creates nor bestows; but faith alone can receive (1· Cor. xi. 27 *sqq.*).

§ 4 seeks to *reduce the prominence given to certain uses of the Eucharist* by pointing out that it **was not by Christ's ordinance reserved, carried about, lifted up, or worshipped,** but instituted primarily for sacrifice and communion. The need for this declaration lay in the fact that, in the popular religion, Reservation, Processions, and Elevation of the Host, all for the purposes of worship, had almost obscured the proper use of the sacrament. The Article does not say that these practices are wholly to be condemned. Reservation for the absent is mentioned by Justin Martyr in his account of the Eucharist as celebrated in the second century. Elevation, or the raising and exhibition of the Gifts as brought out for the people's communion, occurs in the Eastern liturgies by the ninth century. But as soon as the doctrine of Transubstantiation obtained general credence in the eleventh century, the ideas attached to Reservation and Elevation of the Host took a new direction, and it began to be 'carried about' in Procession for the like purpose of worship. Not that worship is not due to the Divine Person of Our Lord wherever He is present, whether, in accordance with His promise, in the sacrament, or, by His Ascension, at the right hand of the Father: but the practical result of these ceremonies was to *localise* worship by directing

EXPLANATION

it solely to this or that centre on earth, wherever, for the moment, the Host might be in sight, whether as reserved in the sanctuary, carried about in procession, or elevated for the adoration of the people in the Mass. This is radically wrong. The Eucharistic elements, wherever found, are not so many separate centres for the worship of the Risen Lord: but His special presence is vouchsafed by their means in order to 'lift up our hearts' to the eternal self-oblation of the Son which is ever going on before the Father (Heb. x. 19-25), and, by thus 'making us to sit with Him in the heavenly places' (Eph. ii. 6), to direct our adoration towards its one centre, the Lamb standing at the right hand of God (*cf.* Rev. iv. v.).

ARTICLE XXIX

‡ De manducatione corporis Christi, et impios illud non manducare.

Impii et viva fide destituti, licet carnaliter et visibilitur (ut Augustinus loquitur) corporis et sanguinis Christ sacramentum dentibus premant, nullo tamen modo Christi participes efficiuntur; sed potius tantae rei sacramentum seu symbolum ad judicium sibi manducant et bibuut.‡

Of the wicked which do not eat the body of Christ, in the use of the Lord's Supper.

The wicked and such as be void of a lively faith, although they do carnally and visibly press with their teeth (as S. Augustine saith) the sacrament of the body and blood of Christ, yet in nowise are they partakers of Christ, but rather to their condemnation do eat and drink the sign or sacrament of so great a thing.

(i) **Source.**—Composed in 1562-3, probably by Archbishop Parker.

(ii) **Object.**—The history of this Article is the key to its purpose. It first appeared in the draft articles presented to Convocation by the Archbishop, which, after various emendations, received the signatures of the Bishops on Jan. 29, 1563. But it was struck out from the series before publication, probably at the bidding of the Queen. She was anxious to conciliate the Roman party, and to retain them, if possible, within the English Church. But in 1570 the papal bull of excommunication was issued, and the policy of comprehension necessarily abandoned. Accordingly, at the last revision of the Articles, No. 29 was re-admitted, and is found in a copy of May 11, 1571, signed by Parker and ten bishops, including Guest of Rochester. But Guest was not

EXPLANATION

satisfied. Believing as he did, not only that Christ is present in the sacrament but also that the wicked eat His body therein, he wrote off at once to Cecil suggesting that in Art. 28 'to avoid offence and contention the word "only" may be well left out,' and, further, that Art. 29 be omitted as likely 'to cause much business.' His advice was not taken. Art. 29 kept its place in the edition ratified by the Queen, and has stood in all subsequent editions. It seems to have been adopted as an appendix to Art. 28 to guard against merely mechanical views of the sacrament.

(iii) **Explanation.**—Its language is open to two interpretations:—

(1) Some, pointing to the fact that the phrase employed in the title, 'Of the wicked which do not eat the body of Christ,' is exchanged in the text for 'in nowise are they partakers of Christ,' contend that, as the titles of the Articles are not always good guides to their meaning,[1] the expression in the heading must be interpreted by that in the body of the Article, and that it is possible to 'eat the body of Christ' without becoming 'a partaker of Christ.' This would mean that the wicked receive the *signum* and the *res* but not the *virtus sacramenti*, which was the ordinary teaching of the Mediæval Church.[2] They eat the body of Christ, but they eat not beneficially. But this view is open to serious objections: (*a*) from the history of the Article. Had it been the natural interpretation of the Article, Guest would have made no effort to get rid of it; (*b*) from its connection with Art. 28, which affirms that 'the mean whereby the body of Christ is received and eaten . . . is faith.' But the **wicked are such as be void of a lively faith.** Therefore they cannot receive it. (*c*) From other expressions in the Article itself. When it is said that **they do carnally and visibly press with their teeth . . . the sacrament of the body and blood of Christ,** 'sacrament' is not here used in the sense of the sign as accompanied by the thing signified, but of the mere sign; for that which **to their**

---

[1] *Cf.* Arts. 4, 10, 13, 31.
[2] *Cf.* S. Thomas Aq., *Summa*, III., lxxx. 3.

condemnation they do eat and drink is described as the sign or sacrament of so great a thing.

(2) Thus the natural sense of the Article is that which stands on its surface. It asserts that the body and blood of Christ, or 'inward part' of the sacrament, is offered to the wicked, but that, in consequence of their spiritual condition, they are not only incapable of receiving it but draw down upon themselves condemnation by profanely approaching it. And this interpretation satisfies the language of Holy Scripture. . In 1 Cor. xi. 27-30, S. Paul's words undoubtedly imply that the elements are by consecration so related to the body and blood of Christ that they cease to be mere bread and wine and thus become capable of profanation; but they do not imply that such profanation arises from the actual eating of the Lord's body by the wicked. 'He that eateth and drinketh, eateth and drinketh judgement unto himself, if he discriminate (*marg.*) not the body' from ordinary food. But to be thus discriminated, it must be there first: *i.e.* in any case there must be a real presence in the sacrament. The words of Our Lord are equally conclusive. In John vi. 50-54, He speaks of 'life' as imparted by 'eating His flesh and drinking His blood'; 'and no such thing is contemplated as a *real* eating of them, which is not a *beneficial* eating of them also.' Admittedly 'the wicked' have not 'life' through the sacrament. So they 'do not eat the body of Christ' in the sacrament. 'Without faith it can only be eaten *sacramentally* by eating the bread which is the sign or sacrament of it.'[1]

[1] *Cf.* Mozley, *Lectures and other Theological Papers*, p. 205.

ARTICLE XXX

De Utraque Specie.

‡ Calix Domini laicis non est denegandus, utraque enim pars Dominici sacramenti, ex Christi institutione et praecepto, omnibus Christianis ex aequo administrari debet.‡

Of Both Kinds.

The Cup of the Lord is not to be denied to the lay people; for both the parts of the Lord's sacrament, by Christ's ordinance and commandment, ought to be ministered to all Christian men alike.

(i) **Source.**—Composed and first inserted in 1563.

(ii) **Object.**—To restore to the laity the participation in the Chalice which had been denied to them since the twelfth century. On July 16, 1562, the Council of Trent had anathematised any one who should say 'that by the precept of God (*ex Dei praecepto*) or by necessity of salvation (*ex necessitate salutis*) all and each of the faithful of Christ ought to receive both species of the most holy sacrament of the Eucharist.'[1] The Article looks like a reply to the challenge. It says that communion in both kinds is *ex Christi praecepto*. But it does not say that it is *ex necessitate salutis*. Thus the difference between England and Rome is dealt with as a question of discipline.

(iii) **Explanation.**—The denial of the Cup to the laity is merely a custom of the Western Church in the Middle Ages. In Scripture, all communicated in both kinds (1 Cor. xi. 24-26, 28; *cf.* x. 21): while the descriptions of the Eucharist, as given by S. Justin Martyr in the second century and by S. Cyril of Jerusalem in the fourth century, afford ample evidence that it was so administered

[1] Sess. xxi., can. 1.

among the Christians of their day. About 1100, the denial of the Chalice to the laity began to creep in from motives of reverence, but it was at once condemned by the popes themselves 'as a human and novel institution.' But the custom spread, chiefly owing to the prevalent belief in Transubstantiation; on the basis of which it was easily justified by the doctrine of Concomitance, *i.e.* that Our Lord is so entirely and indivisibly present in either element that all who partake of the consecrated Host receive therein His blood concomitantly with His body.[1] At the Reformation the demand for the restoration of the Cup to the laity was loud and widespread: but the Roman Church being now committed to the doctrine of Concomitance, which had been accepted by the Council of Constance, 1415, in defence of the denial of the Chalice, could not give way except at the expense of her own infallibility. Her only course is to find arguments in its favour. They are drawn (1) from Scripture. S. Paul says 'eat the bread *or* drink the cup' (1 Cor. xi. 27), and Our Lord speaks of the bread as life-giving (John vi. 51, 58). But the use of one kind cannot be thus defended in the face of 1 Cor. x. 16 and the Words of Institution, 'Drink ye *all* of this.' If it be replied that *all* the Apostles were priests, it is doubtful whether they were priests then; and in any case the fact would be irrelevant, for in the Roman Church only the celebrant communicates in both kinds; (2) from reverence and convenience. But these considerations cannot be set against a Divine command; (3) from the power of the Church to decree rites and ceremonies. But she may not decree any contrary to Scripture.[2]

[1] 'Ex naturali concomitantia.' S. Thomas Aq., *Summa*, III., lxxvi. 1.
[2] *Cf.* Art. 20.

ARTICLE XXXI

De unica Christi oblatione in Cruce perfecta.

(§ 1) Oblatio Christi, semel facta, perfecta est redemptio, propitiatio, et satisfactio pro omnibus peccatis totius mundi, tam originalibus quam actualibus; neque praeter illam unicam est ulla alia pro peccatis expiatio. (§ 2) Unde missarum sacrificia, quibus vulgo dicebatur sacerdotem offerre Christum in remissionem poenae aut culpae pro vivis et defunctis, blasphema figmenta sunt et pernitiosae imposturae.

Of the one oblation of Christ finished upon the Cross.

(§ 1) The offering of Christ once made is the perfect redemption, propitiation, and satisfaction for all the sins of the whole world, both original and actual, and there is none other satisfaction for sin but that alone. (§ 2) Wherefore the sacrifices of Masses, in the which it was commonly said that the priests did offer Christ for the quick and dead to have remission of pain or guilt, were blasphemous fables and dangerous deceits.

(i) **Source.**—Composed by the English Reformers, 1552-3; and maintained, with but slight verbal alterations, since that time.

(ii) **Object.**—To reject later mediæval conceptions of the Eucharistic Sacrifice which conflicted with the sufficiency of Christ's sacrifice upon the Cross; and, as expressed in current practice, led to grave abuses. The tenets in question are not to be hastily identified with the official doctrine of the Roman Church on the sacrifice of the Mass, which was only laid down by the Council of Trent[1] on Sept. 17, 1562. From the title of the Article it might be inferred that it is concerned with the Atonement. But the title is inexact,[2] and only describes the restatement of that doctrine in § 1 which is

[1] Sess. xxii.   [2] *Cf.* Arts. 4, 10, 13.

introduced as a basis for the main affirmation of § 2. The Article deals with the Eucharist, as is clear both from its structure and from its place in the series. The 'Wherefore' of § 2 indicates that its substantive declaration is to be sought in its final clause.[1] Again, it stands last in the group relating to the Church, the Ministry, and the Sacraments (Arts. 19-31); in immediate connection with the two Articles which deal with the Real Presence (Arts. 28, 29); and between two others which broke down the two abuses connected with the Eucharist, of confining Communion in both kinds to the celebrant (Art. 30) and of enforcing celibacy on the clergy (Art. 32), abuses resting for their sanction on an exaggerated isolation ascribed to the priest in the Mass.

(iii) **Explanation.**—§ 1 is *preliminary*. It *restates the doctrine of the Atonement*, so as, by emphasising the sufficiency of the one oblation once made, to provide a rule by which perverted doctrines of the Eucharistic Sacrifice are to be rejected. **The offering of Christ once made is the perfect redemption, propitiation, and satisfaction for all the sins of the whole world both original and actual, and there is none other satisfaction for sin but that alone.** We have already considered the Atonement,[2] and the metaphors of *Redemption* and *Propitiation* by which it is described in Scripture. *Satisfaction* is another figure originating in Latin theology with the barrister Tertullian (c. 200), who borrowed it from the Civil Law.[3] It became a convenient term to cover that aspect of Our Lord's sacrifice in which it may be regarded as payment of human debt or obligation: and acquired a recognised place in later theology, specially through its adoption by S. Anselm (d. 1109). Treating sin as debt (Matt. vi. 12), he laid it down that either satisfaction or punishment must follow every sin.[4] Christ's death, being of infinite worth as the death of God and available for us as the death of our fellow-man, was a payment in full or

---

[1] *Cf.* structure of Arts. 7, 10, 11, 16, 20, 21, 32, 36.
[2] Art. 2, vol. i. pp. 75 *sqq.*
[3] 'Satisfactio pro solutione est.'—Ulpian. It=a release.
[4] 'Necesse est ut omne peccatum satisfactio aut pœna sequatur.'
—*Cur Deus Homo,* i. 15.

entire satisfaction for human sin. Thus the fourfold cycle of figures—Reconciliation, Redemption, Propitiation, and Satisfaction—is completed by which the sufficiency of Christ's sacrifice for sin in all its forms is affirmed: while the universal extent of its efficacy is re-asserted in terms equally familiar. It was for *all the sins of the whole world both original and actual.*[1] As to this perfection of His sacrifice on the Cross, the Epistle to the Hebrews (vii. 26, 27; ix. 11-14, 24-28; x. 10-14) is conclusive. He 'made there (by His one oblation of Himself once offered) a full, perfect, and sufficient sacrifice, oblation, and satisfaction for the sins of the whole world.'[2] But it is equally clear from Scripture that in the Eucharist there is a sacrifice. It was instituted at the Passover (Luke xxii. 15) in language full of sacrificial associations, such as those which would be conveyed by the separate consecration of the bread and the wine, pointing to the severance of Our Lord's Body and Blood in death, and by the use of technical terms, such as 'this is my blood of the covenant (Matt. xxvi. 28; Mark xiv. 24; *cf.* Ex. xxiv. 8) which is shed [better *tr.* being 'poured out,' as Luke xxii. 20] for many,' a phrase which would recall the characteristic act of sacrifice as consisting not in the death of the victim but in its life surrendered, not in the shedding of its blood by the sinner but in the presentation of its blood by the priest (Lev. xvii. 11; xvi. 14; Heb. ix. 24 *sqq.*). Moreover it was as the Christian sacrifice that the Eucharist presented itself to the earliest converts, Gentile or Jewish. The Gentile Christian was appealed to on the ground that through 'the table of the Lord' he had fellowship with his God, as the pagan with his idol through its altar called 'the table of devils' (1 Cor. x. 21): the Jewish Christian on the ground that in it he had 'an altar' or place of sacrifice,[3] 'whereof they have no right to eat which serve the tabernacle' (Heb. xiii. 10). In either case, the point of the appeal is that in the Eucharist Christians have a specific sacrifice of their

---

[1] *Cf.* Arts. 2, 9, 15.
[2] Prayer of Consecration in Holy Communion.
[3] See Westcott, *ad loc.*

own. And the appeal was effective. With both Jew and Gentile, the Eucharist effaced the craving for a system of animal sacrifices, and yet satisfied that belief in worship as essentially sacrificial which belongs to Catholic Christianity in common with the religious instincts of all mankind. How then was the sufficiency of the Sacrifice on the Cross to be reconciled with the reality of a Sacrifice in the Eucharist? By their common relation to the eternal self-oblation of Our Lord in heaven. As in the Levitical sacrifices,[1] the death of the victim was but preliminary to the outpouring of its blood in the sanctuary by the priest, so the death on Calvary is consummated by the entry of the High Priest 'into heaven itself now to appear before the face of God for us' (Heb. ix. 24, *cf.* 12 ; xii. 24), as 'the Lamb' that 'had been slain' (Rev. v. 6), and yet still '*is* the propitiation for our sins' (1 John ii. 2). Thus, as our 'priest for ever' (Heb. vii. 17), Christ approaches the Father for us, with His one offering perpetually available (x. 14) : but we in our turn are invited to 'draw near' (x. 22) in the Eucharist,[2] 'having boldness . . . to enter into the holy place by the blood of Jesus by the way which he dedicated for us, a new and living way, through the veil, that is to say [by the way of[2]] his flesh, and having a great high priest over the house of God' (x. 19-21). Thus the truth is 'that the Eucharistic Sacrifice, even in its highest aspect, must be put in one line (if we may so say) not with what Christ did once for all upon the Cross, but with what He is doing continually in heaven ; that as present naturally in heaven and sacramentally in the Holy Eucharist, the Lamb of God exhibits Himself to the Father, and *pleads* the Atonement as once finished in act but ever living in operation ; that in neither case does He repeat it or add to it. The notion that it was *not* unique or perfect, but could be reiterated or supplemented, in heaven or on earth, was justly denounced as a "blasphemous fable" in Art. 31.'[3]

---

[1] See vol. i. p. 76. *Cf.* Lev. i.-v. ; xvi.
[2] See Westcott, *ad loc.*
[3] Bright, *Ancient Collects*, p. 144, n.

EXPLANATION

§ 2 condemns the popular religion of *sacrifices, priests,* and *Masses* (note the plurals) *as implying that Christ's sacrifice had to be reiterated and supplemented.* It does not condemn every doctrine of the Eucharistic Sacrifice, but only such as may derogate from the all-sufficiency of the one oblation once made upon the Cross, as is implied by the connecting particle, **Wherefore**: nor does it condemn the sacrifice of the Mass but **the sacrifices of Masses**: nor any doctrine authoritatively laid down by the Church but only what was **commonly said**: nor the offering of Christ for quick and dead, *i.e.* the inclusion of a memorial for the departed at the Eucharist, but those services in which **the priests did offer Christ for the quick and dead to have remission of pain or guilt.** What then is the system against which such hard words are flung as that its outstanding features were **blasphemous fables and dangerous deceits?** The Eucharistic Sacrifice was not discussed by the earlier Schoolmen, who were too much occupied with elaborating the theory of Transubstantiation in defence of the Real Presence. But S. Thomas (*d.* 1274) let fall assertions to the effect that sacrifice consists in the physical modification of the victim,[1] and that the chief use of the Eucharist lies not in the Communion of the faithful but in the Consecration by the priest.[2] Thus two new elements acquired undue prominence in the doctrine of the Eucharistic Sacrifice. The destruction of the victim ousted the offering of the blood as the characteristic feature of the sacrifice, and the place of the people was obscured by the stress laid on the function of the priest. Later theology came very near to a reiteration of Christ's death in each Mass, and argued the more priests and Masses the greater the merit or satisfaction obtainable. These tendencies fell in admirably with the beliefs, independently developed, in the power of the sacraments to take effect mechanically[3] and in the penalties[4] of sin that remained to be met by satisfaction in Purgatory. Out of these three elements, namely an erroneous view of sacrifice, a mechanical theory of the efficacy of Masses, and a belief

---

[1] *Summa*, II^{a.} II^{ae.}, lxxxv. 3 ad 3. [2] *Ib.*, III., lxxx. 12 ad 2.
[3] *Cf.* Art. 25. [4] *Cf.* Art. 22.

in 'pain' or penalties to be worked off, grew up a system which found expression in the establishment from the thirteenth century onwards of Chantries, in which priests were endowed to sing 'Masses satisfactory' *for the quick and dead to have remission of pain or guilt.* In the sixteenth century, a further notion prevailed to the effect that Christ died on the Cross for original sin, and instituted the Mass for expiation of actual sins.[1] As every act of sin was held to require its corresponding act of satisfaction, popular religion was mainly occupied in procuring, often in purchasing, Masses as a set-off against sins, whether for oneself or for friends departed. It was this system, with its underlying ideas, that was put down by the Act dissolving the Chantries[2] in 1547, and afterwards denounced in the unsparing language of the Article. The denunciation was deserved, for the popular doctrine obscured the perpetual power of the one sacrifice once offered upon the Cross. But when this had been re-asserted by the Article, the door was re-opened to a recovery of the primitive and Catholic doctrine of the Eucharistic Sacrifice, as 'commemorative, impetrative, and applicative'[3] of Our Lord's High Priestly work.

[1] See vol. i. p. 77.
[2] 1 Ed. VI. c. 14. On the intricacies of the system, so difficult of apprehension by us from whom it is wholly removed, the author may refer to *The Later Mediæval Doctrine of the Eucharistic Sacrifice* (S.P.C.K.), where this Article and its antecedents are examined at length, with full references.
[3] Bramhall, *Works*, i. 54.

Group D. Miscellaneous Articles relating to the discipline of the Church of England. (Arts. 32-39.)

ARTICLE XXXII

‡ De Conjugio Sacerdotum.

(§ 1) Episcopis, Presbyteris et Diaconis nullo mandato divino praeceptum est, ut aut coelibatum voveant aut a matrimonio abstineant. (§ 2) Licet igitur etiam illis, ut caeteris omnibus Christianis, ubi hoc ad pietatem magis facere judicaverint, pro suo arbitratu matrimonium contrahere.‡

Of the Marriage of Priests.

(§ 1) Bishops, Priests, and Deacons are not commanded by God's laws either to vow the estate of single life or to abstain from marriage. (§ 2) Therefore it is lawful also for them, as for all other Christian men, to marry at their own discretion, as they shall judge the same to serve better to godliness.

(i) **Source.**—Composed in 1552-3, when it merely contained the negative statement that a single life is not enjoined on the clergy.[1] This was exchanged in 1563, when the Article was rewritten, for the positive assertion that they may marry. Note the retention of 'sacerdos' as indicative of what is meant by 'priest.'

(ii) **Object.**—To dispel the prejudice against marriage of priests as sinful.

(iii) **Explanation.**—§ 1 lays down as a *premiss* that there is no prohibition of the marriage of the clergy in Scripture. No one would dispute this. The Roman Church has not said more than that this is a question of discipline. The Levitical priesthood were married (Lev. xxi. 13, 14), S. Peter 'was himself a married man'

[1] See Appendix.

(Mark i. 30), and S. Paul both claims the 'right' for himself (1 Cor. ix. 5) and acknowledges it in other clergy (1 Tim. iii. 2, 12; Tit. i. 5, 6). § 2 draws the *conclusion* **that it is lawful also for them, as for all other Christian men, to marry at their own discretion**, etc. But apparently this was not the conclusion drawn by the early Church, whether in East or West. The cases referred to in Scripture imply the existence of a clergy married before ordination, but they are silent as to the right of the clergy to marry, and as to the use of marriage, after it. The clergy were freely allowed the use of marriage in the first three centuries; in the fourth it was forbidden in the West, but prevailed in the East, where it is still permitted to priests and deacons. But marriage after ordination has been universally prohibited[1] from early times. The prohibition, however, was difficult to enforce; and, when enforced, was generally disastrous to clerical morals. It was removed in England by a resolution of Convocation on December 17, 1547, and re-affirmed in this Article. The right of a local Church thus to take her own line in a matter of discipline would be justified by an appeal to the principle of Art. 34.

[1] Except, on conditions, to deacons at Arles, 314.

ARTICLE XXXIII

De Excommunicatis Vitandis.

Qui per publicam Ecclesiae denunciationem rite ab unitate Ecclesiae praecisus est et excommunicatus, is ab universa fidelium multitudine, donec per pœnitentiam publice reconciliatus fuerit arbitrio judicis competentis, habendus est tanquam ethnicus et publicanus.

Of Excommunicate Persons, how they are to be avoided.

That person which by open denunciation of the Church is rightly cut off from the unity of the Church and excommunicated, ought to be taken of the whole multitude of the faithful as an heathen and publican, until he be openly reconciled by penance and received into the Church by a judge that hath authority thereto.

(i) **Source.**—Composed by the English Reformers, 1552-3.

(ii) **Object.**—To vindicate for the Church her right to exercise discipline over her members, a right much disputed, as by the Anabaptists and in the Vestiarian Controversy, under Edward VI.

(iii) **Explanation.**—The right is assumed, and indeed belongs to every self-governing society, which must have power to decide upon its terms of membership and expel offenders. The Article merely deals with the mode in which such power is to be exercised, by Excommunication. The Jewish Church had two forms: (1) temporary exclusion from the congregation, such as was inflicted on Miriam (Num. xii. 14), or on a leper (Lev. xiii. 5), who suffered the same penalty as the Apostles and others when 'separated' (Luke vi. 22), or 'put out of the synagogue' (John ix. 22; xii. 42; xvi. 2), and (2) permanent anathema (Ezra x. 8), cutting off the offender from all intercourse with the faithful (1 Cor. v. 11). Such powers of discipline Our Lord claimed for and bestowed on His Church when He laid down rules for its administration. An offender is to be dealt with, first by private expostulation; next, in company of 'two or three witnesses'; and, if that fails, openly by 'the church,' here apparently the local Church (Matt. xviii. 15-17). Apostolic practice and precept followed these lines. S. Paul excommunicated the incestuous man at Corinth (1 Cor. v. 1-5) to protect others (6-8) as well as to save the man's own soul (5); though, both in his case and in that of Hymenæus and Alexander (1 Tim. i. 20), 'delivery unto Satan' may have implied more than excommunication and have carried with it the infliction of bodily disease, as indeed was not unnatural when, in the miraculous age of the infant Church, the spiritual and moral, was of set purpose enforced by the physical, order (*cf.* Acts v. 1-11; xiii. 10, 11; 1 Cor. xi. 30; Jas. v. 13-15). But precepts indicating the Apostolic practice of excommunication are of frequent occurrence (Rom. xvi. 17; 2 Thess. iii. 14; Titus iii. 10; 2 John 10). The later Church made effective use of the weapon of excommunication for spiritual and moral offences; but it was brought into discredit when the mediæval popes began to wield it for political advantage. From this degradation it has never recovered; and, though retained by the Church of England [1] in the double form of the lesser excommunication,[2] which deprives the offender of sacraments and divine worship, and of the greater excommunication,[3] which, for grave offences against faith and morals, further excludes him from **the whole multitude of the faithful as an heathen and publican** (Matt. xviii. 17), excommunication as an effective part of Church discipline is in abeyance. For its infliction or removal, **the judge that hath authority thereunto** is the Bishop, or an Ecclesiastical Court.

[1] *Cf.* first rubric after Nicene Creed, and before the Order for the Burial of the Dead.
[2] Third rubric before the Order for Holy Communion. *Cf.* Canon 65 of 1604.
[3] Canon 68 of 1604.

ARTICLE XXXIV

De Traditionibus Ecclesiasticis.

(§ 1) Traditiones atque caeremonias easdem non omnino necessarium est esse ubique, aut prorsus consimiles ; nam et variae semper fuerunt et mutari possunt, pro regionum ‡ temporum ‡ et morum diversitate, modo nihil contra verbum Dei instituatur.

(§ 2) Traditiones et caeremonias ecclesiasticas quae cum verbo Dei non pugnant et sunt autoritate publica institutae atque probatae, quisquis privato consilio volens et data opera publice violaverit, is ut qui peccat in publicum ordinem Ecclesiae, quique laedit autoritatem magistratus, et qui infirmorum fratrum conscientias vulnerat, publice, ut caeteri timeant, arguendus est.

(§ 3) † Quaelibet Ecclesia particularis sive nationalis autoritatem habet instituendi mutandi aut abrogandi caeremonias aut ritus ecclesiasticos, humana tantum autoritate institutos, modo omnia ad aedificationem fiant.†

Of the Traditions of the Church.

(§ 1) It is not necessary that traditions and ceremonies be in all places one or utterly alike ; for at all times they have been diverse, and may be changed according to the diversity of countries, times, and men's manners, so that nothing be ordained against God's word.

(§ 2) Whosoever through his private judgment willingly and purposely doth openly break the traditions and ceremonies of the Church which be not repugnant to the word of God, and be ordained and approved by common authority, ought to be rebuked openly that other may fear to do the like, as he that offendeth against the common order of the Church, and hurteth the authority of the magistrate, and woundeth the conscience of the weak brethren.

(§ 3) Every particular or national Church hath authority to ordain, change, and abolish ceremonies or rites of the Church ordained only by man's authority, so that all things be done to edifying.

(i) **Source.**—§§ 1, 2 stood, as at present, in 1552-3, except for the addition of *temporum* in 1563, but are traceable to the Thirteen Articles. § 3 was inserted in 1563, being borrowed from a Latin series of twenty-four 'Heads of Religion' drawn up by Parker in 1559. It is therefore placed between † †.

(ii) **Object.**—To vindicate for the English Church her right to regulate her own order in matters of discipline, regardless of the claims of § 2 Puritans and § 3 Papists.

(iii) **Explanation.**—The Article should be closely compared with Art. 20.

§ 1 lays it down that there is no need for **traditions,** *i.e.* customs, **and ceremonies** to be everywhere alike, and appeals to history in proof of the statement. That they **have been diverse** may be illustrated by the incident of Pope Anicetus and S. Polycarp, in the middle of the second century, who agreed to differ about the time for celebrating Easter, and maintained communion with each other: and that they **may be changed according to the diversity** of circumstances is no more than is covered by the wise eclecticism which Pope Gregory recommended to S. Augustine, 601. Such circumstances vary with **countries,** as when a cold climate makes affusion in Baptism preferable to immersion; with **times,** as when, by the change from persecution to honour which the Church experienced in the fourth century, she was at liberty to replace a simple, by a ceremonious, worship; and with **men's manners,** as when the Kiss of Peace[1] fell out of use because such a mode of salutation, ordinary enough in the common life of orientals and southerners, was not congenial to the manners of the less demonstrative north. So long as the omission or introduction of any custom is **not against God's word,** it is a matter to be ruled by considerations like these.

§ 2 lifts the principle regulating **traditions and ceremonies** on to a higher plane. It condemns wilful disregard of rule in things once **ordered and approved by common authority**[2] as a breach of (1) **the common order of the Church,** (2) the obedience due to **the magistrate,** and (3) charity, or consideration for **the consciences of the**

---

[1] See vol. i. p. 99.
[2] *Cf.* The Prayer Book, Of ceremonies (1549).

EXPLANATION 253

weak brethren. The first and third of these obligations are pointedly set forth in Scripture. Our Lord bade men submit to 'the scribes and the Pharisees' who 'sit on Moses' seat' (Matt. xxiii. 2, 3); and without some such principle of action confusion would be inevitable, and the corporate life of the Church itself be endangered. This to S. Paul is no light offence (1 Cor. iii. 16, 17); and he is equally emphatic that, in things indifferent, charity is the first duty (1 Cor. viii. 1). But the right of the civil power to interfere in the outward order of the Church is bound up with the principle that it is part of the function of the magistrate to maintain religion, a principle recognised in our formularies,[1] but less readily acknowledged now than in the sixteenth century. In that age each of these three sanctions was of special importance when (1) Anabaptists rejected all authority in Church or State, when (2) some bishops, as Ridley in his substitution of Tables for Altars, 1550, anticipated the action of the law to gratify their own preferences;[2] and when (3) Hooper rejected, as an offence to weak consciences, the right of the Church[3] to prescribe observances indifferent in themselves, 1550. The best justification of the position here taken up is the attempt of the Puritans, all but successful, to overthrow the common order on February 13th, 1563,[4] and the confusion that followed, before 1571, on their claiming the right to stay in the Church as nonconformists[5] to it.

§ 3 carries the argument to its conclusion, against the Papists, by adding that such rights of self-government belong to **every particular or national Church**. On this ground rests the justification for most of what had been done in the course of the English Reformation. In that age of national consolidation a *particular* or local *Church* naturally took the shape and name of a *national* Church; though autonomy in 'customs' was freely recognised by the

---

[1] *Cf.* The Litany, and the Prayer for the Church Militant.
[2] Dixon, *History of the Church of England*, iii. p. 206.
[3] *Ib.*, p. 214 *sq.*
[4] See vol. i. pp. 49 *sqq.*
[5] Dixon, iii. pp. 184 *sqq.* 'Nonconformity not separation.'

ancient councils[1] to belong as much to the Churches of a 'diocese,' or administrative division of the Roman Empire such as Egypt, or to a province, as to the independent Churches of Cyprus or Armenia. All that is meant is that no argument can be drawn from Scripture or antiquity in favour of universal uniformity. But this liberty of local Churches is limited by two conditions. The customs they **ordain, change, and abolish** must be such as were **ordained only by man's authority**: and the rule in any action they take must be that **all things be done to edifying** (Rom. xiv. 19; 1 Cor. xiv. 26). It may be added that while we claim this liberty to reform ourselves, we allow it to others. 'In these our doings we condemn no other nations, nor prescribe anything but to our own people only.'

[1] *Cf.* Nicaea, Canon vi.; Constantinople, Canon ii.; Ephesus, Canon viii.

ARTICLE XXXV

De Homiliis.

‡ Tomus secundus Homiliarum, quarum singulos titulos huic Articulo subjunximus,[1] continet piam et salutarem doctrinam et his temporibus necessariam, non minus quam prior tomus Homiliarum, quae editae sunt tempore Edwardi Sexti: itaque eas in Ecclesiis per ministros diligenter et clare, ut a populo intelligi possint, recitandas esse judicamus. ‡

Of Homilies.

The second Book of Homilies, the several titles whereof we have joined under this Article,[1] doth contain a godly and wholesome doctrine and necessary for these times, as doth the former Book of Homilies which were set forth in the time of Edward the Sixth: and therefore we judge them to be read in Churches by the ministers diligently and distinctly, that they may be understanded of the people.

(i) **Source.**—One of the series of 1552-3, rewritten in 1563.

(ii) **Object.**—To commend the doctrine contained in the Books of Homilies, and to secure their being read in Church.

(iii) **Explanation.**—The need of Homilies arose from scarcity of preachers, who were either incapable or intemperate: incapable, owing to the decay of learning in the Universities which followed upon the destruction of the monasteries; and intemperate, because such as could preach were partisans. Two measures were adopted in remedy of the evil. The Crown from time to time silenced all, or all but licensed, preachers. The Church put Homilies, composed by prominent divines, into the hands of the

---

[1] They are omitted here for lack of space, but may be found in the Articles as printed with the Prayer Book. The Homilies are published by the S.P.C.K.

clergy. In 1542 the bishops agreed 'to make certain Homilies for stay of such errors as were then by ignorant preachers sparkled among the people,' which were produced in Convocation, 1543. But the project slept till the next reign, when the First Book of Homilies, 1547, twelve in number, and afterwards, 1549, divided into thirty-two parts, was 'appointed by the King's Majesty to be declared and read by all parsons, vicars, and curates every Sunday in their churches' at High Mass.[1] Under Mary this was exchanged for other Homilies, projected both in Royal Articles, 1554, and in Synod, 1555, but never achieved. Yet the need was thus recognised on both sides. The date of the publication of **The Second Book of Homilies** under Elizabeth is uncertain, but the Article of 1563 commends it along with **the former Book, and orders them to be read in churches . . . diligently and distinctly.** The point of this order lies in the fact that the Homilies were resented by many of the old-fashioned clergy on the score of doctrine, who took their revenge by reading them unintelligibly. Afterwards they were no less distasteful to the Puritans, as restricting the liberty of preaching in favour of 'conceived' utterances. 'Remove Homilies, Articles, Injunctions' was one of their demands in the First Admonition to Parliament, 1572. Considering that the pulpit then took the place of the press, the platform, and the playhouse, as the means of influencing public opinion, the policy of setting forth Homilies by authority was an expedient as certain to be seized in its own interests by the government as to be resented by its opponents among the governed. The addition in 1571 of the Homily against Wilful Rebellion, after the Northern Rebellion of 1569, is a case in point.[2]

It should be observed that *the nature of assent* demanded to the Homilies is but as to documents of *general* authority and *temporary* usefulness. They **contain a godly and wholesome doctrine, and necessary for these times.**

---

[1] *Cf.* rubric after the Nicene Creed in the Prayer Books of 1549, 1552, 1559, 1662.
[2] This made twenty-one Homilies in forty-three parts.

ARTICLE XXXVI

‡ De Episcoporum et Ministrorum Consecratione.

(§ 1) Libellus de Consecratione Archiepiscoporum et Episcoporum et de ordinatione Presbyterorum et Diaconorum, editus nuper temporibus Edwardi Sexti et auctoritate Parliamenti illis ipsis temporibus confirmatus, omnia ad ejusmodi consecrationem et ordinationem necessaria continet; et nihil habet quod ex se sit aut superstitiosum aut impium. (§ 2) Itaque quicunque juxta ritus illius libri consecrati aut ordinati sunt, ab anno secundo praedicti Regis Edwardi usque ad hoc tempus aut in posterum juxta eosdem ritus consecrabuntur aut ordinabuntur, rite, atque ordine, atque legitime statuimus esse et fore consecratos et ordinatos. ‡

Of Consecration of Bishops and Ministers.

(§ 1) The Book of Consecration of Archbishops and Bishops and ordering of Priests and Deacons, lately set forth in the time of Edward the Sixth and confirmed at the same time by authority of Parliament, doth contain all things necessary to such consecration and ordering; neither hath it anything that of itself is superstitious or ungodly. (§ 2) And therefore whosoever are consecrate or ordered according to the rites of that book, since the second year of the aforenamed King Edward unto this time, or hereafter shall be consecrated or ordered according to the same rites, we decree all such to be rightly, orderly, and lawfully consecrate or ordered.

(i) **Source.**—Composed in 1563, and substituted then for an Article of more general character which occupied this position in 1553.

(ii) **Object.**—To vindicate § 1 Anglican Orders against the objections of Papists and Puritans to their spiritual validity, and § 2 to establish the legality of the Ordinal in answer to the cavils of certain Papists against its statutory authority.

(iii) **Explanation.**—§ 1 contends for the spiritual validity of Anglican orders.

(1) In reply to the objections of *Papists*, it asserts that the Ordinal of Edward VI. **doth contain all things necessary.** The Edwardian Ordinal, in its earlier form, appeared in 1550 under the sanction of 3 and 4 Ed. VI. c. 12, and in its later form, in 1552, under cover of the second Act of Uniformity, 5 and 6 Ed. VI. c. 1: but, so far as the spiritual validity of the rite is concerned, the two Ordinals were not materially different. The objections entertained by the Romanensian party against the rite when the Article was framed in 1563 are to be seen in their treatment of Orders conferred under it during the Marian Reaction. Before Pole arrived, Nov. 1554, as Papal Legate with instructions to deal with the question, a policy had been instituted by the Queen and carried out by Bonner in his diocese of London which, 'touching such persons as were heretofore promoted to any orders after the new sort and fashion of order,' was meant to 'supply that thing which wanted in them before.'[1] Among these deficiencies we find mentioned the omission of the anointing of the hands of a priest at his ordination. 'They would have us believe,' writes Pilkington, a contemptuous but contemporary witness afterwards Bishop of Durham, 1561-76, 'that the oil hath such holiness in it that whosoever lacketh it is no priest nor minister. Therefore in the late days of Popery our holy bishops called before them all such as were made ministers without such greasing, and . . . anointed them, and then all was perfect: they might sacrifice for quick and dead.'[2] Some clergy, however, scrupled rehabilitation by any such supplementary proceedings, presented themselves for re-ordination, and received it. But, by Pole's arrival, such re-ordinations had ceased: and the Cardinal appears to have tolerated Edwardian Orders by leaving in their benefices men who

---

[1] The Queen's Injunctions of March 4, 1554, ap. Cardwell, *Documentary Annals*, i. p. 125: and for Bonner's Articles, *ib.*, p. 144.

[2] *Works*, Parker Society, p. 163.

had received them.¹ Yet in his legatine constitution of February 10, 1556, Pole embodied the judgment of Eugenius IV., given in 1439, which lays it down that the 'matter' of ordination to the priesthood consists in the Delivery of the Chalice and Paten, and its 'form' in the sentence, 'Receive the power of offering sacrifice in the Church for quick and dead.' Probably, then, it was on the ground of such omissions as these that the Romanensians rejected the Edwardian rite in 1563.² But these objections are now abandoned by Romanists. The unction of the hands is a local usage dating only from the ninth or tenth century; the Delivery of the Instruments with its formula appears first in the twelfth. The Papal Bull of 1896 condemns Anglican Orders as null and void, on the ground that the rite is defective in (*a*) Intention and (*b*) Form. Thus (*a*) the Ordinal is held to have been 'changed with the manifest intention of introducing another rite not approved by the Church and of rejecting what the Church does.'³ But the preface to the Ordinal is a sufficient answer to this charge. If again (*b*) the rite is condemned as failing to make mention in its 'Form' either of the order to be conferred or of the power of offering sacrifice,⁴ our reply is that it is impossible to maintain by a comparison of other rites admittedly valid that either the one or the other of these conditions is invariably satisfied.⁵ The Article, however, is content to use a moderate though firm tone in defence of the Ordinal: and no scholar who has well surveyed its history and contents side by side with those of other Ordinals will wish to do more. But as 'public prayer with imposition of hands'⁶ (Acts vi. 6, etc.) constitutes the sole essentials of ordination, it is abundantly plain that the Ordinal which prays for the ordinand in Our Lord's own words (John xx. 22) at the moment of his ordination *doth contain all things necessary to such consecration and ordering.*

¹ Frere, *The Marian Reaction*, pp. 118 *sqq.* ² Dixon, iv. p. 462.
³ Bull of Leo XIII., *Apostolicae Curae*, p. 21.   ⁴ *Ib.*, p. 16.
⁵ Cf. *The Answer of the Archbishops of England*, § xii. p. 21; and *Priesthood in the English Church* (No. xli. of the Church Historical Society's publications), p. 42, n. 3.
⁶ Preface to the Ordinal.

(2) If the Papists thus charged the Ordinal with defect, the *Puritans* accused it of excess: and in answer to them the Article proceeds, **neither hath it anything that of itself is superstitious or ungodly**. Probably the complaints urged in 1563 were anticipations of such as were formulated by Cartwright, after the revision of 1571, and eventually answered by Hooker. If so, they concerned (*a*) the formula of Ordination, 'Receive the Holy Ghost: whose sins thou dost forgive, etc.' This was denounced as a 'ridiculous and ... blasphemous saying,' and it was held that 'the Bishop may as well say to the sea, when it rageth and swelleth, Peace, be quiet; as to say, "Receive, etc."'[1] The Puritans meant that there was something as profane in claiming that the Spirit can be bestowed through man as in claiming that man can work miracles. But this is to beg the question. Spiritual powers were exercised by Christ as man (Matt. ix. 6 and 8); and the words 'Receive, etc.,' were immediately preceded by words bestowing on men the very commission which He himself had received from the Father (John xx. 21). Further, unless 'Holy Spirit' (*ib.*, 22, marg.) can be ministered through human and material agencies, the whole truth of the Incarnation, the Church, and the Sacraments is done away. (*b*) A second and graver objection was directed against Episcopacy. Originally prompted by resentment at the action of the Bishops in enforcing the ceremonies, and gathering force largely in opposition to 'the lordship and civil government of Bishops,'[2] *i.e.* the coercive authority with which they were invested for the purpose, the Puritan movement broke out into a demand for 'a true ministry and regiment of the Church according to the word.'[3] Their cry was for a 'parity of ministers,' and their ideal 'the Genevan platform' of Church discipline. This alone they held to be of 'divine right,' and they rejected Episcopacy as unscriptural. This raises a large question, not really in controversy when the Article was composed. Enough that a system of the nature of Episcopacy appears at the

---

[1] Hooker, *E. P.*, V. lxxvii. 5.
[2] Prothero, *Statutes and Constitutional Documents*, p. 197.
[3] The First Admonition to Parliament, *ib.*, p. 199.

EXPLANATION

beginning of the Apostolic age in the Church of Jerusalem (Acts xii. 17; xv. 13-21; xxi. 18; Gal. ii. 9, 12; Acts xi. 30; vi. 6), and at its close in the Churches of Ephesus (1 Tim. i. 3; iii. 1-7; and 8-13) and Crete (Titus i. 5-9). In the Churches founded by S. Paul during the interval, organisation appears in varied stages of development (1 Thess. v. 12; Rom. xii. 6-8; *cf.* Heb. xiii. 7, 17, 24): and an itinerant ministry of Apostles and Prophets (1 Cor. xii. 28; Eph. iv. 11), existed side by side with local officers called 'bishops and deacons' (Phil. i. 1). The Puritan objections to the Ordinal rested upon a double mistake. From the fact that 'bishop' and 'presbyter' are convertible terms (*cf.* Acts xx. 17 with 28; and Tit. i. 5 with 7) they argued for a 'parity of ministers,' forgetting that the question was not one of names but of things: and they took an organisation which was only in process of development as possessing the authority of an institution permanently and divinely fixed. It cannot now be denied either that Episcopacy was the goal of such development or that it was reached under the guidance of S. John, *i.e.* inferentially, of Our Lord Himself.[1]

§ 2, which contains the real point of the Article, answers an objection raised by Bonner and his party, after the accession of Elizabeth, to the statutory legality of the Ordinal. It was only a cavil. By 1 Mary st. ii. c. 2, 1553, which abolished the Prayer Book, the Ordinal had been repealed by name; but when the Prayer Book was restored by 1 Eliz. c. 2, 1559, the Ordinal was not so specified, being regarded as part of it. Bonner, to defend himself against Horne, who, as bishop of the diocese of Winchester in which he was then imprisoned, was enjoined to administer the oath of supremacy to him under 5 Eliz. c. i. § 6, refused to take it on the plea that 'Dr. Horne is no lawful bishop,' having been 'made Bishop according to the Book of King Edward, not yet authorised in Parliament.' Nothing is objected

---

[1] *Cf.* Lightfoot, *Dissertations on the Apostolic Age*, pp. 241 sqq. On modern questions relating to the Ministry, see Bright, *Some Aspects of Primitive Church Life*, c. 1: Moberly, *Ministerial Priesthood*: Sanday, *The Conception of Priesthood*.

as to the spiritual validity of Horne's consecration, but simply to his legal status as bishop. The matter was set at rest, first by the affirmation of the Article that **whosoever are consecrate or ordered according to the rites of that book . . . be . . . lawfully consecrated and ordered**, and afterwards by 8 Eliz. c. 1, 'An Act declaring the making and consecration of the Archbishops and Bishops of this realm to be good, lawful, and perfect, A.D. 1565-6.'[1]

[1] Cf. *The Elizabethan Bishops and the Civil Power* (No. xxii. of the Church Historical Society's publications).

ARTICLE XXXVII

De Civilibus Magistratibus.

(§ 1) ‡ Regia Majestas in hoc Angliae regno ac caeteris ejus dominiis summam habet potestatem, ad quam omnium statuum hujus regni, sive illi ecclesiastici sive civiles, in omnibus causis suprema gubernatio pertinet, et nulli externae jurisdictioni est subjecta, necesse debet. Cum Regiae Majestati summam gubernationem tribuimus, quibus titulis intelligimus animos quorundam calumniatorum offendi, non damus regibus nostris aut verbi Dei aut sacramentorum administrationem, quod etiam Injunctiones ab Elizabetha Regina nostra nuper editae apertissime testantur: sed eam tantum prerogativam quam in Sacris Scripturis a Deo ipso omnibus piis principibus videmus semper fuisse attributam, hoc est, ut omnes status atque ordines fidei suae a Deo commissos, sive illi ecclesiastici sint sive civiles, in officio contineant, et contumaces ac delinquentes gladio civili coerceant. ‡

(§ 2) Romanus Pontifex nullam habet jurisdictionem in hoc regno Angliae.

(§ 3) Leges regni possunt Christianos propter capitalia et gravia crimina morte punire.

(§ 4) Christianis licet ex mandato Magistratus arma portare et justa bella administrare.

Of the Civil Magistrates.

(§ 1) The Queen's Majesty hath the chief power in this realm of England and other her dominions, unto whom the chief government of all estates of this realm, whether they be ecclesiastical or civil, in all causes doth appertain, and is not nor ought to be subject to any foreign jurisdiction.

Where we attribute to the Queen's Majesty the chief government, by which titles we understand the minds of some slanderous folks to be offended, we give not to our princes the ministering either of God's word or of sacraments, the which thing the Injunctions also lately set forth by Elizabeth our Queen doth most plainly testify: but only that prerogative which we see to have been given always to all godly princes in Holy Scriptures by God himself, that is, that they should rule all estates and degrees committed to their charge by God, whether they be ecclesiastical or temporal, and restrain with the civil sword the stubborn and evil-doers.

(§ 2) The Bishop of Rome hath no jurisdiction in this realm of England.

(§ 3) The laws of the realm may punish Christian men with death for heinous and grievous offences.

(§ 4) It is lawful for Christian men at the commandment of the Magistrate to wear weapons and serve in the wars.

(i) **Source.**—Composed by the English Reformers, 1552-3, but rewritten 1563. The first paragraph originally consisted of the bald statement that 'the King of England is Supreme Head in earth, next under Christ, of the Church of England and Ireland.' In 1563 it was exchanged for (1) *an affirmation* assigning to the Crown no such Supreme Headship but **the chief power or chief government**, and (2) a *denial*, based on the Queen's Injunctions of 1559, refusing to princes any share in the spiritual functions of the clergy.

(ii) **Object.**—To assert the rights of the Crown (1) as against the Papists who rejected the Royal Supremacy, § 1, as incompatible with the Papal claims, § 2 ; and (2) as against the Anabaptists who, by denying to the Crown the right to punish its subjects, § 3, and to enlist them in defence of their country, § 4, would have rendered civil government impossible.

(iii) **Explanation.**—§ 1 is a guarded statement of the *Royal Supremacy.* **The Queen's Majesty hath . . . the chief government of all estates of this realm, whether they be ecclesiastical or civil.** During the Middle Ages the Crown claimed and maintained two principles of action, (1) a regulative authority over the internal affairs of the kingdom, and (2) a defensive authority used to protect the body politic against aggression from without. Thus (1) its regulative powers were used, in the interests of its subjects, to see that the Spiritualty and the Temporalty, or administrative officers of Church and State respectively, did their duty each in their own sphere and did not encroach upon the domain of each other. For example, King Edgar claimed the right of visitation. 'It appertaineth unto us,' he says, ' to enquire into the lives' of the clergy : but he was careful to exercise it through the Spiritualty, headed by Archbishop Dunstan (959-988). The Conqueror, by forbidding synods to debate or promulgate their decisions without his consent, allowed the Spiritualty legislative freedom within its own sphere as he allowed it a judicature of its own, and supported it in both with the authority of the Crown. His successors, by issuing prohibitions to stay the proceedings of Church synods and courts where they seemed

EXPLANATION

to encroach upon the rights of the subject or the sphere of the Temporalty which claimed all questions of person and property, as also by forbidding attempts of Parliament to tax the clergy, kept both Spiritualty and Temporalty to their several duties, and prevented either part of the body politic from interfering with the functions of the other. But (2) the Crown also exercised a defensive authority as champion of the Church and realm. Thus the Conqueror laid down the rule that no papal legate should be allowed to land in England unless he had been appointed at the request of the King and the Church; while both as to legates and as to appeals, his successors, though they accepted both, maintained their right to admit them only at their pleasure. Hence the Crown vindicated for itself the right to exercise *government* over all its subjects, which was at the same time a *chief*, sovereign, imperial, or supreme government as subject to no other foreign authority. This, in brief, was what was meant by the Royal Supremacy before the Reformation, an authority older than the name used to describe it. But it was quite consistent with the ascription of government in things spiritual to the Pope as Head of the Church according to the mediæval theory: and in practice, with his exercise, by connivance of or collusion with the Crown, of a large measure of jurisdiction, in appeals, episcopal appointments, and Church administration generally.

At the Reformation it was to the interest of Henry VIII. and the nation to resist the papal claims. Hence the Crown revived, and temporarily exaggerated, its old prerogatives. Not content with reviving the old constitutional theory, stated in the preamble of 24 H. VIII. c. 12, that England is an empire whose subjects are a body politic divided into Spiritualty and Temporalty, each governing itself under the Crown by its proper officers, Henry, in 1531, forced the clergy to acknowledge him 'only Supreme Head on earth of the Church of England,' and then, after embodying his new title in the Act of Supreme Head (26 H. VIII. c. 1), 1534, proceeded to exercise, in virtue of it, a Headship that was more than regulative; for, when it was put into

commission in the hands of Cromwell, 1535, the bishops
found their authority, both to govern and to visit their
dioceses, immediately superseded. For all this Henry
never went so far as to intrude upon their spiritual
functions, an intrusion which he expressly disclaimed
in reply to the protestation of Tunstal in 1531. But
for twenty years this Headship was attached to the
Crown, and exercised by Henry VIII., Edward VI., and
Mary in succession. Mary repudiated the title, 1554.
It was not revived by Elizabeth, who, however, had
restored to the Crown its 'ancient jurisdiction over
the estate ecclesiastical and spiritual' by 1 Eliz. c. 1,
which describes 'the Queen's Highness' as 'the only
Supreme Governor of this realm . . . as well in all . . .
ecclesiastical causes as temporal.' The Act certainly
gave to the Crown powers of government over the Church
which were directive and more than regulative: but they
were (a) now for the first time limited by statutory definition; (b) entrusted, for visitatorial and corrective purposes, to an organised court of justice;[1] and (c) carefully
safeguarded by the Injunction of 1559, repeated in the
second paragraph of § 1 of this Article so as to preclude
all possibility of supposing that the Crown is possessed
of purely spiritual authority. **We give not to our princes
the ministering either of God's word or of sacraments.**

§ 2 *repudiates the jurisdiction of the Pope.* The
papal claims as they have affected England are of two
kinds. (1) The popes claimed a temporal suzerainty.
This was based on forgeries like the Donation of Constantine (eighth century); on fictions, as that islands belong
as such to the see of the Fisherman; or on precedents,
such as that afforded by John's tribute to Innocent III.
in 1213. It was a claim easily disposed of. In 1076
William I. refused to do homage to Gregory VII. In
1366 Parliament repudiated the tribute promised by
John. In 1399 it declared, as again in 1533, that 'the
Crown of England and the rights of the same Crown
have been from all past time so free, that neither chief
pontiff, nor any one else outside the kingdom, has any
right to interfere in the same.' But (2) the popes have

---

[1] The Court of High Commission, abolished 1641.

also claimed a spiritual authority, in virtue of their office as Head of the Church by Divine appointment. They have based their claim on the promise to S. Peter (Matt. xvi. 18), who certainly held a primacy among the Apostles (Matt. x. 2; Acts i. 15; ii. 14, etc.), but as certainly refrained from vindicating for himself any pre-eminence of jurisdiction (Acts xi. 1-4; Gal. ii. 11; 1 Pet. v. 1). There is no reason to think that he was Bishop of Rome; and, even if he were, there is nothing to show that the authority supposed to be his was meant for his successors in that see. Yet the Roman See was the only Apostolically founded see of the West, as well as the see of the capital of the empire. On both grounds it acquired great prestige: and when the English Church was founded, 597, the papal authority was highly esteemed in England. Authority grew into jurisdiction, moral influence into legally recognised rights. Protests from time to time were raised against the exercise of such rights by the State, but rarely by the Church of England; for in the Middle Ages it was never questioned that the Pope was the successor of S. Peter and Head of the Church by Divine appointment. In 1534 the Convocations resolved that 'the Bishop of Rome has not in Scripture any greater jurisdiction in the kingdom of England than any other foreign bishop.' The Article, in re-affirming this declaration that **the Bishop of Rome hath no jurisdiction in this realm of England**, has denied his authority as Head, *jure divino*, over the whole Church: but not his primacy, *jure ecclesiastico*, nor his authority as Patriarch of the West.

§ 3 merely affirms that capital punishment, advisable or not, is lawful, *cf.* Gen. ix. 6.

§ 4, proceeding on the principle that Christianity accepted the institutions of society, *e.g.* slavery, as it found them, with a view not to revolutionise and overturn (Eph. vi. 5; Philemon), but to reform and leaven them, asserts the lawfulness of war. Cornelius was baptized without being required to give up his profession (Acts x. 47, 48), and S. Paul adopts the figure of the Christian's armour (Eph. vi. 11) without any sense of its unfitness to describe the Christian life.

ARTICLE XXXVIII

De illicita bonorum communicatione.	Of Christian men's goods which are not common.
Facultates et bona Christianorum non sunt communia quoad jus et possessionem, ut quidam Anabaptistae falso jactant; debet tamen quisque de his quae possidet, pro facultatum ratione, pauperibus eleemosynas benigne distribuere.	The riches and goods of Christians are not common, as touching the right, title, and possession of the same, as certain Anabaptists do falsely boast; notwithstanding every man ought of such things as he possesseth liberally to give alms to the poor, according to his ability.

(i) **Source.**—Composed by the English Reformers, 1552-3, and since unchanged.

(ii) **Object.**—To condemn the Communism advocated by some Anabaptists.

(iii) **Explanation.**—The notion that Christianity inculcates Communism is derived from the two summaries of the inner life of the Christian Church at Jerusalem preserved in Acts ii. 42-47 and iv. 32-35. But the assertion that they 'had all things common' (ii. 44) will not bear this meaning. (*a*) If so, the Apostles would have been introducing a social revolution, which would have been contrary to Our Lord's precepts (Matt. xxii. 21; xxiii. 2) and example (Luke xii. 14; John xviii. 36), as well as out of harmony with their own practice, *e.g.* in regard to slavery. Everywhere Christians were warned as good citizens to respect the established institutions of society (Rom. xiii. 1-7; 1 Pet. ii. 13-17; iii. 1, 16, etc.). (*b*) No rule of surrendering private property was enforced (Acts v. 4). Communism moreover is (*c*) not only incompatible with the permanent obligation of the eighth and tenth commandments (Rom. xiii. 9), but (*d*) with the 'need' (Acts ii. 45 and iv. 35) and the duty of almsgiving, both of which Our Lord assumes (Matt. xxvi. 11; vi. 2-4); while almsgiving was a duty recognised on a very large scale by the Christian Church (1 Cor. xvi. 2; 1 Pet. iv. 9, 10). (*e*) Further, the Christian principle about property is not that '*la propriété c'est le vol*,' but that property is a trust. We are not bound to a community of possession but we are bound to some community of use (Eph. iv. 28).

ARTICLE XXXIX

De Jurejurando.

Quemadmodum juramentum vanum et temerarium a Domino nostro Jesu Christo et Apostolo ejus Jacobo Christianis hominibus interdictum esse fatemur, ita Christianorum religionem minime prohibere censemus quin, jubente magistratu in causa fidei et caritatis jurare liceat, modo id fiat juxta Prophetae doctrinam in justitia, in judicio, et veritate.

Of a Christian man's Oath.

As we confess that vain and rash swearing is forbidden Christian men by our Lord Jesus Christ, so we judge that Christian religion doth not prohibit but that a man may swear when the magistrate requireth in a cause of faith and charity, so it be done according to the Prophet's teaching in justice, judgment, and truth.

(i) **Source.**—Composed by the English Reformers, 1552-3, and unchanged since.

(ii) **Object.**—To combat the scruples of Anabaptists against oaths.

(iii) **Explanation.**—Two passages (Matt. v. 33-7 ; James v. 12) have seemed to others, beside the Anabaptists, *e.g.* to some of the Fathers and the Quakers, to forbid the taking of oaths in any case. But what is there under consideration is not oaths in a court of law, but the Christian's rule of conversation. He is to speak as one perpetually living in the presence of God. "The essence of the oath is the solemnly putting oneself *on special occasions* in the presence of God."[1] For such oaths on solemn occasions we have not only the sanction of the Apostolic writers who saw nothing wrong in the practice (Heb. vi. 17) and used it themselves (2 Cor. i. 23), though ordinarily a Christian's word should be enough (*ib.*, i.

---

[1] Gore, *Sermon on the Mount*, pp. 74-8—*q.v.* on 'Oaths.'

17, 18), but the example of Our Lord Himself who, when adjured by the High Priest, did not refuse to answer (Matt. xxvi. 62-64). But there are obvious conditions attaching to oaths before a judge. 'When a Christian goes to take an oath in a court of law he should only go to profess openly that motive to truthfulness which rules all his speech':[1] and *according to the Prophet's teaching* he will swear 'in truth, in judgement, and in righteousness' (Jer. iv. 2).

[1] Gore, *loc. cit.*

THE RATIFICATION

Confirmatio Articulorum.

Hic Liber antedictorum Articulorum jam denuo approbatus est per assensum et consensum Serenissimae Reginae Elizabethae Dominae nostrae, Dei gratia Angliae, Franciae, et Hiberniae Reginae, Defensoris Fidei, etc., retinendus, et per totum regnum Angliae exequendus. Qui Articuli et lecti sunt et denuo confirmati subscriptione Domini Archiepiscopi et Episcoporum superioris domus, et totius cleri inferioris domus in Convocatione, A.D. 1571.

The Ratification.

This Book of Articles before rehearsed is again approved and allowed to be holden and executed within the realm by the assent and consent of our Sovereign Lady Elizabeth, by the grace of God, of England, France, and Ireland Queen, Defender of the Faith, etc. Which Articles were deliberately read and confirmed again by the subscription of the hands of the Archbishop and Bishops of the upper house, and by the subscription of the whole clergy in the nether house in their Convocation, in the year of our Lord God, 1571.

HIS MAJESTY'S DECLARATION

BEING by God's Ordinance, according to Our just Title, *Defender of the Faith, and Supreme Governour of the Church, within these Our Dominions,* We hold it most agreeable to this Our Kingly Office, and Our own religious Zeal, to conserve and maintain the Church committed to Our Charge, in the Unity of true Religion, and in the Bond of Peace; and not to suffer unnecessary Disputations, Altercations, or Questions to be raised, which may nourish Faction both in the Church and Commonwealth. We have therefore, upon mature Deliberation, and with the Advice of so many of Our Bishops as might conveniently be called together, thought fit to make this Declaration following:

That the Articles of the Church of *England* (which have been allowed and authorized heretofore, and which Our Clergy generally have subscribed unto) do contain the true Doctrine of the Church of *England* agreeable to God's Word: which We do therefore ratify and confirm, requiring all Our loving Subjects to continue in the uniform Profession thereof, and prohibiting the least difference from the said Articles; which to that End We command to be new printed, and this Our Declaration to be published therewith.

That We are Supreme Governour of the Church of *England*: And that if any Difference arise about the external Policy, concerning the *Injunctions, Canons,* and other *Constitutions* whatsoever thereto belonging, the Clergy in their Convocation is to order and settle them, having first obtained leave under Our Broad Seal so to do: and We approving their said Ordinances and Constitutions; providing that none be made contrary to the Laws and Customs of the Land.

That out of Our Princely Care that the Churchmen may do the Work which is proper unto them, the Bishops and Clergy, from time to time in Convocation, upon their humble Desire, shall have Licence under Our Broad Seal to deliberate of, and to do all such Things, as, being made plain by them, and assented unto by Us, shall concern the settled Continuance of the Doctrine and Discipline of the Church of *England* now established; from which We will not endure any varying or departing in the least Degree.

That for the present, though some differences have been ill raised, yet We take comfort in this, that all Clergymen within Our Realm have always most willingly subscribed to the Articles established; which is an argument to Us, that they all agree in the true, usual, literal meaning of the said Articles; and that even in those curious points, in which the present differences lie, men of all sorts take the Articles of the Church of *England* to be for them; which is an argument again, that none of them intend any desertion of the Articles established.

That therefore in these both curious and unhappy differences, which have for so many hundred years, in different times and places, exercised the Church of Christ, We will, that all further curious search be laid aside, and these disputes shut up in God's promises, as they be generally set forth to us in the holy Scriptures, and the general meaning of the Articles of the Church of *England* according to them. And that no man hereafter shall either print, or preach, to draw the Article aside any way, but shall submit to it in the plain and full meaning thereof: and shall not put his own sense or comment to be the meaning of the Article, but shall take it in the literal and grammatical sense.

That if any publick Reader in either of Our Universities, or any Head or Master of a College, or any other person respectively in either of them, shall affix any new sense to any Article, or shall publickly read, determine, or hold any publick Disputation, or suffer any such to be held either way, in either the Universities or Colleges respectively; or if any Divine in the Universities shall preach or print any thing either way, other than is already established in Convocation with Our Royal Assent; he, or they the Offenders, shall be liable to Our displeasure, and the Church's censure in Our Commission Ecclesiastical, as well as any other: And We will see there shall be due Execution upon them.

APPENDIX

NOTE.—(1) Blank spaces enclosed in [ ] indicate points at which new matter was afterwards inserted.
(2) Words between † † were subsequently dropped.
(3) Clauses, etc., between * * were subsequently re-written.

1553.

VIII

Peccatum Originale.

Peccatum originis (non est ut fabulantur Pelagiani, † et hodie Anabaptistae repetunt †) in imitatione Adami situm, sed est vitium et depravatio naturæ cuiuslibet hominis ex Adamo naturaliter propagati, qua fit, ut ab originali justitia quam longissime distet, ad malum sua natura propendeat, et caro semper adversus spiritum concupiscat; unde in unoquoque nascentium, iram Dei atque damnationem meretur. Manet etiam in renatis hæc naturæ depravatio; qua fit, ut affectus carnis, græce φρόνημα σαρκὸς (quod alii sapientiam, alii sensum, alii affectum, alii studium [   ] vocant), legi Dei non subjiciatur. Et quanquam renatis et credentibus nulla propter Christum est condemnatio, peccati tamen in sese rationem habere concupiscentiam fatetur Apostolus.

1563.

IX

Peccatum Originale.

Peccatum originis non est (ut fabulantur Pelagiani) in imitatione Adami situm, sed est vitium et depravatio naturæ cujuslibet hominis ex Adamo naturaliter propagati, qua fit, ut ab originali justitia quam longissime distet, ad malum sua natura propendeat, et caro semper adversus spiritum concupiscat; unde in unoquoque nascentium, iram Dei atque damnationem meretur. Manet etiam in renatis hæc naturæ depravatio; qua fit, ut affectus carnis, græce φρόνημα σαρκὸς (quod alii sapientiam, alii sensum, alii affectum, alii studium [   ] interpretantur), legi Dei non subjiciatur. Et quanquam renatis et credentibus nulla propter Christum est condemnatio, peccati tamen in sese rationem habere concupiscentiam fatetur Apostolus.

1553.

IX

De Libero Arbitrio.

[

]

Absque gratia Dei, quae per Christum est, nos praeveniente ut velimus, et cooperante dum volumus, ad pietatis opera facienda, quae Deo grata sint et accepta, nihil valemus.

X

† De Gratia.

Gratia Christi, seu Spiritus Sanctus qui per eundem datur, cor lapideum aufert, et dat cor carneum. Atque licet ex nolentibus quae recta sunt volentes faciat, et ex volentibus prava nolentes reddat, voluntati nihilominus violentiam nullam infert: et nemo hac de causa, cum peccaverit, seipsum excusare potest, quasi nolens aut coactus peccaverit, ut eam ob causam accusari non mereatur aut damnari.†

XI

De Hominis Justificatione.

* Justificatio ex sola fide Jesu Christi, eo sensu quo in Homilia de Justificatione explicatur, est certissima et saluberrima Christianorum doctrina.*

.

1563.

X

De Libero Arbitrio.

Ea est hominis post lapsum Adae conditio, ut sese, naturalibus suis viribus et bonis operibus, ad fidem et invocationem Dei convertere ac praeparare non possit. Quare absque gratia Dei, quae per Christum est, nos praeveniente, ut velimus, et cooperante dum volumus, ad pietatis opera facienda, quae Deo grata sint et accepta, nihil valemus.

XI

De Hominis Justificatione.

Tantum propter meritum Domini ac Servatoris nostri Jesu Christi, per fidem, non propter opera et merita nostra, justi coram Deo reputamur. Quare sola fide nos justificari, doctrina est saluberrima, ac consolationis plenissima: ut in Homilia de Justificatione hominis fusius explicatur.

APPENDIX

1553.

1563.

XII
De Bonis Operibus.

Bona opera, quæ sunt fructus fidei et justificatos sequuntur, quanquam peccata nostra expiari et divini judicii severitatem ferre non possunt, Deo tamen grata sunt et accepta in Christo, atque ex vera et viva fide necessario profluunt, ut plane ex illis æque fides viva cognosci possit atque arbor ex fructu judicari.

]

XII
Opera ante Justificationem.

Opera quae fiunt ante gratiam Christi et Spiritus ejus afflatum, cum ex fide Jesu Christi non prodeant, minime Deo grata sunt, neque gratiam (ut multi vocant) de congruo merentur: imo cum non sint facta ut Deus illa fieri voluit et praecepit, peccati rationem habere non dubitamus.

XIII
Opera ante Justificationem.

Opera quæ fiunt ante gratiam Christi, et spiritus ejus afflatum, cum ex fide Jesu Christi non prodeant, minime Deo grata sunt, neque gratiam (ut multi vocant) de congruo merentur: imo cum non sint facta ut Deus illa fieri voluit et præcepit, peccati rationem habere non dubitamus.

XIII
Opera Supererogationis.

Opera quae Supererogationis appellant, non possunt sine arrogantia et impietate praedicari. Nam illis declarant homines non tantum se Deo reddere quae tenentur, sed plus in ejus gratiam facere quam deberent: cum aperte Christus dicat, Cum feceritis omnia quaecunque praecepta sunt vobis, dicite, Servi inutiles sumus.

XIV
Opera Supererogationis.

Opera quæ Supererogationis appellant, non possunt sine arrogantia et impietate prædicari. Nam illis declarant homines non tantum se Deo reddere quæ tenentur, sed plus in ejus gratiam facere quam deberent: cum aperte Christus dicat, Cum feceritis omnia quæcunque præcepta sunt vobis, dicite, Servi inutiles sumus.

XIV
Nemo praeter Christum est sine peccato.

Christus in nostrae naturae veritate, per omnia similis factus

XV
Nemo præter Christum sine peccato.

Christus in nostræ naturæ veritate per omnia similis factus est

1553.

est nobis, excepto peccato, a quo prorsus erat immunis, tum in carne tum in spiritu. Venit ut agnus absque macula esset, qui mundi peccata per immolationem sui semel factam tolleret: et peccatum (ut inquit Joannes) in eo non erat. Sed nos reliqui, etiam baptizati et in Christo regenerati, in multis tamen offendimus omnes: et si diximus quia peccatum non habemus, nos ipsos seducimus, et veritas in nobis non est.

1563.

nobis, excepto peccato, a quo prorsus erat immunis, tum in carne tum in spiritu. Venit, ut agnus absque macula esset, qui mundi peccata per immolationem sui semel factam tolleret: et peccatum (ut inquit Joannes) in eo non erat. Sed nos reliqui, etiam baptizati et in Christo regenerati, in multis tamen offendimus omnes: et si dixerimus quia peccatum non habemus, nos ipsos seducimus, et veritas in nobis non est.

XV

* De peccato in Spiritum Sanctum.*

Non omne peccatum mortale post baptismum voluntarie prepetratum, est peccatum in Spiritum Sanctum et irremissibile. Proinde lapsis a baptismo in peccata, locus poenitentiae non est negandus. Post acceptum Spiritum Sanctum possumus a gratia data recedere atque peccare, denuoque per gratiam Dei resurgere ac resipiscere. Ideoque illi damnandi sunt, qui se quamdiu hic vivant, amplius non posse peccare affirmant, aut vere resipiscentibus poenitentiae locum denegant.

XVI

De Lapsis post Baptismum.

Non omne peccatum mortale post baptismum voluntarie perpetratum, est peccatum in Spiritum Sanctum et irremissibile. Proinde lapsis a baptismo in peccata, locus poenitentiae non est negandus. Post acceptum Spiritum Sanctum, possumus a gratia data recedere atque peccare, denuoque per gratiam Dei resurgere ac resipiscere. Ideoque illi damnandi sunt, qui se quamdiu hic vivant, amplius non posse peccare affirmant, aut vere resipiscentibus poenitentiae locum denegant.

XVI

† Blasphemia in Spiritum Sanctum.

Blasphemia in Spiritum Sanctum, est cum quis verborum Dei manifeste perceptam veritatem, ex malitia et obfirmatione animi, convitiis insectatur, et hostiliter insequitur. Atque

1553.

hujusmodi, quia maledicto sunt obnoxii, gravissimo sese astringunt sceleri: unde peccati hoc genus irremissibile a Domino appellatur, et affirmatur.†

XVII
De Praedestinatione et Electione.

Praedestinatio ad vitam est aeternum Dei propositum, quo ante jacta mundi fundamenta suo consilio, nobis quidem occulto, constanter decrevit eos quos [   ] elegit ex hominum genere, a maledicto et exitio liberare, atque ut vasa in honorem efficta, per Christum ad aeternam salutem adducere. Unde qui tam praeclaro Dei beneficio sunt donati, illi, Spiritu ejus opportuno tempore operante, secundum propositum ejus vocantur; vocationi per gratiam parent; justificantur gratis; adoptantur in filios; unigeniti Jesu Christi imagini efficiuntur conformes; in bonis operibus sancte ambulant; et demum ex Dei misericordia pertingunt ad sempiternam felicitatem.

Quemadmodum Praedestinationis et Electionis nostrae in Christo pia consideratio, dulcis, suavis, et ineffabilis consolationis plena est vere piis et his qui sentiunt in se vim Spiritus Christi, facta carnis et membra quae adhuc sunt super terram mortificantem, animumque ad coelestia et superna rapientem, tum quia fidem nostram de aeterna salute consequenda per Christum plurimum stabilit atque confirmat, tum quia amorem nostrum in Deum

1563.

XVII
De Prædestinatione et Electione.

Prædestinatio ad vitam, est æternum Dei propositum, quo ante jacta mundi fundamenta, suo consilio, nobis quidem occulto, constanter decrevit, eos quos in Christo elegit ex hominum genere, a maledicto et exitio liberare, atque ut vasa in honorem efficta, per Christum ad æternam salutem adducere. Unde qui tam præclaro Dei beneficio sunt donati, illi, Spiritu eius opportuno tempore operante, secundum propositum eius vocantur; vocationi per gratiam parent; justificantur gratis; adoptantur in filios; unigeniti Jesu Christi imagini efficiuntur conformes; in bonis operibus sancte ambulant; et demum ex Dei misericordia pertingunt ad sempiternam felicitatem.

Quemadmodum Prædestinationis et Electionis nostræ in Christo pia consideratio, dulcis, suavis, et ineffabilis consolationis plena est vere piis et his qui sentiunt in se vim Spiritus Christi, facta carnis et membra quæ adhuc sunt super terram mortificantem, animumque ad cœlestia et superna rapientem, tum quia fidem nostram de æterna salute consequenda per Christum plurimum stabilit atque confirmat, tum quia amorem nostrum in Deum vehementer

1553.

vehementer accendit: ita hominibus curiosis, carnalibus, et Spiritu Christi destitutis, ob oculos perpetuo versari Praedestinationis Dei sententiam, perniciosissimum est praecipitium, unde illos diabolus pertrudit vel in desperationem vel in aeque perniciosam impurissimae vitae securitatem.

Deinde † licet Praedestinationis decreta sunt nobis ignota†, promissiones † tamen † divinas sic amplecti opertet, ut nobis in sacris literis generaliter propositae sunt; et Dei voluntas in nostris actionibus ea sequenda est, quam in verbo Dei habemus diserte revelatum.

XVIII

Tantum in nomine Christi speranda est aeterna salus.

Sunt et illi anathematizandi qui dicere audent, unumquemque in lege aut secta quam profitetur esse servandum, modo juxta illam et lumen naturae accurate vixerit: cum sacrae literae tantum Jesu Christi nomen praedicent, in quo salvos fieri homines oportcat.

XIX

† Omnes obligantur ad moralia Legis praecepta servanda.

Lex a Deo data per Mosen, licet quoad caeremonias et ritus Christianos non astringat, neque civilia ejus praecepta in aliqua republica necessario recipi debeant; nihilominus ab obedientia mandatorum quae moralia vocantur nullus quantumvis Christianus est solutus. Quare illi non sunt audiendi, qui sacras

1563.

accendit: ita hominibus curiosis, carnalibus, et Spiritu Christi destitutis, ob oculos perpetuo versari Praedestinationis Dei sententiam, perniciosissimum est praecipitium, unde illos diabolus protrudit, vel in desperationem vel in aeque perniciosam impurissimae vitae securitatem.

Deinde promissiones divinas sic amplecti oportet, ut nobis in sacris literis generaliter propositae sunt; et Dei voluntas in nostris actionibus ea sequenda est, quam in verbo Dei habemus diserte revelatam.

XVIII

Tantum in nomine Christi speranda est aeterna salus.

Sunt illi anathematizandi qui dicere audent, unumquemque in lege aut secta quam profitetur esse servandum, modo juxta illam et lumen naturae accurate vixerit: cum sacrae literae tantum Jesu Christi nomen praedicent, in quo salvos fieri homines oporteat.

1553.

literas tantum infirmis datas esse perhibent, et Spiritum perpetuo jactant, a quo sibi quae praedicant suggeri asserunt, quanquam cum sacris literis apertissime pugnent.†

XX
De Ecclesia.

Ecclesia Christi visibilis est coetus fidelium, in quo verbum Dei purum praedicatur et sacramenta, quoad ea quae necessario exiguntur, juxta Christi institutum recte administrantur. Sicut erravit Ecclesia Hierosolymitana, Alexandrina, et Antiochena, ita et erravit Ecclesia Romana, non solum quoad agenda et caeremoniarum ritus, verum in his etiam quae credenda sunt.

XXI
De Ecclesiae auctoritate.

[   ] Ecclesiae non licet quicquam instituere, quod verbo Dei scripto adversetur, neque unum Scripturae locum sic exponere potest, ut alteri contradicat. Quare licet Ecclesia sit divinorum librorum testis et conservatrix, attamen, ut adversus eos nihil decernere, ita praeter illos nihil credendum de necessitate salutis debet obtrudere.

XXII
De auctoritate Conciliorum Generalium.

Generalia Concilia sine jussu et voluntate principum congre-

1563.

XIX
De Ecclesia.

Ecclesia Christi visibilis est cœtus fidelium, in quo verbum Dei purum prædicatur et sacramenta, quoad ea quæ necessario exiguntur, juxta Christi institutum recte administrantur. Sicut erravit Ecclesia Hierosolymitana, Alexandrina, et Antiochena, ita et erravit Ecclesia Romana, non solum quoad agenda et cæremoniarum ritus, verum in his etiam quæ credenda sunt.

XX
De Ecclesiæ auctoritate.

Habet Ecclesia ritus statuendi jus, et in fidei controversiis auctoritatem, quamvis Ecclesiæ non licet quioquam instituere, quod verbo Dei scripto adversetur, nec unum Scripturæ locum sic exponere potest, ut alteri contradicat. Quare licet Ecclesia sit divinorum librorum testis et conservatrix, attamen, ut adversus eos nihil decernere, ita præter illos nihil credendum de necessitate salutis debet obtrudere.

XXI
De auctoritate Conciliorum Generalium.

Generalia Concilia sine jussu et voluntate principum congregari

1553.

gari non possunt; et ubi convenerint, quia ex hominibus constant qui non omnes Spiritu et verbis Dei reguntur, et errare possunt et interdum errarunt, etiam in his quae ad normam pietatis pertinent. Ideo quae ab illis constituuntur, ut ad salutem necessaria, neque robur habent neque auctoritatem, nisi ostendi possunt e sacris literis esse desumpta.

XXIII
De Purgatorio.

Scholasticorum doctrina de Purgatorio, de Indulgentiis, de veneratione et adoratione tum Imaginum tum Reliquiarum, nec non de Invocatione Sanctorum, res est futilis, inaniter conficta, et nullis Scripturarum testimoniis innititur, imo verbo Dei perniciose contradicit.

XXIV
Nemo in Ecclesia ministret nisi vocatus.

Non licet cuiquam sumere sibi munus publice praedicandi aut administrandi sacramenta in Ecclesia, nisi prius fuerit ad haec obeunda legitime vocatus et missus. Atque illos legitime vocatos et missos existimare debemus, qui per homines, quibus potestas vocandi ministros atque mittendi in vineam Domini publice concessa est in Ecclesia, cooptati fuerint et asciti in hoc opus.

XXV
Agendum est in Ecclesia lingua quae sit populo nota.

*Decentissimum est et verbo Dei maxime congruit, ut nihil

1563.

non possunt; et ubi convenerint, quia ex hominibus constant, qui non omnes Spiritu et verbis Dei reguntur, et errare possunt, et interdum errarunt, etiam in his quæ ad normam pietatis pertinent. Ideo quæ ab illis constituuntur, ut ad salutem necessaria, neque robur habent, neque auctoritatem, nisi ostendi possint e sacris literis esse desumpta.

XXII
De Purgatorio.

Doctrina Romanensium de Purgatorio, de Indulgentiis, de veneratione et adoratione tum Imaginum tum Reliquiarum, nec non de Invocatione Sanctorum, res est futilis, inaniter conficta, et nullis Scripturarum testimoniis innititur, imo verbo Dei contradicit.

XXIII
Nemo in Ecclesia ministret nisi vocatus.

Non licet cuiquam sumere sibi munus publice prædicandi aut administrandi sacramenta in Ecclesia, nisi prius fuerit ad hæc obeunda legitime vocatus et missus. Atque illos legitime vocatos et missos existimare debemus, qui per homines, quibus potestas vocandi ministros atque mittendi in vineam Domini publice concessa est in Ecclesia, cooptati fuerint et asciti in hoc opus.

XXIV
Agendum est in Ecclesia lingua quæ sit populo nota.

Lingua populo non intellecta publicas in Ecclesia preces pera-

APPENDIX

1553.

in Ecclesia publice legatur aut recitetur lingua populo ignota, idque Paulus fieri vetuit, nisi adesset qui interpretaretur.*

XXVI
De Sacramentis.

† Dominus noster Jesus Christus sacramentis numero paucissimis, observatu facillimis, significatione praestantissimis, societatem novi populi colligavit, sicuti est Baptismus et Coena Domini.†

[

]

Sacramenta non instituta sunt a Christo ut spectarentur aut circumferrentur, sed ut rite illis uteremur: et in his duntaxat qui digne percipiunt, salutarem habent effectum, † idque non ex opere (ut quidam loquuntur) operato, quae vox ut peregrina est et sacris literis ignota, sic parit sensum minime pium, sed admodum superstitiosum †, qui vero indigne percipiunt damnationem (ut inquit Paulus) sibi ipsis acquirunt.

Sacramenta per verbum Dei instituta, non tantum sunt notae professionis Christianorum, sed certa quaedam potius testimonia et efficacia signa gratiae atque bonae in nos voluntatis Dei, per quae invisibiliter ipse in nobis operatur, nostramque fidem in se non solum excitat, verum etiam confirmat.

1563.

gere, aut sacramenta administrare, verbo Dei et primitivæ Ecclesiæ consuetudini plane repugnat.

XXV
De Sacramentis.

Sacramenta a Christo instituta, non tantum sunt notæ professionis Christianorum, sed certa quædam potius testimonia, et efficacia signa gratiæ atque bonæ in nos voluntatis Dei, per quæ invisibiliter ipse in nobis operatur, nostramque fidem in se, non solum excitat, verum etiam confirmat.

Duo a Christo Domino nostro in Evangelio instituta sunt Sacramenta, scilicet Baptismus et Coena Domini.

Quinque illa vulgo nominata Sacramenta, scilicet, Confirmatio, Poenitentia, Ordo, Matrimonium, et Extrema Unctio, pro Sacramentis Evangelicis habenda non sunt, ut quæ partim a prava Apostolorum imitatione profluxerunt, partim vitæ status sunt in Scripturis quidem probati, sed Sacramentorum eandem cum Baptismo et Coena Domini rationem non habentes: quomodo nec Poenitentia, ut quæ signum aliquod visibile seu cæremoniam a Deo institutam non habeat.

Sacramenta non in hoc instituta sunt a Christo, ut spectarentur, aut circumferrentur, sed ut rite illis uteremur: et in his duntaxat qui digne percipiunt, salutarem habent effectum: qui vero indigne percipiunt, damnationem (ut inquit Paulus) sibi ipsis acquirunt.

1553.

XXVII

Ministrorum malitia non tollit efficaciam institutionum divinarum.

Quamvis in Ecclesia visibili, bonis mali sint semper admixti, atque interdum ministerio verbi et sacramentorum administrationi praesint, tamen cum non suo sed Christi nomine agant, ejusque mandato et auctoritate ministrent, illorum ministerio uti licet, cum in verbo Dei audiendo, tum in sacramentis percipiendis. Neque per illorum malitiam effectus institutorum Christi tollitur, aut gratia donorum Dei minuitur quoad eos, qui fide et rite sibi oblata percipiunt, quae propter institutionem Christi et promissionem efficacia sunt, licet per malos administrentur. Ad Ecclesiae tamen disciplinam pertinet, ut in eos inquiratur, accusenturque ab iis, qui eorum flagitia noverint, atque tandem, justo convicti judicio, deponantur.

XXVIII

De Baptismo.

Baptismus non est tantum signum professionis ac discriminis nota, qua Christiani a non Christianis discernuntur, sed etiam est signum regenerationis, per quod tanquam per instrumentum recte Baptismum suscipientes, Ecclesiae inseruntur, promissiones de remissione peccatorum atque adoptionis nostra in filios Dei per Spiritum Sanctum visibiliter obsignantur, fides confirmatur, et vi divinae invocationis, gratia augetur.

1563.

XXVI

Ministrorum malitia non tollit efficaciam institutionum divinarum.

Qvamvis in Ecclesia visibili bonis mali semper sint admixti, atque interdum ministerio verbi et sacramentorum administrationi praesint, tamen cum non suo sed Christi nomine agant, ejusque mandato et auctoritate ministrent, illorum ministerio uti licet, cum in verbo Dei audiendo, tum in sacramentis percipiendis. Neque per illorum malitiam effectus institutorum Christi tollitur, aut gratia donorum Dei minuitur, quoad eos qui fide et rite sibi oblata percipiunt, quæ propter institutionem Christi et promissionem efficacia sunt, licet per malos administrentur. Ad Ecclesiæ tamen disciplinam pertinet, ut in malos ministros inquiratur, accusenturque ab his, qui eorum flagitia noverint, atque tandem, justo convicti judicio, deponantur.

XXVII

De Baptismo.

Baptismus non est tantum professionis signum ac discriminis nota, qua Christiani a non Christianis discernantur, sed etiam est signum regenerationis, per quod tanquam per instrumentum recte Baptismum suscipientes, Ecclesiæ inseruntur, promissiones de remissione peccatorum atque adoptionis nostra in filios Dei, per Spiritum Sanctum visibiliter obsignantur, fides confirmatur, et vi divinæ invocationis, gratia augetur.

APPENDIX

1553.

* Mos Ecclesiae baptizandi parvulos et laudandus est, et omnino in Ecclesia retinendus.*

XXIX

De Coena Domini.

Coena Domini non est tantum signum mutuae benevolentiae Christianorum inter sese, verum potius est sacramentum nostrae per mortem Christi redemptionis: atque adeo rite, digne et cum fide sumentibus, panis quem frangimus est communicatio corporis Christi; similiter poculum benedictionis est communicatio sanguinis Christi.

Panis et vini transubstantiatio in Eucharistia, ex sacris literis probari non potest, sed apertis Scripturae verbis adversatur [   ] et multarum superstitionem dedit occasionem.

† Quum naturae humanae veritas requirat, ut unius ejusdemque hominis corpus in multis locis simul esse non posset, sed in uno aliquo et definito loco esse oporteat, idcirco Christi corpus in multis et diversis locis eodem tempore praesens esse non potest. Et quoniam, ut tradunt sacrae literae, Christus in coelum fuit sublatus, et ibi usque ad finem saeculi est permansurus, non debet quisquam fidelium carnis ejus et sanguinis realem et corporalem (ut loquuntur) praesentiam in Eucharistia vel credere vel profiteri. †

Sacramentum Eucharistiae ex institutione Christi non servabatur, circumferebatur, elevabatur, nec adorabatur.

1563.

Baptismus parvulorum omnino in ecclesia retinendus est, ut qui cum Christi institutione optime congruat.

XXVIII

De Coena Domini.

Coena Domini non est tantum signum mutuae benevolentiae Christianorum inter sese, verum potius est sacramentum nostrae per mortem Christi redemptionis: atque adeo rite, digne et cum fide sumentibus, panis quem frangimus est communicatio corporis Christi; similiter poculum benedictionis est communicatio sanguinis Christi.

Panis et vini transubstantiatio in Eucharistia, ex sacris literis probari non potest, sed apertis Scripturae verbis adversatur, sacramenti naturam evertit, et multarum superstitionum dedit occasionem.

Corpus Christi datur, accipitur, et manducatur in Coena, tantum coelesti et spirituali ratione. Medium autem quo corpus Christi accipitur, et manducatur in Coena, fides est.

Sacramentum Eucharistiae ex institutione Christi non servabatur, circumferebatur, elevabatur, nec adorabatur.

1553.

[

]

XXX
De unica Christi oblatione in Cruce perfecta.

Oblatio Christi semel facta, perfecta est redemptio, propitiatio, et satisfactio pro omnibus peccatis totius mundi, tam originalibus quam actualibus; neque praeter illam unicam est ulla alia pro peccatis expiatio. Unde missarum sacrificia, quibus vulgo dicebatur sacerdotem offerre Christum in remissionem poenae aut culpae pro vivis et defunctis, [   ] figmenta sunt et perniciosae imposturae.

XXXI
* Coelibatus ex verbo Dei praecipitur nemini.

Episcopis, Presbyteris et Diaconis non est mandatum ut coelibatum voveant; neque jure divino coguntur matrimonio abstinere.*

XXXII
Excommunicati vitandi sunt.

Qui per publicam Ecclesiae denuntiationem rite ab unitate Ecclesiae praecisus est et excommunicatus, is ab universa

1563.

XXIX
De Utraque Specie.

Calix Domini laicis non est denegandus: utraque enim pars Dominici sacramenti ex Christi institutione et praecepto, omnibus Christianis ex aequo administrari debet.

XXX
De unica Christi oblatione in Cruce perfecta.

Oblatio Christi semel facta, perfecta est redemptio, propitiatio, et satisfactio pro omnibus peccatis totius mundi, tam originalibus quam actualibus; neque praeter illam unicam est ulla alia pro peccatis expiatio. Unde missarum sacrificia, quibus vulgo dicebatur sacerdotem offerre Christum in remissionem poenae aut culpae pro vivis et defunctis, blasphema figmenta sunt et perniciosae imposturae.

XXXI
De Coniugio Sacerdotum.

Episcopis, Presbyteris et Diaconis, nullo mandato divino praeceptum est, ut aut coelibatum voveant, aut a matrimonio abstineant. Licet igitur etiam illis, ut caeteris omnibus Christianis, ubi hoc ad pietatem magis facere judicaverint, pro suo arbitratu matrimonium contrahere.

XXXII
Excommunicati uitandi sunt.

Qui per publicam Ecclesiae denuntiationem rite ab unitate Ecclesiae praecisus est et excommunicatus, is ab universa fidelium

1553.

fidelium multitudine, donec per poenitentiam publice reconciliatus fuerit arbitrio judicis competentis, habendus est tanquam ethnicus et publicanus.

XXXIII
Traditiones Ecclesiasticae.

Traditiones atque caeremonias easdem non omnino necessarium est esse ubique aut prorsus consimiles; nam et variae semper fuerunt et mutari possunt pro regionum [ ] et morum diversitate, modo nihil contra Dei verbum instituatur.

Traditiones et caeremonias ecclesiasticas, quae cum verbo Dei non pugnant, et sunt auctoritate publica institutae atque probatae, quisquis privato consilio volens et data opera publice violaverit, is, ut qui peccat in publicum ordinem Ecclesiae, quique laedit auctoritatem Magistratus, et qui infirmorum fratrum conscientias vulnerat, publice, ut caeteri timeant, arguendus est.

[

]

XXXIV
* Homiliae.

Homiliae nuper Ecclesiae Anglicanae per injunctiones Regias traditae atque commendatae, piae sunt atque salutares, doctrinamque ab omnibus amplectendam continent; quare, populo diligenter, expedite clareque recitandae sunt.*

1563.

multitudine, donec per poenitentiam publice reconciliatus fuerit, arbitrio judicis competentis, habendus est tanquam ethnicus et publicanus.

XXXIII
Traditiones Ecclesiasticæ.

Traditiones atque cæremonias easdem, non omnino necessarium est esse ubique aut prorsus consimiles; nam et variæ semper fuerunt, et mutari possunt, pro regionum, temporum, et morum diversitate, modo nihil contra verbum Dei instituatur.

Traditiones et cæremonias ecclesiasticas, quæ cum verbo Dei non pugnant, et sunt auctoritate publica institutæ atque probatæ, quisquis privato consilio volens et data opera publice violaverit, is, ut qui peccat in publicum ordinem Ecclesiæ, quique lædit auctoritatem Magistratus, et qui infirmorum fratrum conscientias vulnerat, publice, ut cæteri timeant, arguendus est.

Quælibet Ecclesia particularis, sive nationalis, auctoritatem habet instituendi, mutandi, aut abrogandi cæremonias aut ritus ecclesiasticos, humana tantum auctoritate institutos, modo omnia ad ædificationem fiant.

XXXIV

Tomus secundus Homiliarum, quarum singulos titulos huic Articulo subjunximus, continet piam et salutarem doctrinam, et his temporibus necessariam, non minus quam prior Tomus Homiliarum quæ editæ sunt tempore Edwardi sexti. Itaque eas in ecclesiis per ministros diligenter et clare, ut a populo intelligi possint, recitandas esse judicamus.

1553.

1563.

Catalogus Homiliarum.

De recto Ecclesiæ usu.
Adversus idolatriæ pericula.
De reparandis ac purgandis Ecclesiis.
De bonis operibus.
De jejunio.
In gulæ atque ebrietatis vitia.
In nimis sumptuosos vestium apparatus.
De oratione sive precatione.
De loco et tempore orationi destinatis.
De publicis precibus ac sacramentis, idiomate vulgari omnibusque noto, habendis.
De sacrosancta verbi divini auctoritate.
De eleemosyna.
De Christi nativitate.
De Dominica passione.
De resurrectione Domini.
De digna corporis et sanguinis Dominici in cœna Domini participatione.
De donis Spiritus Sancti.
In diebus, qui vulgo Rogationum dicti sunt, concio.
De matrimonii statu.
De otio seu socordia.
De pœnitentia.

xxxv

*De Libro Precationum et Caeremoniarum Ecclesiae Anglicanae.

Liber qui nuperrime auctoritate Regis et Parliamenti Ecclesiae Anglicanae traditus est, continens modum et formam orandi et sacramenta administrandi in Ecclesia Anglicana, similiter et libellus eadem auctoritate editus de ordinatione ministrorum Ecclesiae, quoad

xxxv

Libellus de Consecratione Archiepiscoporum et Episcoporum et de ordinatione Presbyterorum et Diaconorum editus nuper temporibus Edwardi sexti, et auctoritate Parliamenti illis ipsis temporibus confirmatus, omnia ad ejusmodi consecrationem et ordinationem neces-

1553.

doctrinae veritatem pii sunt et salutari doctrinae Evangelii in nullo repugnant sed congruunt, et eandem non parum promovent et illustrant; atque ideo ab omnibus Ecclesiae Anglicanae fidelibus membris, et maxime a ministris verbi, cum omni promptitudine animorum et gratiarum actione recipiendi, approbandi, et populo Dei commendendi sunt.*

XXXVI
De Civilibus Magistratibus.

† Rex Angliae est Supremum Caput in terris, post Christum, Ecclesiae Anglicanae et Hibernicae.†

[

]
Romanus Pontifex nullam

1563.

saria continent, et nihil habet quod ex se sit aut superstitiosum aut impium. Itaque quicunque juxta ritus illius libri consecrati aut ordinati sunt ab anno secundo praedicti Regis Edwardi, usque ad hoc tempus, aut in posterum juxta eosdem ritus consecrabuntur aut ordinabuntur rite, ordine, atque legitime, statuimus esse et fore consecratos et ordinatos.

XXXVI
De Civilibus Magistratibus.

Regia Majestas in hoc Angliae regno ac cæteris ejus Dominiis, jure summam habet potestatem, ad quam omnium statuum hujus regni sive illi ecclesiastici sunt sive non, in omnibus causis suprema gubernatio pertinet, et nulli externae jurisdictioni est subjecta, nec esse debet.

Cum Regiae Majestati summam gubernationem tribuimus, quibus titulis intelligimus animos quorundam calumniatorum offendi, non damus regibus nostris aut verbi Dei aut sacramentorum administrationem, quod etiam Injunctiones ab Elizabetha Regina nostra nuper editae, apertissime testantur: sed eam tantum praerogativam, quam in Sacris Scripturis a Deo ipso omnibus piis principibus, videmus semper fuisse attributam, hoc est, ut omnes status atque ordines fidei suae a Deo commissos, sive illi ecclesiastici sint sive civiles, in officio contineant, et contumaces ac delinquentes, gladio civili coërceant.

Romanus Pontifex nullam ha-

1553.

habet jurisdictionem in hoc regno Angliae. †Magistratus civilis est a Deo ordinatus atque probatus, quamobrem illi non solum propter iram, sed etiam propter conscientiam, obediendum est.†

Leges civiles possunt Christianos propter capitalia et gravia crimina morte punire.

Christianis licet ex mandato Magistratus arma portare et justa bella administrare.

1563.

bet jurisdictionem in hoc regno Angliæ.

Leges civiles possunt Christianos propter capitalia et gravia crimina morte punire.

Christianis licet ex mandato Magistratus arma portare et justa bella administrare.

XXXVII

Christianorum bona non sunt communia.

Facultates et bona Christianorum non sunt communia, quoad jus et possessionem, ut quidam Anabaptistae falso jactant; debet tamen quisque de his quae possidet, pro facultatum ratione, pauperibus eleemosynas benigne distribuere.

XXXVII

Christianorum bona non sunt communia.

Facultates et bona Christianorum non sunt communia quoad jus et possessionem, ut quidam Anabaptistæ falso jactant; debet tamen quisque de his quæ possidet, pro facultatum ratione, pauperibus eleemosynas benigne distribuere.

XXXVIII

Licet Christianis jurare.

Quemadmodum juramentum vanum et temerarium a Domino nostro Jesu Christo et ab Apostolo ejus Jacobo Christianis hominibus interdictum esse fatemur, ita Christianam religionem minime prohibere censemus, quin, jubente Magistratu, in causa fidei et charitatis jurare liceat, modo id fiat juxta Prophetae doctrinam in justitia, in judicio, et veritate.

XXXVIII

Licet Christianis jurare.

Quemadmodum juramentum vanum et temerarium a Domino nostro Jesu Christo, et Apostolo ejus Jacobo Christianis hominibus interdictum esse fatemur, ita Christianam religionem minime prohibere censemus, quin, jubente Magistratu, in causa fidei et charitatis, jurare liceat, modo id fiat juxta Prophetæ doctrinam in justitia, in judicio, et veritate.

XXXIX

† Resurrectio mortuorum nondum est facta.

Resurrectio mortuorum non adhuc facta est, quasi tantum

1553.

ad animum pertineat qui per Christi gratiam a morte peccatorum excitetur, sed extremo die quoad omnes qui obierunt expectanda est; tunc enim vita defunctis (ut Scripturae manifestissime testantur) propria corpora carnes et ossa restituentur ut homo integer, prout vel recte vel perdite vixerit, juxta sua opera sive praemia sive poenas reportet.†

1563.

XL

†Defunctorum animae neque cum corporibus intercunt, neque otiose dormiunt.

Qui animas defunctorum praedicant usque ad diem judicii absque omni sensu dormire, aut illas asserunt una cum corporibus mori et extrema die cum illis excitandas, ab orthodoxa fide quae nobis in sacris literis traditur prorsus dissentiunt.†

XLI

†Millenarii.

Qui Millenariorum fabulam revocare conantur sacris literis adversantur et in Judaica deliramenta sese praecipitant.†

XLII

†Non omnes tandem servandi sunt.

Hi quoque damnatione digni sunt qui conantur hodie perniciosam opinonem instaurare quod omnes, quantumvis impii, servandi sunt tandem, cum definito tempore a justitia divina poenas de admissis flagitiis luerunt.†

INDEX

Admonition, *The First*, 256.
Adrian VI., Pope, 194.
All Souls, Feast of, 192.
Anabaptism, 180.
Anabaptists, the, 122, 128, 131, 147, 149, 158 ff, 162, 175, 204, 211, 218, 221 f, 249, 253, 264, 269, 271.
Anglican Orders, 258 f.
Anicetus, Pope, 252.
Antinomianism, 137 f.
Antioch, Council of, 186.
Apollinarianism, 181.
Articles (1538), the Thirteen, 165, 203, 210, 217, 252.
—— (1552), the Forty-five, 141, 191.
—— (1553), the Forty-two, 141, 149, 191, 227, 275 ff.
—— (1559), the Heads of Religion, 252.
—— (1563), the Thirty-nine, 275 ff.
—— (1595), the Lambeth, 156.
Arundel, Archbishop, 196.
Athanasius, Saint, 186 f.
Atonement, the, 242.
Augustine of Canterbury, Saint, 252.
Augustine of Hippo, Saint, 122 f, 125, 129, 164, 201, 210, 219.

BAPTISM, 126 f, 221 ff.
Basil, Saint, 176, 201.
Bellarmine, 201.
Berengarius, 230, 232.
Bishops' Book, The, 126, 165.
Blasphemy against the Holy Ghost, 149.
Boniface VIII., Pope, 144.
Bonner, Bishop, 258, 261.
Burnet, Bishop, 186.

CALVIN, 121, 149, 156 f.
Calvinism, 156.
Calvinists, 152.
Catacombs, 191.
Catechism, the, 227 ff.
Catechismus Romanus, 193, 201, 233 n.
Celibacy of the clergy, 242.
Ceremonies, 176 f.
Chalcedon, Council of, 184, 187.
Chalice, denial of, to the laity, 177, 239 f.
Chantries, 192, 246.
Chaucer, 194.
Cheke, Sir John, 232.
Chrysostom, Saint, 176.

INDEX 293

Church, the, 161 ff, 218; authority of, 174 ff; relation of, to the Kingdom of God, 169; to the Scriptures, 181.
Clement VI., Pope, 145.
Clermont, Council of, 144.
Colet, Dean, 199.
Communion in both kinds, 239, 242.
Communism, 269 f.
Concomitance, 240.
Concupiscence, 127.
Confessions: Augsburg, 203, 210, 218; Lutheran and Reformed, 126 f; Westminster, 127; Würtemberg, 131, 138, 174.
Confirmation, 214 f.
Congregation, the, 162, 170.
Constance, Council of, 240.
Constantine Pogonatus, 184.
Constantinople, Councils of (381), 181, 184; (553), 184.
Conversion, 223.
Convocation, 175, 179 f, 227, 236, 248, 256, 267.
Corpus Christi, Feast of, 215.
Cranmer, Archbishop, 141, 228, 232.
Cromwell, 266.
Crusades, the, 144, 198.
Culpa and poena, 145, 192, 245.
Cyril of Jerusalem, Saint, 199, 239.

DECLARATION, His Majesty's, 179, 273 f.
Departed, Prayer for the Faithful, 176, 191 f, 245.
Discipline, 172, 214.
Donatism, 219.
Dunstan, Archbishop, 264.

EDWARD VI., 266.
Elect, the, 155.
Election, 154 ff.
Elizabeth, Queen, 175, 237, 256.
Elvira, Council of, 195.
Ephesus, Councils of (431), 254 n; (449), 187.
Episcopacy, 203, 260 f.
Erasmus, 196, 199.
Establishment, 178.
Eucharist, connection of, with early hours of the Lord's Day, 178; object of, 215; sacrifice of, 229, 241 ff.
Eugenius IV., Pope, 259.
Eutychianism, 184.
Excommunication, 249 ff.
Ex opere operato, 210.

FAITH, meaning of, 134 f.
'Faithful, the,' meaning of, 171.
'Faith only,' meaning of, 135, 137.
Fall, the, 124 f, 128.
Final Perseverance, 152.
Florence, Council of, 192.
Freewill, 128 ff.

GARDINER, Bishop, 227.
General Councils, 183 ff.
Good works, 129, 138 f.
Grace, meaning of, 123, 129; irresistibility of, 152.
Gregory the Great, Pope, 192, 195, 201, 252.
Gregory VII., Pope, 266.
Guest, Bishop, 236 f.

HELENA, Empress, 198.
Henry VIII., 227, 265 f.

Homilies, the, 255 f.
Honorius, Pope, 173.
Hooper, Bishop, 149 n, 160, 165, 253.
Horne, Bishop, 261.
Host, Procession of the, 215, 234 ; Elevation of the, 234 ; Reservation of the, 234.
Hundred Grievances, the, 194.
Hus, 165.

ICONOCLASTIC CONTROVERSY, the, 195 ff.
Images, 195 ff.
Immaculate Conception of Our Lady, the, 147 f.
Indulgences, 144, 193 ff.
Infallibility, Claim of the Popes to, 162, 173.
Infant Baptism, 221, 225.
Innocent III., Pope, 266.
Intermediate State, the, 190 f, 199.
Invisible Church, the, 164 f.

JAMES, relation of SS. Paul and, 136.
John, King, 266 f.
Judicial power of the Church, the, 179 ff.
Julius, Pope, 186.
Jurisdiction of the Pope, the, 266 f.
Justification, 121, 129, 131 ff.
Justinian, 184.
Justin Martyr, Saint, 234, 239.

KINGDOM OF GOD, the, 168 ff; relation of, to the Church, 169 f.
Kiss of Peace, the, 252.

LATERAN COUNCIL, the, 187, 231.
Latitudinarianism, 159 f.
Latria, 196.
Laud, Archbishop, 175.
Legislative power of the Church, the, 175 ff.
Leo the Great, Pope, 184.
Leo the Isaurian, 196.
Leo XIII., Pope, 259 n.
Liberius, Pope, 173.
Liturgies, the primitive, 176, 191, 200, 208, 234.
Local Churches, the rights of, 176, 253 f.
Lollards, the, 231.
Luther, 121, 137 f, 175, 211.
Lutherans, 203.

MACEDONIANISM, 181, 184.
Marcian, 184.
Marriage of the clergy, 247 f.
Mary, Queen, 256, 266.
Mass, sacrifice of the, 241.
Matrimony, 215.
Matter and Form, 172.
Mechanical theory of the operation of the sacraments, 216, 245.
Mediæval system, the, 134, 141 f, 191 ff, 198, 202, 230, 237, 241 ff.
Melanchthon, 165.
Merit, 148 ; de condigno, 141 ; de congruo, 140 ff; Treasury of, 145, 193.
Ministry, the, 203 ff.
Monophysitism, 184.
Monothelitism, 173, 185.
Montanism, 180.
More, Sir Thomas, 196, 202.
Mortal and venial sin, 151.

INDEX

NESTORIANISM, 184.
Nicaea, Councils of (325), 176, 184, 186 f, 202; (787), 196.
Nominalists, the, 231.
Nonconformists, 253.
Notes of the Church, the, 171 f.

OATHS, 270 f.
Oldcastle, Sir John, 231.
Orange, Council of, 180.
Orders, 215.
Ordinal, the, 204, 257 ff.
Original and actual sins, 243, 246.
Original righteousness, 124.
Original sin, 121 ff, 147.

PAPAL CLAIMS, the, 266 f.
Papists, 252, 257 ff, 264 (see Romanensians).
Pardons, 193 ff (see Indulgences).
Parker, Archbishop, 149, 227, 236, 252.
Particular redemption, 156.
Paul, relation of SS. James and, 136.
Pelagianism, 130, 180.
Pelagians, the, 122 f.
Pelagius, 123, 129, 173.
Penance, 214 f.
Penitential system, the, 144.
Peter Lombard, 201.
Pilkington, Bishop, 258.
Poena and culpa, 145, 192, 245.
Pole, Cardinal, 258 f.
Polycarp, Saint, 198, 252.
Prayer Book, The, 227.
Precepts and counsels, 145.
Predestination, 121, 154 ff.

Propitiation, 242 f.
Protestantism, 137, 181, 196, 228.
Purgatory, 145, 190 ff, 245.
Puritans, the, 152, 175, 177, 219, 227, 252, 260.

QUAKERS, the, 270.

RATIFICATION, the, 272.
Realists, the, 231.
Real Presence, the, 227, 232 ff, 238, 242, 245.
Reconciliation, 243.
Redemption, 242 f.
Reformatio Legum, the, 122, 149, 154, 159, 184, 227.
Regeneration, 222 f.
Relics, 197 ff.
Renewal, 223 f.
Reprobation, 154 ff.
Ridley, Bishop, 253.
Rites, 176.
Romanensians, the, 189, 236, 258 (see Papists).
Rome, Church of, 173, 207, 214; Court of, 173.

SACRAMENTARIES, the, 211.
Sacraments, the, 209 ff, 218 ff.
Sacrifices of Masses, 192 f, 245.
Saints, Invocation of, 199 ff.
Sanctification, 131 ff.
Satisfaction, 242.
Scholasticism, 140.
Schoolmen, the, 141, 143, 145, 147, 192, 231, 245.
Scotists, the, 125.
Semi-Pelagianism, 181.
Solifidianism, 137 f.

'Spiritual,' meaning of, 233 f.
Spiritualty and Temporalty, 264.
'Substance,' meaning of, 231.
Sunday not the Sabbath, 178.
Supererogation, Works of, 143 ff.
Supremacy, the Royal, 264 ff.
Swiss reformers, the, 175.

TERTULLIAN, 126, 195.
Tetzel, 194.
Theodosius, I. and II., 184.
Thomas Aquinas, Saint, 196, 201, 219 n, 240 n, 245.
Thomas of Canterbury, Saint, 198.
Thomists, the, 125.
Titles of the Articles, inexact, 140 f, 159, 237, 241.
Traditions and ceremonies, 251 ff.
Transubstantiation, 187, 230 ff, 245.
Trent, Council of, 125, 131, 134, 138, 149, 175, 187, 189, 193 f, 196, 202, 207, 210, 231, 239, 241.
Tunstal, Bishop, 266.

UNCTION, EXTREME, 214 f.
Unworthiness of the Minister, 217 ff.

VENIAL AND MORTAL SIN, 151.
Vestiarian controversy, the, 249.
Visible Church, the, 164 ff.
Vulgar tongue, service in, 207 f.

WESTMINSTER ASSEMBLY, the, 126 n, 141.
William the Conqueror, 264 ff.
Works before Justification, 140.
Wyclif, 165.

ZOSIMUS, Pope, 173.
Zwingli, 165, 211.
Zwinglianism, 228.
Zwinglians, 222.

www.ingramcontent.com/pod-product-compliance
Lightning Source LLC
Chambersburg PA
CBHW022026240426
43667CB00042B/1208